Wallis & Edward

Letters
1931~1937

ALSO BY MICHAEL BLOCH

The Duke of Windsor's War
Operation Willi

Wallis & Edward

Letters
1931-1937

THE INTIMATE CORRESPONDENCE
OF THE DUKE AND DUCHESS OF WINDSOR

Edited by Michael Bloch

Weidenfeld & Nicolson

LONDON

First published in Great Britain by
George Weidenfeld & Nicolson Limited
91 Clapham High Street, London SW4 7TA

ISBN 0 297 78804 3
Printed in Great Britain by
Butler & Tanner Ltd
Frome and London

CONTENTS

ILLUSTRATIONS

Wallis and Aunt Bessie being photographed by the King at the Fort at the end of November 1936 (*Popperfoto*)
At the Villa Lou Viei at Cannes, 10 December 1936 (*Keystone*)
Edward arrives in Vienna to begin his exile, 13 December 1936 (*Daily Mail*)
The Château de Candé (*Duchess of Windsor's collection*)
Wedding party at Candé, 3 June 1937 (*Duchess of Windsor's collection*)
WE are one (*Duchess of Windsor's collection*)

ACKNOWLEDGEMENTS

Quotations from *Norman Birkett* by H. Montgomery Hyde (Hamish Hamilton, 1964) reprinted by kind permission of the author.
Quotations from *Walter Monckton* by Lord Birkenhead (Weidenfeld and Nicolson, 1969) reprinted by kind permission of the publisher.
Quotations from *The Abdication of Edward VIII* by Lord Beaverbrook (Hamish Hamilton, 1966) reprinted by kind permission of the publisher.

PREFACE

This book relates the most celebrated love story of modern times –
that of Wallis Simpson (*née* Warfield) of Baltimore, who became
Duchess of Windsor, and Edward, Prince of Wales, who succeeded to
the throne as King Edward VIII and, having abdicated in order to marry
her, became Duke of Windsor. It is a story which has already been
told many times and in many forms. Wallis and Edward have written
their memoirs, as have many of the others involved; there have been
numerous films on the subject, books by the hundred, newspaper and
magazine articles by the tens of thousand. But here the tale is told
with an extraordinary new intimacy, revealing a hitherto completely
unknown picture. For here are the intimate letters of the lovers themselves, from the moment of their first meeting in January 1931 up to
the moment they became man and wife in June 1937.

These letters – now in the ownership of the Duchess's estate – come
from two sources. First, there is the regular series of letters Wallis
wrote throughout the period to her much-loved Aunt Bessie, Mrs D.
Buchanan Merryman. These papers – returned to the Duchess of
Windsor on Mrs Merryman's death in 1965 at the age of one hundred
– constitute a fascinating, month-by-month record of Wallis's developing relations with the man born to be King. (Sadly, Aunt Bessie's
replies to her niece appear, with a few exceptions, to be lost.) Secondly,
there is the exchange of correspondence, lovingly preserved on both
sides, which took place between Wallis and Edward before, during
and after his reign, and which, growing steadily in interest and importance, enables one to penetrate into the very heart of their relationship.
As well as being great human documents, these letters are of considerable historical significance: in particular they illustrate the extent to
which, in 1936, Wallis tried to escape from the King and so keep him
on his throne.

It was the wish of the Duchess of Windsor that these letters
be published upon her death. She was distressed by a number of

biographies which appeared after the Duke died in 1972 giving an impression of their characters and their relations with one another which she found distorted beyond recognition. She was determined that, at the right moment, the truth should be known to the world in the form of the authentic contemporary record. In the autumn of 1975 the Duchess fell seriously ill, and it was left to Maître Suzanne Blum, her lawyer and friend, to give effect to her instructions.

I have tried to be faithful to the Duchess's intention. I have sought not to write a new biography of her, but to present the correspondence as a coherent whole in its historical and personal context. It was necessary to edit the letters considerably, if only on grounds of space; but I have only removed what seemed dull, repetitive, unclear or legally objectionable. I do not believe I have omitted anything of real importance. I have tried to make the story tell itself, and keep the commentary to the minimum necessary to enable the reader to understand the background. Wherever possible, I have described events in the words of the Duke and Duchess rather than my own; where appropriate, I have quoted from their memoirs, while pointing out that the letters often reveal those memoirs (written in the 1950s, when there was much that could not be said and even more that had been forgotten) to be incomplete and inaccurate. I have done my best to identify the persons mentioned in the letters, most of whose names appear in no works of reference; inevitably, there are a number of cases in which my researches have failed to yield result.

I have tried to keep the letters in their original form, save where this would have made them difficult to read. In brisk personal correspondence, the Duchess paid little attention to punctuation. A kind of dash served her as full stop, comma, hyphen or question-mark. I have tried to interpret these ubiquitous dashes according to the context; but I have respected the fact that almost all her letters, written as it were in one deep breath, consist of a single long paragraph. The Duke for his part was particularly weak in the use of the apostrophe, which he tended either to misplace (as in 'did'nt') or omit altogether. I have retained these errors without comment, and have indicated his occasional mis-spellings and ungrammatical expressions with a 'sic'. Reading the letters published herein, one must not pass too harsh a judgement on the literacy of the Duke and Duchess. These missives were dashed out freely for the eyes of loved ones; in their more formal correspondence, they wrote with considerably more care.

In their letters to one another, Wallis and Edward use a number of curious private expressions; and in most cases the meaning of these must be left to the imagination of the reader.

I am grateful to the Duchess of Windsor's *major-domo*, Georges Sanègre; to Peter Bloxham, Posy Guinness, Betty Hanley, Jim Lees-Milne, Anita Leslie, Brian Masters, Stuart Preston and Terry Sheppard; to Tony Friis and Paul Proctor of Prefis Limited, on whose new word-processing system, *Book Machine*, the manuscript was written; and to Andrew Best, my guide, literary agent and friend. But above all I am grateful to Maître Blum, but for whose chivalrous and unremitting efforts the Duchess's wishes might never have been realized and this book would not have appeared in its present form.

MICHAEL BLOCH
PARIS
24 April 1986

Introduction 1896~1930

In January 1931, Wallis Simpson, the American wife of a conventional London businessman, realized the daydream of every middle-class woman in England: in the course of a week-end country house party in the English Midlands, she was introduced socially to the great idol of the day, Edward, Prince of Wales. The encounter (which had come about through accident rather than design) was understandably thrilling for her; but there is no evidence that, on that occasion, she made any impression on the heir to the throne.

It would have been surprising if she had, for she was a very ordinary woman. At thirty-four, she was no longer young; she could not be considered beautiful; nor was she in particularly robust health. She was neither rich nor well-educated. There was nothing outstanding about her manners or conversation. She had no sporting, artistic or intellectual achievements to her name. Of politics, history, the great movements of the day, she knew nothing. For that matter, she knew remarkably little of the traditions and habits of mind of her adopted country, in which she had been living for two and a half years. Her principal daily preoccupations, as with countless other women of her time and class, were with the running of a household at a time of economic depression. Her friends (mostly American) were the wives of diplomats and businessmen. Her principal hobby was playing cards.

To be fair, she had her qualities too. She was a witty and lively woman with an original and forthright manner; she had a somewhat adventurous history, and a healthy curiosity about people and things; she possessed perfect clothes sense and food sense; and, in a modest way, she had acquired a reputation as a hostess at the modern flat which she occupied with her husband in the West End of London, in the prosperous if not especially fashionable district north of Marble Arch. There was, however, no reason why the Prince should pay the slightest attention to this unexceptional married woman into whose company he was briefly and fortuitously thrown that week-end early in 1931, save as required by good manners; nor was there any reason for her to suppose she would ever see him again.

But they did see each other again – and, as time passed, she did become the object of his attentions. By the beginning of 1932, he liked her well enough to invite her and her husband to spend a week-end at his country retreat, Fort Belvedere. By the middle of 1933 the Simpsons were regular visitors there, and could count themselves among the Prince's circle of friends. By the middle of 1934 he had decided that she mattered more to him than anyone he had ever known. By the time he succeeded as King Edward VIII at the beginning of 1936 he had long been desperately in love with her and dependent on her, and he had become obsessed with the idea of eventual marriage to her. And at the end of that same year – in the most dramatic romantic gesture of modern times – he gave up his throne in order that they might become man and wife.

The first part of this work will trace the slow evolution of that historic relationship – through Wallis Simpson's journal in the form of her regular letters to her aunt, and eventually through her intimate correspondence with the Prince himself. Through these vivid contemporary documents, her personality will reveal itself with extraordinary clarity. But first it is necessary to show how she became the woman that she was.

Bessiewallis Warfield (known from her infancy as Wallis) was born at Blue Ridge Summit, Pennsylvania, on 19 June 1896, only child of Teackle Wallis Warfield and his wife Alice Montague. In spite of the accident of her 'Northern' birth, her background was firmly rooted in the American South. The family home was in Baltimore, a bastion of Southern sympathies and Southern life. Both her parents came from well-known Southern families: the stern Warfields had long been associated with the public life of Maryland, where they had done well in business in the nineteenth century; the Montagues, though much reduced in circumstances since the Civil War, were an old Virginia clan, noted for their wit, charm and good looks. But the two families did not get on. The Montagues regarded the Warfields as *nouveaux riches*. The Warfields regarded the Montagues as frivolous aristocrats. When Teackle married Alice for love in 1895, therefore, it was regarded as a *mésalliance*, and they received little support from their relations. This was unfortunate, for Alice Montague had no money to her otherwise distinguished name, while Teackle Warfield had few prospects since he was in an advanced stage of tuberculosis. It was hoped that the mountain air of Pennsylvania might help him; but he died only five months after his daughter's birth, leaving his widow penniless.

It is impossible to understand the personality of the future Duchess of Windsor unless one bears in mind this background. It explains almost everything about her. All her life, she profoundly believed that, through her parents, she had inherited two conflicting strains of character: the Warfield calculating toughness and practical ability, and the Montague gentleness and *joie de vivre*. The two elements constantly battled within her; sometimes one would be ascendent, sometimes the other. This may have been mere imagination, but it is what she believed and it conditioned the way she thought. She was also strongly conditioned by her Southern identity and upbringing. Her flirtatiousness, her wit, her fatalism, her notions of hospitality and good living – all these were Southern characteristics, and they were deeply ingrained within her. Ingrained too was the consciousness that her ancestors had been fine people, that the circumstances of her birth, and the way of life which had been forced upon her mother, did not befit their rank. Here was the root of her ambition – a desire to avenge early struggles, to prove herself in the eyes of rich and snobbish cousins, to restore herself to a social and material level which, in her heart, she felt to be rightfully hers.

Wallis's childhood in Baltimore was that of a poor relation. She and her mother clung to each other in a lonely and unfriendly world. They were dependent for their existence on a small and irregular allowance from Alice's eccentric brother-in-law, the railway tycoon Solomon D. Warfield ('Uncle Sol'). At first they lived with Wallis's forbidding Warfield grandmother, who barely tolerated Alice; later with Alice's elder sister, the kindly Bessie Merryman, also a widow. When Alice finally installed herself in a flat of her own, she had to take in paying dinner guests to make ends meet. She trained her daughter to laugh at adversity and make the best of things, and to master those pleasing social arts which are necessary in those dependent on the charity of others. Wallis was sent to the best local schools her mother could afford. Holidays were spent on the estate of her mother's first cousin Lelia Montague Barnett ('Cousin Lelia') at Wakefield in the hunting country of northern Virginia, or on the farm of her uncle, General Henry Warfield ('Uncle Harry'), at Timonium near Baltimore.

3

When Wallis was twelve, Alice married again; her new husband was John Raisin, an indolent middle-aged bachelor with a comfortable private income. Financial cares temporarily vanished, and Wallis was sent to Oldfields, a fashionable girls' boarding-school in the Baltimore hills. Its motto was 'gentleness and courtesy are expected of girls at all times'; like all similar establishments, its purpose was to prepare its pupils for the marriage market. Wallis seems to have been happy and popular there and formed many friendships, the closest of which was with the pretty and high-spirited Mary Kirk. But when she was not quite seventeen her stepfather died, and with him the income which had sustained the family.

Alice's dream was that her daughter should find a well-heeled and well-born Southern husband. Though again destitute, she made sacrifices to have Wallis brought out as a debutante in the social season of 1914–15. At the exclusive Bachelors' Cotillon at Baltimore, and the coming-out tea dance given for her by Cousin Lelia in Washington, Wallis cut a striking figure. She was not beautiful as her mother had once been, but already showed unusual poise and dress sense and knew how to make herself attractive. If somewhat coquettish, she possessed good manners and a lively, original, outgoing personality. She attracted a host of suitors, and seemed to have every prospect of making a glittering match with a suitable 'beau'.

But fate decreed otherwise. Early in 1916, she went on an extended holiday to stay with her cousin Corrine Mustin (younger sister of Cousin Lelia), whose husband commanded a naval station in California. There she succumbed to the charms of a dashing navy aviator from Chicago, Earl Winfield Spencer. He was a Northerner, he was eight years her senior, he possessed neither wealth nor social position, and he was a mere junior grade lieutenant. For all her disappointment, Alice did not oppose the marriage. It took place that November.

Wallis's marriage to 'Win' was a disaster from the start. It was not long before the seductive lieutenant proved himself to be a moody alcoholic, brutal and sadistic in his cups, and suffering from a pathological jealousy. One of his practices was to go out alone for an evening, having locked her in a room or tied her to the bed. Matters seemed to improve with America's entry into the First World War in the spring of 1917: promoted to lieutenant-commander and put in charge of an important air training-station, Spencer sobered up for a

4

while. It was at this period that Wallis - a commanding officer's wife at twenty-one and seeking escape from private unhappiness - began to immerse herself in the arts of housekeeping and entertaining. With the war's end, however, Spencer disintegrated rapidly. He was passed over on account of his intemperate habits and relegated to a desk job at the Navy Department in Washington, where he was maddened by inactivity. His wife bore the brunt of his frustrations. By the end of 1921 - after five years of torment - she could stand it no longer. After a night which she had spent locked in a hotel bathroom, she left him, determined to seek a divorce.

Both the Warfields and the Montagues were scandalized. Divorce was unheard of in either family, and socially unthinkable. Uncle Sol warned her that she would be treated as an outcast, that she could expect no help or inheritance from him. Her mother and Aunt Bessie pleaded with her. Wallis was persuaded to return to her husband; but after a repetition of familiar scenes, they agreed to separate. Wallis went to live with her mother, who had moved to Washington, and Spencer continued to allow her $225 a month out of his navy pay. 'Whatever his faults', she wrote in her memoirs, 'he was essentially a gentleman.'

For six years (1922-8) Wallis led the insecure existence of a married woman living apart from her husband - 'a kind of female Crusoe', as she later put it, 'a castaway upon an emotional sea'. But these were in many ways the happiest years of her life. Having been liberated from a nightmare, she was determined to enjoy what remained of her youth. Well-bred and still attractive, with a lively and winning manner, she was soon surrounded by friends and suitors and much in demand as an 'extra woman' at parties of the Washington diplomatic set. She was elected to the *Soixante Gourmets,* an exclusive dining club whose leading light was her friend Willmott Lewis, the witty Washington correspondent of the London *Times.* Amidst this jolly society she developed from a lonely and suppressed young woman into a gay and amusing companion. She had at least one serious romance during this period - with Felipe Espil, the sensuous First Secretary at the Argentine Embassy (subsequently Argentine Ambassador to the United States). They discussed marriage, but Espil finally decided on a match more likely to advance his career.

In 1924, she travelled abroad for the first time, spending several weeks in Paris with her recently widowed cousin Corrine. She con-

5

sidered applying for a divorce there – when she suddenly received a letter pleading for a reconciliation from Winfield Spencer, now commanding an American gunboat at Hong Kong. Wallis sailed out to join him that July; but after a brief second honeymoon, he resumed his old ways – even forcing her to accompany him to the Chinese brothels he frequented – and so she left him for good. But she remained for almost a year in China; the country fascinated her, and life there was cheap for a European. In Peking she came across an old friend from navy days – the former Katherine Moore Bigelow, now married to Herman Rogers, a delightful and patrician New Yorker. Wallis joined them, and together they enjoyed several months of thrilling experiences (some of them hair-raising, China being in the throes of civil war). It was with regret that she sailed for home in the summer of 1925, after 'what was without doubt the most delightful, the most carefree, the most lyrical interval of my youth – the nearest thing to a lotus-eater's dream that a young woman brought up the "right" way could expect to know'. On the sea voyage she contracted a serious illness from which it took her several months to recover; this was the beginning of the nervous stomach trouble which was to plague her intermittently for the rest of her life.

Wallis was now determined to put an end to her moribund marriage. In order to take advantage of the liberal divorce laws of Virginia, she resided during 1926 and 1927 at a commercial hotel in the pleasant country town of Warrenton. It was near the estate of her Cousin Lelia, which gave her an entrée to the local society; and it was not far from Washington, where she was able intermittently to resume her social life. She also visited New York quite often, where her old schoolfriend Mary Kirk now lived with her French husband, Jacques Raffray. She got to know the Raffrays' friends – and among them was Ernest Simpson.

Ernest was twenty-nine when he first met Wallis late in 1926, one year younger than her. His father was a British subject (said to be of Jewish origin) who had spent most of his life in America and founded a successful firm of shipping brokers with offices in New York and London; he had married an American, from whom he had long since separated, preferring the company of attractive young women. Ernest was the second child of the marriage, and a somewhat belated one; his much older sister, Maud Kerr-Smiley, had married a well-to-do

British politician at the turn of the century and was a well-known figure in London Society. Ernest was brought up in America, but spent long holidays in England and Europe, and was told that he would one day have to choose between his parents' two nationalities. He chose to be British, and in 1918 abandoned his studies at Harvard in order to go to England to join the Coldstream Guards. He was commissioned in this prestigious regiment too late for service in the First World War – but it was an association of which for the rest of his life he remained inordinately proud. After the war he joined the New York office of the family shipping firm. He took an American wife, Dorothea ('Dodie'), and had a daughter by her, Audrey; but they were not happy together, and in 1926 – after only three years of marriage – she commenced divorce proceedings against him.

It was around this time that Ernest met Wallis at the Raffrays' – and took to her immediately. In writing her memoirs, Wallis was always generous to Ernest, who was then still alive.

> Reserved in manner, yet with a gift of quiet wit, always well-dressed, a good dancer, fond of the theatre, and obviously well-read, he impressed me as an unusually well-balanced man.... I was attracted to him and he to me.... However ... the friendship was for a long time nothing more than one of those casual New York encounters between the extra man and the out-of-town woman who find pleasure in each other's tastes.

In 1927, Wallis visited Italy and France as the companion of her Aunt Bessie, who paid for the trip out of an inheritance. As always, it was thrilling for her to see new places, and she made many new friends. She was at Paris in October when she learned of the sudden death of her Uncle Sol. In his will, that dour bachelor left the bulk of his estate – valued at five million dollars – to set up a home for indigent gentlewomen in memory of his mother. Wallis, once thought to have been his principal heiress, was bequeathed the income from a small trust fund of $15,000, to cease in the event of her remarriage.

A few weeks later – on 10 December 1927 – Wallis received her divorce decree at Warrenton. Ernest, who was about to be transferred to his firm's London office, promptly proposed to her. To reflect upon his proposal, she accepted an invitation from her friends the Rogers to

7

— blessed never-to-be-forgotten years.
We have built much — pray God
we destroy nothing. During those
years my love for you has grown
till even I do not know the
depth or the breadth of it, save
that it is something vast and
seemingly immeasurable.

Good-night, my Darling One.

Ernest

A sample of the handwriting of Ernest Simpson.

stay with them at their recently acquired villa at Cannes in the South of France.

She was in no hurry to accept him. He had been an agreeable city escort, but they were utterly dissimilar in personality and outlook. She was gay, carefree, extravagant and spontaneous; he was dull, precise, cautious and pretentious. She looked upon life as an adventure; his attitude was wholly middle class. She was agile in movement, thought and speech; he was a slow, heavy man and something of a bore. One only needs to compare their handwriting – his stiff and jerky copperplate with its over-precise punctuation, her round free hand dashing across the page with barely any punctuation at all – to appreciate the gulf between them. But Ernest offered Wallis something she had come to value above all things – security. After five tormented years with Winfield Spencer, followed by six amusing but rootless years as a single woman, there seemed much to be said for the homely virtues and bourgeois comforts of life with the solid and predictable Ernest.

Following her stay with the Rogers at Cannes, Wallis moved to London, which she now saw for the first time. It was from there that she wrote to her mother in Washington on 15 July 1928, in a tone which can only be described as one of resignation.

Dearest Mother,

I've decided definitely that the best and wisest thing for me to do is to marry Ernest. I am very fond of him and he is *kind* which will be a contrast. He has promised that I can come home once a year for a 3 months visit to see you. I decided finally Friday and we made some arrangements yesterday, so hope to have everything completed so as to be married Saturday. It is simple here, we just go to a Registry Office and the deed is done in 15 minutes. We will then have lunch with his father and small nephew aged 22[1] and afterwards motor to Dover the next day crossing to France – car – chauffeur. We will motor a bit in Northern France arriving Paris the 24 and be there to meet Aunt Bessie. We may motor to Barcelona and if so can take Aunt Bessie as far as Biarritz. I am so crazy to see her. Ernest's sister is really so attractive and has been too lovely to me and introduced me to quite a lot of people. Unfortunately she goes to the hospital today for an operation so will not be able to be at the large wedding breakfast. Mummie I shall miss having you with me terribly but the second

1. Peter Kerr-Smiley, whom Wallis did not afterwards wish to know.

Wallis

Stanmore Court
29, St. James's St

July 15<u>th</u>

Dearest Mother —

I've decided definitely that
the best and wisest thing for me to do
is to marry Ernest — I am very fond
of him and he is kind which will be
a contrast — he has promised that I
can <u>come</u> home once a year for a
3 months' visit to see you — I decided
finally Friday and we made some
arrangements yesterday — so hope to
have everything completed so as to
be married Saturday — It is simple
here we just go to a Registry office

time doesn't really somehow seem so important – and I shall come home after Christmas. I wish I could persuade Aunt B to come to London until then and return with her. London is fairly gloomy – I'm sure I shall be lonely next winter and homesick. However, I can't go wandering on the rest of my life and I really feel so tired of fighting the world all alone and with no money. Also 32 doesn't seem so young when you see all the really fresh youthful faces one has to compete against. So I shall just settle down to a fairly comfortable old age. I hope you just announced my marriage to Ernest Simpson of NY. Do you think necessary to send out cards? I don't. I hope this hasn't upset you darling – but I should think you would feel happier knowing somebody was looking after me. The heat here is appalling at the moment and it is hard to think.

All my love to you – and do send wishes for success this time.

WALLIS

PS I sent Uncle Harry a cable and have written a note.

Ernest then sent a telegram to Alice:

REALISE YOUR NATURAL ANXIETY WALLIS HASTEN ASSURE YOU MY GREATEST DESIRE DO UTMOST HER HAPPINESS WELFARE WILL BRING HER HOME SOON WRITING.

ERNEST

and on 21 July, Alice received another telegram:

EVERYTHING PASSED OFF SMOOTHLY SAFELY RETRANSFERRED TO MATRIMONY LOVE

WALLIS ERNEST

The marriage began under good auspices. He was in love with her; and she was conscious of 'a security that I had never really experienced since early childhood'. They discovered that they enjoyed doing the simple things of life together. They were also blessed with prosperity. Ernest's shipping firm was booming; and Wallis received an unexpected capital of $37,500 (in the form of American shares) from Uncle Sol's executors, who were buying off various members of the Warfield family who had threatened to challenge his eccentric will. They were able to start life in London by renting a handsome West End town house for a year, fully furnished and staffed. Wallis found that it was cheaper to live in England than in America on an equivalent income.

London in 1928 was a bustling metropolis of over four million people, whose famous squares and parks, fine domestic architecture and imposing public buildings befitted the capital of an empire which encompassed one quarter of the world. The aristocracy (though chill winds had begun to blow about them) still lived in their great houses, and there was a large and prosperous middle class. The City, where Ernest's firm had its offices, remained the world's principal financial and trading centre. But London was also badly planned, dirty and overcrowded. There was misery (though traditionally assuaged by a philosophical cheerfulness) in some quarters; and in winter, heavy fogs combined with the smoke of numerous chimneys to produce notoriously disgusting atmospheric conditions.

Economically it was quite a stable time, though Britain had never recovered her trading position after the First World War, and unemployment (while modest compared with the heights to which it would soar in the 1930s) remained fairly high. There was growing industrial unrest: 1926 had seen a long coal strike and a general strike. In the aftermath of war, there had been a loosening of old-fashioned morals and a general spirit of enjoyment. It was the era of jazz, cocktails and cigarettes, of women's emancipation and the 'bright young things'. At the same time, however, it was quite a reactionary period: post-war governments had retained much repressive wartime legislation, and took a tough line on such matters as censorship, immigration and 'offences concerning morals'. The times therefore represented something of a mixture between puritanism and hedonism – a paradox which will be familiar to readers of the novels of Evelyn Waugh. A Conservative Government was then in power under Stanley Baldwin, to be replaced by Socialists under Ramsay MacDonald the following year. It was popularly believed that war had been abolished by the League of Nations, the Washington Disarmament Conference, and the Locarno Pact. The Church of England was in the midst of a great campaign to consolidate its hold over its followers. The monarchy, represented by the dull and conservative King George V and Queen Mary with their life of blameless routine, was more popular than it had ever been, being regarded as a symbol of order and tradition at a time of uncertainty and change.

This was the world in which Wallis came to live on her marriage to Ernest Simpson. Although it seemed to promise her a good standard of life and a reasonably happy domestic existence, it at first seemed frightening and unfamiliar. The English struck her as cold and difficult to get to know, and hidebound by custom and tradition. She found the city 'all cold, grey stone and dingy brick, ancient dampness and drabness, and a purposeful hurry and push in the streets', its climate giving it an air of 'incredible greyness and gloominess', the fogs covering everything with 'a sooty grey dinginess'. In time she came to admire these peculiarities of London and the English; but in the first winter of her marriage, they depressed her. And fond though she undoubtedly was of her husband, she cannot have found the early experience of life with Ernest Simpson – with his intense seriousness, clockwork routine, and characteristic insistence that they spend one evening a week going through household accounts – altogether enlivening. As she had predicted in her letter to her mother before her marriage, she felt lonely and homesick. Her sister-in-law, Maud Kerr-Smiley, tried to introduce her to English people and English ways, but Wallis found her snobbish and patronizing, and the two women did not get on.

Nor did she have much love for her parents-in-law, of whom she was obliged to see far more than she would have wished. Their marriage had long since broken down, and their anxiety to avoid each other's company was such that they generally made a point of never being in England at the same time, the arrival of one heralding the departure of the other. In her memoirs, Wallis – doubtless having regard to the susceptibilities of her still-living ex-husband – writes of them with mild affection. In the letters which will be quoted here, however, she depicts Ernest's father as a miserly and cantankerous old satyr, his mother as a tedious frump. Both demanded much attention; and Wallis came to resent this, and the fact that, despite their apparently ample means, they did so little to help Ernest materially.

Every week, Wallis exchanged letters with her own mother, who was now living in Washington with her third husband, Charles Gordon Allen ('Charlie'), a minor civil servant whom she had married in 1926.

Alice's side of the correspondence has survived: barely legible, and consisting mostly of family gossip interspersed with culinary recipes, it cannot be said to be particularly interesting. It does, however, reveal three significant facts. The first is that Alice sorely missed her daughter. ('I dreamed about you last night and was so upset as you looked so thin and badly.... This worries me all the time.') The second is that the now quite affluent Wallis was supporting her mother with regular cheques. The third is that Alice (as one might gather from the messages with which the couple had tried to reassure her in the summer of 1928) did not approve of Wallis's marriage to Ernest, whom she had never met. Indeed, in Alice's letters the name of Ernest is conspicuous by its absence: even her good wishes for the new year of 1929 are pointedly addressed to Wallis alone.

Wallis, however, was passionately devoted to her mother, and on hearing in May 1929 that she had suffered a stroke, crossed the Atlantic by the next boat to be at her bedside. The spectacle which awaited her was a shock: at fifty-nine, Alice, who had never known a day's illness and had always been a gay and youthful spirit, had suddenly become an old woman and a half-blind, bedridden invalid. Wallis wished to remain with her; but Ernest pleaded with her to return, which after two months she did, satisfied that her mother's condition was stable and that she would be looked after by Aunt Bessie. The summer which followed was an anxious one. 'I can't help but be sad underneath everything', she wrote to Aunt Bessie, 'and I know Ernest does not find me as gay and carefree a companion as before. He is sweet and understanding and marvellous to me and realises how hard it is to be torn between two people and places....' Meanwhile Alice's condition deteriorated. 'It was so terribly disappointing to get your letter tonight with its news of mummy', Wallis wrote to Aunt Bessie in October. 'I feel desperate being so far away and knowing she is not getting better and wants and needs me there with her and to think of you having to bear it all alone. I don't think I am much use here as I'm really so sad the majority of the time I'm not a fit companion.' Wallis returned to Washington, but by the time she got there her mother was in a coma. She died at the beginning of November.

Alice's illness and premature death was a trauma for Wallis and intensified her feelings of inner loneliness. The memory of her mother and of the sacrifices she had endured was to haunt her and to act as a spur to success in her social career. As she wrote to Aunt Bessie in April 1934, when she suddenly found herself the favourite of the Prince of Wales and sought after by the best society: 'Wouldn't mother have loved it all?'

It was to Aunt Bessie that Wallis now transferred her filial affections. Mrs D. Buchanan Merryman was then sixty-six. She was plump, kindly, witty and forthright; born during the American Civil War, she was the epitome of an old-fashioned Southern woman and revered by numerous friends. She lived in Washington, where since 1914 she had been employed on generous terms as companion to Miss Mary B. Adams, a newspaper heiress. It was to this worldly-wise and affection-ate relative that Wallis now looked up as her guardian angel and confidante. For the next twenty years, she was to address a constant stream of letters to her, spontaneous and gossipy accounts of her life and her feelings and thoughts. Though often banal (for they relate a largely banal existence), they are fascinating documents of social his-tory; and they eventually amount to nothing less than a diary of her slowly developing relationship with the man who would give up king-ship for her.

At the end of 1929 Wallis and Ernest found a place of their own in London – Number 5, Bryanston Court, a modest but comfortable first-floor flat in a fashionable new block near the bustling shopping precincts of Oxford Street and the Edgware Road. It consisted of drawing-room, dining-room, three bedrooms and a modern kitchen, with four rooms for servants elsewhere in the building. Wallis threw herself with delight into the task of doing it up, which she did with the help of the well-known decorator Syrie Maugham, wife of the novelist. Modern colours and fabrics contrasted agreeably with a few well-chosen pieces of antique furniture. She began to collect silver, china and glass. She engaged servants: the matter of servants (now becoming less freely available) was to exercise her considerably over the next few years, as with all middle-class women in England. Her staff ultimately consisted of a chauffeur, Hughes (paid for by Ernest's firm); her personal maid, Mary Burke; a housemaid, Agnes; an excel-lent Scottish parlourmaid, Mary Cain; and a cook. This was a fairly normal London household at that period for a 'professional' couple with an income of about £1,500 a year. Wallis was a perfectionist and an exacting mistress, though those who stayed the course received a training which served them well in their future careers.

Thus established, the Simpsons soon formed a circle of friends. It was largely drawn from the United States Embassy, where Wallis already knew a number of people from her days as a service wife and her Washington period. These included the Naval Attaché, William ('Billy') Galbraith, and his wife Katherine; the Air Attaché, Martin ('Mike') Scanlon; and the Second Secretary, Walter Prendergast. Then, in the middle of 1930, Wallis's cousin Corrine came to live in London with her second husband George Murray, who had been appointed Assistant Naval Attaché and Galbraith's deputy.

Most of the Simpsons' other friends belonged to the then large American business community in London. Their only good English friends were Bernard Rickatson-Hatt, editor-in-chief of Reuters, Ernest's old comrade-in-arms from his brief service in the Guards, and his wife Frances; and George and Kitty Hunter, a jolly couple introduced by Maud Kerr-Smiley before she and Wallis drifted apart.

By the end of 1930, Wallis had already acquired something of a reputation as a hostess among this rather limited circle. Though her flat was little different from hundreds of others of its type, she had managed to create an unusually warm and welcoming atmosphere there. She was known for her good food, and for the smooth and efficient way she ran her household. She had initiated the agreeable custom, not especially common in England, of being at home to all comers every evening at the cocktail hour – and many came.

Wallis felt infinitely happier than she had done two and a half years earlier, when she had first settled in London. But two factors marred life's pleasant prospect. Her health was uncertain: she suffered periodic attacks from a duodenal ulcer. And the easy prosperity which had marked the early days of her marriage had vanished. Following the Wall Street Crash of October 1929, the economic crisis had arrived. Ernest's family shipping firm found itself in serious difficulties. The American shares Wallis had inherited from Uncle Sol rapidly dwindled in value; by the time she had settled the bills of the doctors and nurses who had looked after her mother during her protracted illness, not much remained. The Simpsons' comfortable existence, with nightly dinner parties, a flatful of servants, a car and driver, and foreign travel, was becoming increasingly difficult to sustain.

On 28 December 1930, Wallis wrote a somewhat dispirited seasonal letter to Aunt Bessie, from whom she had received a Christmas cheque.

'You're much too good and generous and I'm ashamed to accept any more from you. You really spoil me as much as mother did yet you know how rotten I am!' The gift was much appreciated: for their financial situation was grimmer than ever, and Ernest's family not disposed to help.

> The best yet for Xmas cheer was a stiff letter from Mr Simpson wishing us the usual bunk and saying due to hard times he was not giving any presents this year. Really can you think of anything quite so small? I think the girl [the elder Simpson's young French mistress] most dangerous and he'll probably leave or give all his money to her – but the family are powerless to intervene.

She made some wry comments on the news that her stepfather Charlie was remarrying only a year after Alice's death. Other complaints were of the London weather ('... foul fogs and everything is getting so dirty in the flat ...') and her health: her ulcer had been causing trouble, and she feared she would have to have her tonsils out in 1931.

She concluded with the news that Benjamin Thaw, the new First Secretary at the US Embassy, would be coming to dinner the following evening. She already knew him quite well: his brother had been a navy colleague of Winfield Spencer, and she had met him during her days with the Washington diplomatic set. He would be bringing his wife, Consuelo *née* Morgan, and also her sister, Thelma, Viscountess Furness. Thelma, as Wallis presumably knew, had for the past three years been the mistress of the Prince of Wales.

PART ONE

Wallis and the Prince

JANUARY 1931–JANUARY 1936

CHAPTER ONE
1931: Acquaintance

With the aid of Wallis's letters to her Aunt Bessie, it is now at last possible to establish the exact date of her first meeting with the Prince of Wales. Writing in the 1950s, the Duchess of Windsor placed the event in November 1930; the Duke thought it might have been in the autumn of 1931.[1] Both their memories were at fault. The fateful encounter took place at Burrough Court, Lady Furness's country house at Melton Mowbray in Leicestershire, on Saturday, 10 January 1931.

In her memoirs, the Duchess has described the circumstances of the meeting. The Prince was to spend the second week-end of 1931 with Thelma Furness at Melton Mowbray; and Thelma's sister, Consuelo Thaw, was due to travel down with her husband Benjamin as chaperon. But at the last moment 'Connie' was called away to Paris, to the bedside of her sick mother-in-law. She asked Wallis to go with Ernest in her stead; 'Benny' would accompany them.

Wallis tells us that, though thrilled, she was not a little agitated at the prospect of spending a week-end in the company of the heir to the throne, and hesitated accepting. She was terrified by the advice of her patronizing sister-in-law, Maud Kerr-Smiley, on how to behave with royalty. She was also in the throes of a feverish cold. Ernest, however, would not hear of their refusing; and so they went.

Edward, Prince of Wales, was then in his thirty-seventh year, though he looked much younger. He was known for his melancholy good looks, his democratic sentiments and his unconventional habits. Since 1928 his father had been in poor health, and the prospect of succession to the throne – a prospect which he seemed to regard with a strange foreboding – loomed before him. He was a leader of fashion, and through his journeyings abroad and throughout the Empire had

---

1. The Duchess of Windsor, *The Heart has its Reasons* (Michael Joseph, London, 1956); the Duke of Windsor, *A King's Story* (Cassels, London, 1951).

become an international superstar. In a few days' time he was due to embark on a four-month goodwill tour of South America, on which he would be accompanied by his handsome and lively brother Prince George, then twenty-eight.

Thursday, Jan 8th   5, Bryanston Court, Bryanston Square, W.1.

Dearest Aunt Bessie

We are fog bound and ice bound at the same time – there is no excuse for such a climate. Both Katherine [Galbraith] and myself are struggling with colds. She has had hers since before Xmas. Mine is new. So I'm staying in bed today to try and lose it. Be patient with my handwriting as a result. I can't remember exactly where I left off with my news in my last letter. We have been quite busy since New Years the eve of which passed off pleasantly at the Savoy. NY's day the Grants had eggnog[1] and that week-end we went to the country getting home Sunday in time for a KT [cocktail] party George [Murray][2] was having. Monday I had 10 for dinner including George. Gordon [Mustin][3] has been in bed for a week with a rotten cold but is up and much better now. Tuesday we dined with the Galbraiths and last night the Holts and tonight was to be the Andersens[4] but I've backed out as I want to lose this cold.

Tuesday, Jan 13th. I never finished the letter as Friday I got up and spent the entire day on hair and nails etc as Saturday we were going to Melton Mowbray to stay with Lady Furness (Mrs Thaw's sister) and the Prince of Wales was also to be a guest. In spite of cold we took the 3.20 train with Ben Thaw Saturday, Connie being in Paris. We arrived at 6.30 and the Prince & Thelma Furness came about 7.30, also Prince George and the Prince's equerry Gen. Trotter.[5] Prince

1. Lester E. Grant (1884–1965), an American mining engineer based in London, where he was local representative of Guggenheim Bros. His wife was Roberta Hamilton. Eggnog: a rich American punch made with brandy and cream, traditionally drunk cold at the Christmas season.
2. Commander George Murray of the US Embassy, married to Wallis's cousin Corrine who was in America at this moment.
3. Corrine's adolescent son by her earlier marriage.
4. Reginald Andersen, a London businessman, and his American wife, Mildred.
5. Brigadier-General G. F. ('G') Trotter (1871–1945), Groom-in-Waiting to the Prince of Wales, 1921–36. A jovial and rakish character devoted to his master, he had lost an arm in the Boer War.

and to-night was to be the
Andersens **5 BRYANSTON COURT** but I've
Lacked **BRYANSTON SQUARE.W.1.** not as
AMBASSADOR 2215.
I want to lose the cold.

———————

Tuesday, Jan 13

I never finished the letter
as Friday I got up and
spent the entire day on
hair and nails etc as
Saturday we were going
to Melton Mowbray to stay
with Lady Furness (Thelma's
sister) and the Prince
of Wales was also to be a guest.

George stayed a while and then went on to Lady Wodehouse where he was staying. That left just 7 of us – so you can imagine what a treat it was to meet the Prince in such an informal way. There was no dinner party Sat night but Sunday she had 10 for dinner, Prince George returning for that. We came back yesterday at lunch time. It was quite an experience and as I've had my mind made up to meet him ever since I've been here I feel relieved. I never expected however to accomplish it in such an informal way and Prince George as well.

Think it's grand about Willmott [Lewis].[1] The Thaws and ourselves sent them a poem by cable – hope it didn't arrive garbled. We told the Prince what the King had done regarding Ethel![2] Am having an awful domestic upheaval so life is not too pleasant. Hughes was impudent to Ernest so was sacked on the spot. We have a new man tomorrow, entirely different type. I also dismissed my maid 'for age' yesterday upon my return and have a new one coming Monday. The cook is *hopeless* so I'm dismissing her on the 18th which means she will be leaving February 18th and I'm afraid to get the sort of cook I want I shall have to come to a kitchen maid. Can you beat it? Kitty Hunter[3] has *no one* can't find anyone without a kitchen maid – all so absurd. You haven't told me whether you have sent the table and what I owe for it. Give Corrine [Murray] a cheese scoop for me and the Arts & Crafts on Conn. Ave have some bridge scores with your initials on top – I should like 4 of these initialed in red – and a set of fillers for them. You must have some recipes – entrees and egg dishes especially. Going to George's for KTs this p.m., he's busy with that sort of party but otherwise very quiet and faithful to the last ditch. Mildred Andersen wants to present me at Court this year[4] and though I would rather have someone else do it I don't think it matters just so you go. The

1. The well-known Washington correspondent of *The Times*, who had received a knighthood in the New Year's Honours of 1931. He was a good friend of Wallis from her Washington days, as was his second wife Ethel Noyes.
2. The crack was that it had taken George v to 'make a lady' of Ethel.
3. George and Kitty Hunter were Wallis's best English friends in London. She described them in her memoirs as 'very British, very charming, and wonderful hosts. Florid, portly and hearty, George was the epitome of an English country squire; a man of means, he never had to work, so far as I could judge. ... Both he and Kitty, having travelled widely, knew as much about food as any amateurs I have had the good fortune to meet.'
4. Presentation at Court – a curtsey to the sovereign wearing formal dress – was a picturesque ceremony which, up to the Second World War, marked the official admission of a debutante into London Society. It was necessary to be sponsored by a woman who had herself been presented. Divorced women had once been ineligible, but could now be presented provided they could show they had been the innocent party.

Lord Chamberlain asked for my divorce decree as they have to be sure who did the divorcing. I can't find it – must have mislaid it so have asked Madge Larrabee[1] for a copy to be sent at once as the longer held up the later the Court one gets. You might just ring her up and see if she has got it off to me. We miss you – and it's so silly having the ocean between us – though the winter is too harrowing here. It's my last if I have the money to get out next year. All love,

WALLIS

Such was the manner in which Wallis signalled to her aunt her first encounter with the man who, within six years, would renounce a throne in order to be married to her – a banal few lines sandwiched between an account of her cold and an account of her servant troubles.

In her memoirs, the Duchess of Windsor gives a more detailed account of the episode. There she described the train journey to Leicester with Ernest and 'Benny' Thaw, in the course of which she practised her curtsey; their arrival at Melton Mowbray to find the countryside shrouded in freezing fog; the long and nerve-racking wait for Thelma and the two Princes, in the course of which her cold turned streaming and she began to run a temperature. She told of how she thought the Prince surprisingly small but otherwise like his famous photographs, and of how enchanting she found his 'utter naturalness' and his 'gaiety and joie de vivre'. She wrote that she and Ernest felt thoroughly out of place as the strangers among a large aristocratic company interested mainly in horses; but that the Prince put her at ease, conversing with her casually but pleasantly about the American way of life. She wondered whether he was happy, and why he had not married. She concluded her account by remarking that she had found him

an altogether charming but remote figure, not quite of the workaday world – a figure whose opportunities and behaviour were regulated by laws different from those to which the rest of us responded. I had already dismissed from my mind the possibility of our ever meeting again. A woman with the sniffles and a croaking voice would scarcely be judged a desirable addition to the bright company that revolved around the Prince of Wales.

Wallis's other letters to her aunt that winter certainly suggest that she had regarded her meeting with the Prince as no more than a

1. Mrs Sterling Larrabee, a friend who lived near Warrenton where Wallis had received her divorce.

thrilling chance encounter, unlikely to be repeated. They mention his name only in passing. For the most part, they deal with the mundane fabric of her everyday life – problems with servants; purchases; entertaining and being entertained; the struggle to keep up living standards amidst economic depression; the saga of Ernest's family; disenchantment with London and homesickness for America. Where she does write about the Prince, it is in a jocular and schoolgirlish vein. She is coyly uncertain whether to break the news of her seeing him to her friends in America – though she is glad to note that it has made her sister-in-law jealous. She wistfully doubts whether she will 'ever hear of or see any of them again' – though perhaps she might come across the Prince at Thelma's after his return frm South America, or in connection with her forthcoming presentation at Court. . . .

The Prince of Wales, delightful but unreal, belongs for her to a dream world, a world utterly different from her 'real' world as the wife of Ernest Simpson, the humdrum, middle-class world of Bryanston Court. What is fascinating, in her letters to Aunt Bessie over the next five years, is to observe the counterpoint between these two worlds. At first the Prince only makes an occasional appearance as a note of fairy tale in the midst of a very ordinary life. But eventually – very gradually, and quite unexpectedly – the fairy tale will take over.

Thursday, Jan 22nd   Bryanston Court

Dearest Aunt B

The hams have just arrived and are being unpacked at the moment. Please let me know what I owe, including shipping table. Speaking of the latter, have you heard from Win whether he received it? I am sorry for his wife if he has started drinking, also I am sorry for him.[1] Sent you a wire as I would not like it put in paper I had been on a houseparty with HRH. I hear from Kitty [Hunter] that Maud is in a state over our having got that far. Serves her right. Can't help but feel we are better off without her anyway. My cold has gone but Katherine and Billy can't get rid of theirs so go to the south somewhere for the month of February. There is no news really – dinner and bridge continue and Ernest and myself have lost constantly – in fact £14 together last week – *rather awful*. I have a terrible longing for the sight of the

1. Through her aunt, Wallis had returned some furniture to her previous husband, Winfield Spencer, who had recently remarried.

sea and something green – this really has been a winter – electric light the entire day – it does weaken the morale. Let me know what I owe otherwise I can't ask you to get anything more for me. All love

WALLIS

Wednesday the 28th [January]   Bryanston Court

Dearest Aunt B

Can't think of anything to tell you. Am in such a gale over domestics – you know how I go to pieces. Have my second chauffeur since Hughes was sacked and I think I have got a grand one this time. As to cooks it's too awful – this single handed business and wages are going up each day. We are going to have to come to a kitchen maid without doubt and how we'll afford the extra expense we can't figure out. I do think it worth while to give up something for a really good cook but E says I never do the giving up! Kitchen maids are £35-40 per year and cooks £85 – then food, washing & insurance added makes the 2 come up to American wages. I would have to put the k.m. in Agnes' room and buy furniture for her. Sorry to bore you but can think of nothing else....

Thursday, Feb. 5th   Bryanston Court

Dearest Aunt Bessie

Am sure the cat is out of the bag about HRH as I wrote Mary Raffray[1] the news and I have a letter from her today saying she was in Baltimore when she received my letter and couldn't resist telling Dr Taylor! So you may as well have the fun of telling Cousin L[elia]. You could say I did not want it put in the paper however. Should also like Ethel [Lewis] to know we were travelling high for once in our London life. My cold completely gone. Thanks loads for the recipes – will try them on my next effort. Mary R says she is coming over in the spring – she is always on her way but nothing happens. I have bought a black satin evening dress – the first thing to wear I've bought since our orgy in Paris.[2] Not bad for me. I do hope Thelma Furness will ask us again

1. Wallis's old schoolfriend, somewhat loosely married to her French husband, Jacques ('Jackie') Raffray.
2. A spending spree of the previous summer, when Aunt Bessie was holidaying on the Continent with the Simpsons.

27

with the Prince when their respective trips are over. Probably we will never hear of or see any of them again however. Take care of yourself. I do wish we were nearer to each other and both didn't have to remain so glued to the source of supply. All my love

WALLIS

Was Wallis socially ambitious? She thought the English notions of 'class' most peculiar, and treated her coming Presentation at Court as a mildly exciting joke. But there can be no doubt that she was highly enthusiastic about the prospect of meeting interesting and fashionable new people, and moving in more exalted circles – as was Ernest, who 'dearly loved a lord'. Both of them were keen to 'get on'.

At a bridge party at the house of their friend 'Mike' Scanlon, the attractive bachelor of forty-one who was air attaché at the US Embassy, they met Anne, Lady Sackville, the American chatelaine of one of the great houses of England. . . .

Tuesday, Feb 10th   Bryanston Court

Dearest Aunt B

Thanks for cable. It was cheering to know you were thinking of me. I am expecting the new cook a week from tomorrow and am now frantically searching a kitchen maid. We have not done much lately – nearly everyone has gone in search of sun. Sunday we motored to Knole to have tea with Lord and Lady Sackville.[1] I've met them since you left. I suppose Knole is the most famous house in England. It's immense and really wonderful. We hope now that we have been looked over we'll be asked for a week-end. We have spent the last 2 nights deciding whether to borrow on E's insurance or put a mortgage he holds up – he has to put money back into the firm this year and we don't want to change our way of living now we are all installed and meeting new people ever so often – so we must borrow about 12 or 14 thousand $ to continue in said form and also return to the firm what he has to. He is going to try Pa first but I think that will be a crash. Everyone here thinks things are going to be even worse and that nothing bright will happen before 1935. Isn't it too depressing? What

1. Major-General Charles Sackville-West, 4th Baron Sackville (1870–1962), and his second wife Anne Meredith, an American actress. Uncle of the writer Vita Sackville-West, Charles Sackville had succeeded to the title and to the Knole estate in Kent in 1928.

do people think in your part of the world? The fogs have been awful and made things so dirty in the flat – you should see the curtains – am having them cleaned room by room. Am having a time with the divorce things. Have got the copy of the [divorce] decree OK. Now they [the Lord Chamberlain's Office] ask for the shorthand notes of the case – the idea being to prove nothing was said against me. They showed E reams of divorce notes they had there of others. So I've written away for the evidence. In the meantime if I ever see the Prince again I shall ask him to help – though I'm not mad to go. All love

WALLIS

Friday the 6th [March]   Bryanston Court

Dearest Aunt B

Nothing new here except I've got a grand cook, if she'll only stay and we can afford to keep her as she is extravagant.[1] Mrs Simpson *threatens* to come over the end of March or April to talk Pa over with the children.[2] Won't it be too awful? I would go to Paris for clothes if I had the cash and miss most of the rioting as E foresees the whole thing ending in a grand row. We may have to make the gesture of asking her here. E says she won't come. I hate taking the chance however. Mildred is doing my portrait, not bad so far. The Grants are giving an advertisement party the 21st and I can't think what ad to go as. Don't know what I'll do for spring clothes as have put everything in the flat. We are having table made for 12 now as it's cheaper to have 3 tables of bridge than two dinners of 8. I am concentrating on visiting you in the fall with or without E. Love

WALLIS

Saturday the 21st [March]   Bryanston Court

Dearest Aunt B

Tonight is Berta Grant's advertisement party. I am going as a tube of Odol tooth paste in blue oil cloth with silver oil cloth yoke and round silver cap and Odol in white letters across the dress. Ernest goes

1. Formerly Lady Curzon's kitchen-maid, Mrs Ralph proved herself under Wallis's guidance to be an outstanding cook.
2. Ernest's aged father had shocked his children and his estranged wife by taking a young French mistress.

as Guinness. It's been a lot of trouble so I hope it's fun. Katherine is to be Dutch cleanser and Billy Dewars scotch. Yesterday at Tamar [Consuelo] Thaw's I met Miss Frazer.[1] She is stopping at the Park Lane. Seems to be at a loose end but came to be near her friend Mrs Shane Leslie[2] and she has invited Tamar and self to the latter's house for bridge next Thursday so I am having them lunch here first. My papers are here and I have been OKed by the Lord Chamberlain so now it remains for a command. You're an angel to offer the dress. I may ask your help for the train and headdress – the dress I can use as an evening dress all year. We don't want to go unless he can get us into a June Court. Take care of yourself and have plenty of people to see you. I am of course sorry for Charlie[3] but can't be surprised. I am more than thankful mother is not here to have to face his long illness and debts, aren't you? As for that old rice pudding I don't give a damn. All my love Aunt Bessie darling

WALLIS

Good Friday [10 April]   Bryanston Court

Dearest Aunt Bessie

Thanks a 1000 times for the Easter present. I don't know what I'll invest it in at the moment – possibly something for my table. Anyway it will be in something that will last and not go towards clothes. We are spending Easter at home – that is until Sunday when we go to the Crimmies in Kent for a night. They return with us also for the night and to the theatre. We had a grand invitation to go to the Osbornes (Polly Reyburn's ex) from today until Monday but unfortunately had accepted the Crimmies first. Today we are dining with the Thaws and Mrs Vanderbilt[4] who arrived from the USA yesterday. I hope to be able to have a month at Cannes with Tamar and Mrs V. I think I would probably meet some interesting people through them. Loads of love and many thanks for my Easter egg. You know how much I appreciate all you do for me and us.

WALLIS

1. A friend of Aunt Bessie whose brother was to become US Consul-General in London. An enormous woman, she was the mistress of the war correspondent Ashmead Bartlett.
2. The American wife of Shane Leslie, the eminent Irish eccentric and man of letters.
3. Wallis's stepfather, Charles Gordon Allen.
4. Thelma's twin sister, the widowed Gloria Vanderbilt, who was to be involved three years later in the most famous custody case of American history.

The Prince of Wales was due to return from his South American tour at the end of April. Having got on so well with the Morgan sisters and their friends, Wallis began to wonder whether she might not soon have the chance to see him again.

Meanwhile her letters reflect her anxieties about money and her health.

Thursday, April 16th   Bryanston Court

Darling

We had a rainy Easter at the Crimmies, cold and clammy and the bathroom miles from the rooms. However I went to an English point-to-point for the first time and now understand the pictures of women in boots, tweeds etc. We got covered with mud and the Costa shoes stood it well. Nothing exciting here. Too much gloom about in No. 5. The business seems to be going to the bow-wows. They have cut salaries in the office here (not E's) and laid off people in the NY office. I think our car will go next. It's a bit of a strain until things pick up. Tamar's sister Mrs Vanderbilt is grand. We have been to a party she gave and also to spend last Sunday with Lady Milford Haven[1] in the country. She is Lady Mountbatten's sister-in-law. It is nice for us to meet all these swell people even if we can't keep up their pace! I have had the latter [Lady Milford Haven] for luncheon etc and she is to be in the Cannes party which consists of Tamar, Lady M. Haven, Gloria V., starting July first. Tamar and self have figured we can do 5 weeks there for $500 including taking her Ford and getting a French chauffeur. I have decided to borrow from the bank as poor old E can't help me. By all laws I should not move this summer but I feel it would be worth it to go with those girls as I would meet such nice people, English as well which would help here, and I do crave some hot sun. Had a stomach attack just before Easter and found a grand Dr who has me feeling better than I have for ages on some machine and a reasonable diet that is possible to keep to. E very leery about my going to USA, says I spend so much money when I go away. We'll see – and if we're stony you'll have to come here in spite of fogs. I've done nothing – there was no reason to really – and Cain[2] is away

1. Nada, Countess Torby, morganatic daughter of the Grand Duke Michael of Russia. She had married George, 2nd Marquess of Milford Haven, the brother of Lord Louis Mountbatten.
2. The Simpsons' parlourmaid.

and the pink sofa cover being cleaned. My dining room curtains fell
to bits when cleaned and I don't think drawing room ones and my
room will stand another so am having Peter Jones make new ones out
of celanese voile which I hear is the rage in America. We are invited
by Lady Sackville for the week-end of the 16th of May to stay at
Knole. It will be divine to stay in such a house. Gloria V. and the
Thaws are giving a party May 24th and I'm hoping HRH will be
there. I would like to be given the once-over without the cold. Mr
Simpson and 2 partners arrive next Tuesday then I shall probably run
into Maud. I hear she is wild because we have got about a bit this
winter and without her assistance. No word about Court as yet but I
believe they only give 3 weeks' notice. All my love and in spite of
depression we will see each other somewhere in the fall. The complication of my coming to you is the fact that this place has to run and
then I have expenses there. You know how money can be spent by me
in the USA.

WALLIS

Tuesday night [28 April]   Bryanston Court

Dearest Aunt Bessie
    I am spending the evening alone as Ernest has gone to a business
dinner with the partners who have all been here a week tonight,
including Pa. The latter seems well but has some pain in the face at
the moment. The French hussy is not being asked to the house. E and
Maud had one conference but we have not made up. I haven't seen
her. So far there has been no time for E to have a talk with Mr S
about our finances so I am not able to make any plans until we know
where we are. Business gets no better. Only R. Andersen is prosperous
– electrical things are at last being installed in England. Mildred has
car & chauffeur, champagne flows, and many parties at that dreary
Hungaria[1] where we went. Corrine had a party at last – 10 for Sunday
night supper. Bob Dickey[2] was here yesterday – had tea with him at
Corrine's. He was operated on this a.m. for his back. We think it too
bad it wasn't the other side. Minerva and Johnnie starting to fight
have had the results of several scenes brought over here. Can you beat
it though I knew nothing so 100% could continue. One butter plate

1. A well-known restaurant of the period with a gipsy orchestra.
2. Married to a daughter of Wallis's Cousin Lelia.

has been thrown. Isn't it grand. E and self seem to be the turtle doves. It's cold here. Am still wearing my fur coat and rain each day. Mary [Raffray] wrote she may sail about May 20th and would stay with us if OK 2 or 3 weeks. It is not a gala year for her visit unless she catches a beau and I don't know anyone for her except [Mike] Scanlon who is still in America. My table works quite well with 12 and the room not too crowded. May 6 I'm having Lord & Lady Sackville, Lady Milford Haven, Lady Fitzherbert,[1] Tamar and Mrs Vanderbilt with men for dinner and bridge. Haven't had any KT parties – it's so ruinous to everything. Hope everything all right with you. All love

WALLIS

Hope I thanked you for the Easter cable. You should not have sent it in these days of depression.

Sunday the 11th [May]   Bryanston Court

Darling

I was sorry about poor old Charlie. That's all there seems to be to say, he didn't really have much of a time of this earth did he? I hope you kept well away from that dreadful house during it all. Write me what you will do with our furniture. If you think it wise to sell all except the chair which I have sentiment about it's all right by me. Also the black lacquer table with lamp could be used in my room here. I might arrange to bring it back with me in the winter. Mary cabled she sails on the Caronia May 22nd. Isn't it awful? What am I to do with her for a month? We had a nice dinner party last Wed and now I'll rest until the Lewises' arrival next week and hope to do something for them Friday night. Nothing about Court as yet. Let me know what I owe for Charlie's flowers. Mrs Kendall now [Betty] Lawson Johnston[2] is having a huge KT party on the 21st, same day as Corrine's for Ethel [Lewis]. We shall take in both. I am feeling very well but expect Mary to knock me off my feet. All my love

WALLIS

1. Wife of a Derbyshire landowner.
2. A rich American from the Deep South, married to an Anglo–Argentine and prominent as a London hostess. Her parties were attended by the Prince of Wales.

Thursday the 14th [May]   Bryanston Court

Dearest Aunt B

I can't help but think that moving Charlie out of the house when he was dying was awful. Couldn't they have held on for a few more days? Wasn't it all terrible, pathetic and tragic? Darling you are quite wrong about my Cannes idea. I'm borrowing on my securities for the trip and it has nothing to do with my trip to Washington. The hitch in latter is the continued running expenses of this flat while I'm away the 4 servants eating heads off – but anyway I hope to make the grade anyway and am trying to borrow enough money for both 'doings'. We are very gay at the moment – many KT parties and tomorrow one at Lady Furness's with the 2 Princes. I had one for the Lewises today who arrived 2 days ago and when I telephoned [name illegible] to ask him [Felipe] Espil[1] was in the office so asked to come and he did. E[rnest] not pleased but Thelma Furness so pleased she asked him tomorrow to meet HRH who of course is interested in everything Argentine at the moment. Had a cable from Mary saying sailing in the Mauretania now – which puts her here the 26 – our blankest week. So must hustle for men. We go to Knole Saturday and Whitsun is the week-end of the 23rd so we go with the Thaws to the hotel next door to the Milford Havens as they are giving a series of parties. We return London Monday to greet Mary Tues. It's 12 o'clock so must stop. Just wanted you to know it isn't a question of a choice of trips because if I can only raise enough for one I'm coming to you. Love

WALLIS

From the Duchess of Windsor's memoirs:
On the Prince's return from South America, Thelma Furness gave a large afternoon reception at her house on Grosvenor Square at which he was present. Ernest and I were invited. ... Thelma came in with the Prince. All of us rose at his entrance. As they moved through the room he greeted the people he knew. As he passed close by his glance happened to fall on me. He then nudged Thelma, and seemed to be asking her in a whisper: 'Haven't I met that lady before?' In any event he presently came over to say: 'How nice to see you again. I remember our meeting at Melton [Mowbray].' I thought he looked finely drawn, as if the long trip had

1. Wallis's old flame from Washington days. See above, page 5.

exhausted him. He made a remark or two about his trip before moving away. It was a mark of attention flattering to us both.

[Letter begun late May]

Darling

I am being presented June 10th by Mildred Andersen and I'm borrowing the whole outfit – Tamar Thaw's white satin dress which fits me perfectly – Thelma Furness's white satin embroidered train & her feathers and fan – so I shall only have to get some sort of head ornament. Isn't that marvellous?

June 4th. I've never had a chance to finish this until now due to the rush of Mary's visit. Everyone has been really kind and done things for her. I've given 2 dinners and a large luncheon – and the success of all was taking her to tea at Mrs Lawson Johnston's and Thelma Furness brought the Prince and Mary shook hands with him. I think I wrote you that we saw both the Prince and Prince George at Thelma's at tea one afternoon before Mary came. I am buying an aquamarine & crystal ornament and large aquamarine cross to wear around the neck which hangs about center front of bust – really lovely on the white dress. These I need not add are imitations but effective. Will send you the pictures of the event as soon as ready. We have the Grants' car for Court so all in all are [remainder of letter missing]

Wednesday, June 10th

Darling

Such a check. I am speechless. You know how much too much it is. What a person you are and I feel all queer inside about your sending me such a present. Tonight is the night! I feel slightly nervous but hope that will pass. My borrowed clothes look quite well. We are having the pictures taken tomorrow morning. Mary I think is having a grand time – all my friends have been wonderful about giving her parties. I hope she will leave by the end of the month as I need a few days to straighten out the flat put things away etc. As it is I can't get off before the first week in July and hope to stay until Aug 15th. Ethel is coming with us for about 10 days. I am sharing a room with Tamar. We pay 100 francs per day for it.

Friday 12th. Am going to write you in detail about the Court – but want to catch tomorrow's boat as I've been so bad about writing since having a house PEST. Thank you again & again for all your goodness to me. You know I'm not worth it. All love,

WALLIS

Saturday, June 13th

Dearest Aunt Bessie

We have been lunching and dining at such a pace and I've been trying to get the South of France trousseau together between drinks that I have not been able to write you half enough. Everyone I know has done something for Mary in the way of a party and I feel quite set up over the fact as I never expected it though rather set the stage by doing a lot of asking of people here before her arrival. No beau has become attentive but there have been extra men for her at the dinners. Wednesday I was assisted into my borrowed finery by about 15 people who came to see us dressed. We left early enough to get a good place in the Mall. My aquamarine jewellery really looked divine with the white and Thelma's train is very handsome and longer than regulations. Also her feathers were higher which helps a lot. When we got into the Palace I ran into General Trotter at the entrance to the throne room and he helped get us good seats and we were in one of the first rows to be presented which got the agony over quickly. I was a bit nervous while waiting my turn but not during the actual 'bobbing' to the King and Queen. After Court we went to Thelma Furness' for a party. The Prince was there and brought Ernest and self home in his car at 3 a.m. which threw the porters here into a gale to say nothing of Cain who heard it next morning on her way to the flat. I hope I can have HRH here for a KT some afternoon – but you have to work up to those things gradually and of course through Thelma. We had our pictures taken next morning. We couldn't afford the best photographer – they are so dear here. We went to Bertram Park considered very good 14 gns the dozen. I have mostly pyjamas for Cannes and 3 silk dresses, 3 bathing suits, 3 evening dresses – that is all. Have 2 town day dresses, one coat, 2 evening dresses for the [London] season and have spent quite a bit but badly selected I think, also the new country outfit. Mary has been a very good guest really – but of course Ernest is dead on his feet from the late nights. I am having Thaws,

Lewises, Murrays, Lady Fitzherbert, Prendergast[1] and a man named
Hynes for my birthday dinner. I can't get over your check – you have
given me $225 this spring. You never lose your family do you and I
never do anything for you. I have arranged to borrow $500 so some
time in October I'll be over. E is not taking any holiday which I think
too awful as he is dead tired – should like to get him to America in
the fall, the trip itself would do him good. All my love

WALLIS

Have the fact I was presented put in a paper – just a small notice you
know. Enjoy the fun and tell Cousin L[elia] the driver brought me
home.

From the Duchess of Windsor's memoirs:
The presentation was a magnificent set-piece of pageantry.... As
the Prince of Wales walked past, I overheard him mutter to his
uncle, the Duke of Connaught: 'Uncle Arthur, something ought to
be done about the lights. They make all the women look ghastly.'

Thelma had invited Ernest and me to drop in at her house
afterwards, and we did. Perhaps a dozen people were there....
Presently the Prince arrived, accompanied by 'G' Trotter. Over a
glass of champagne, which he barely touched, he spoke admiringly
of my gown.

'But Sir,' I responded with a straight face, 'I understood that you
thought we all looked ghastly.'

He was startled. Then he smiled. 'I had no idea my voice carried
so far.'

The custom when Royalty is present is for all others to remain
until Royalty has left. After a brief stay, the Prince departed with
General Trotter.... After what we judged to be a reasonable interval, Ernest and I took our leave. To our surprise, the Prince and
'G' were standing by their car, engaged in conversation. Catching
sight of us, the Prince hastened forward to ask whether he could
not give us a lift. I said, 'Thank you, Sir, very much.'

.... Chatting easily, and obviously in high spirits, the Prince
mentioned that they were on their way to his country place, Fort
Belvedere, near Windsor Great Park.... 'All the time I was in South
America', he said laughingly, 'I kept thinking how much work

1. Walter Prendergast (born 1898), Second Secretary at the United States Embassy. A good-
looking, bridge-playing bachelor.

remains to be done at the Fort. And tomorrow morning I want to put in two or three hours in the garden before going back to my work in London.' I was utterly absorbed, and all too soon the car arrived at Bryanston Court.

As the Prince helped me out of the car, I asked whether he and General Trotter might not like to come up for a moment and have a drink before continuing on to Sunningdale. The Prince, I had observed at Melton, had occasionally taken a night-cap. However, the Prince declined. 'I'd very much like to see your flat one day,' he said. 'I'm told it's charming, and seeing it might give me some ideas for brightening up the Fort. But I have to be up so early. Still, if you would be so kind as to invite me again, I'd like to do so.' Then he drove off.

But it was to be six months before they next saw each other.

Meanwhile Wallis enjoyed the London season with the highly social Mary Raffray, and busily prepared for her holiday on the Riviera with her other friends. On 19 June she celebrated her thirty-fifth birthday.

Monday night, June 22nd

Dearest Aunt Bessie

At last a moment to write you and a night to rest in, hence this letter written in bed. My birthday was exhausting – 12 for dinner here and then back to Corrine's for music and much whoopee lasting until 3.30. I sent the liquor and sandwiches. The next night we went to the Aldershot Tattoo[1] in a picnic party consisting of the Grants, Galbraiths, George [Murray] who arrived Thursday and Steens. It was really quite a lot of fun but we didn't get home until 2.30 and Sunday night we went to a subscription party at Bray[2] with the Thaws, Milford Haven etc. Today I had 8 women for lunch and am having 8 more Wednesday. All debts will then be cleared before going away. Mary's visit has been a success I should think. We have certainly been asked to a lot of things. Everything has happened except my getting the P of W here. She had a letter to Lady L. Mountbatten[3] and we went for tea with her. I am sorry E has no holiday but hope we can manage 10 days in Scotland in August. The Court pictures are not too

1. The annual pageant at the military camp of Aldershot in Hampshire.
2. A village on the Thames not far from London, with a well-known hotel.
3. Edwina, the rich and glamorous wife of Lord Louis Mountbatten, who was rarely seen with her husband at this period.

good but definitely fair and will send you 3, one of E and self and the two poses of me alone to add to the Wallis collection! Do you think I should have my heavy curtains cleaned or wait until early next spring when the fogs are over? Don't forget to answer as I don't know how often the custom is to clean them. I have certainly done well by Ethel – but don't imagine she'll do the same by me. Isn't it marvellous Espil being made [Argentine] Ambassador [to the United States]? Do forgive me for not having written as much as I wanted to, it hasn't been that I haven't thought of you every day and don't love you more than anyone else.

WALLIS

At the end of June Wallis set out for the holiday in the South of France to which she had so much been looking forward, both as a change from housekeeping in London and as a step in her social career. Her companions, as we have seen, were the sisters 'Tamar' Thaw and Gloria Vanderbilt, her old friend Ethel, Lady Lewis, and her new friend Nada, Marchioness of Milford Haven. Wallis was to share a room with Tamar; Nada was to share with Gloria. Mary Raffray accompanied the party as far as Paris. To her aunt, Wallis wrote of the jaunt as innocent and enjoyable, but one must read between the lines.

There can be no doubt that, all her life, Wallis – with her rather masculine appearance, her brittle and self-possessed manner – exercised a great fascination on lesbians. Nada Milford Haven was a well-known lesbian of the period; and it would seem that all three of the Morgan sisters shared homosexual inclinations to some degree. Three years later the internationally sensational Vanderbilt case would begin in America, in which Gloria Vanderbilt would try to recover custody of her daughter from her sister-in-law Gertrude Whitney. It would then be alleged that Gloria was morally unfit to bring up her daughter on account of her sexual proclivities; and in support of this, evidence would be produced of a lesbian affair conducted between Gloria and Nada Milford Haven in a Cannes hotel in August 1931 – that is, during the holiday in which Wallis participated. When, therefore, Wallis writes to her aunt that in the South of France men were 'very scarce' but that 'no one cared', she may have been saying more than she intended.

However, Wallis ended her French trip abruptly and returned earlier than planned. To her aunt she gives a reason for this, but one may ask whether it was the true reason. The fact is that the names of Nada Milford Haven and Gloria Vanderbilt practically cease to be mentioned in the letters after this date. Tamar remained Wallis's good friend for a while – but even she, as the letters eventually relate, was finally shunned by Wallis on account of her reputation. Wallis's friendship with Thelma Furness, however, which as time passed would bring her increasingly into the orbit of the Prince of Wales, was destined to flourish for some years yet.

Sunday, July 12th   Miramar, Cannes

Dearest Aunt Bessie

There is so much to tell you it's hard to begin. Mary & self arrived in Paris the night of the 30th and went to stay at Gloria's house with Tamar, Gloria having already left with Nada Milford Haven for here. The second night in Paris Mary and myself went to dine with old Mr Simpson and afterwards went to the Colonial Exposition. Mademoiselle was along also. We had to cross a wide street upon leaving and I took hold of Mr Simpson and hurried across – Mad followed – Mary behind her. When I arrived on the sidewalk I looked around to see where the others were. I was met with the sight of Mary shooting through the air. It was awful. She had been hit by a taxi. We picked her and took her back to Gloria's – an awful ride. Her back hurt most terribly and she was fainting. Then hysterics etc. She was in such pain the doctor could hardly examine her but thought her ribs broken and possibly a kidney injury. We spent an awful night and finally when she passed water there was much blood so we knew then it was kidney. By 5 a.m. we were on our way in the ambulance to the American Hospital. They had five doctors in consultation and by one they decided not to operate but to take the chance it was a bruised kidney not lacerated. You can imagine my state of mind – cabling the family, speaking to NY on the telephone. For 48 hours she was still in danger. However she has staged a marvellous recovery. Her aunt came from Aix-les-Bains and took over from me and we left Monday the 6th for here arriving last Wed. It is really divine – hot and sun, sun everywhere. I am loving it. We swim at Antibes or go to the islands. We have seen no men – 5 women rather terrifying – but we do all the things. The [Herman] Rogers and Sara Elkin are here and we dine with the former tonight, my 3rd appearance. Ethel will sail for the USA on the 27th and I will leave about the first – spend a week in Paris then back to London and poor lonely Ernest who is camping in the flat stranded with no car. I hope you're having a grand summer and haven't been caught in the awful heat. Loads of love

WALLIS

Sunday, August 9th   Knole, Sevenoaks, Kent

Darling

I've been a beast about writing to you from Cannes but really it was a life which simply didn't leave time for pen and paper. My communications to Ernest were by wire – much to his extreme annoyance as you know the complex he has about spending money that way. We did the same things each day, that is either to Eden Roc for lunch and swim or to the islands for picnic lunch and swim with the Rogers in their boat. Ellen Yuille now Blair was there with her husband[1] – such fun to see her again. Also some people from Peking and with Tamar's and Gloria's friends also we were kept going – men very scarce but no one cared. I managed a beau for a few days named Sydney Smith who was there with Willy Vanderbilt[2] but too much effort to keep him in face of the competition. I got brown and filled with health not a nerve and when I tell you I motored 370 miles in one day on our return to Paris and never felt it you know I'm in condition. We had hoped to stay until the 8th but I got a restless wire from E saying we were invited here for the week-end – both or none and would I come as it was the second invitation here while I had been in Cannes and always for a couple not the extra man. I felt a pig not to come so Tamar and self left on the 4th arriving Paris the 5th spent one day buying stockings scent etc and came by the Golden Arrow Friday sending the car with the chauffeur.

Home was gloom. Ernest looking white and wan. The money question is serious and we have to give up the car and pull our horns in in every way. Business foul and no hopes. Ernest looks so badly that his father said at last that he *may* contribute to his taking 10 days' holiday. Unless he does it entirely we can't go. Ernest wants to go to Scotland

---

1. An old schoolfriend of Wallis from a well-known North Carolina family.
2. Probably William Kissam Vanderbilt II (1878-1944), a first cousin of Gloria's late husband.

by car sightseeing again. I fail to see the rest but he says it relaxes him. Everyone has his way. So we may leave next Friday provided the money appears. I still hope to come to you in the fall on borrowed wealth but don't dare mention anything upsetting at the moment as E is so nervous, worried etc. I hope the trip will help – certainly Pa won't or E says can't. I hope you have had a nice time. I have had lovely one and would like to feel you have been happy. Don't punish me and not write. I'll do well now it's too cold to go out after being baked for a month. I'm back in tweeds and furs. All my love

WALLIS

In contrast to Ernest's mean and eccentric father, Aunt Bessie was the fairy godmother of the Simpsons. Though her life was led in the dependent role of paid companion, she had recently inherited money from a friend, and her generous cheques and gifts to her niece helped alleviate the gloom at Bryanston Court. She now offered to pay for Wallis and Ernest to visit America that autumn. But Wallis reluctantly had to refuse.

Saturday the 12th [September]   Bryanston Court

Darling

We were naturally overcome with your generosity. I've never seen anything like you or 'it' before. Here is our position. Ernest is only entitled to a month a year. He has had already 11 days leaving roughly 3 weeks more. To come to America for that length of time at your expense would be utterly absurd especially as some of it would have to be spent with the old devil Ma and to have anything there we would have to take a 6 day boat or something near that as 10 day ones would be useless to E. Anyway we couldn't consider letting you do it under the circumstances it could be arranged at the moment. You know I am itching to get back but I feel that it is impossible to run the flat fully staffed while I am away and secondly it seems wrong to leave Ernest at this particular moment of business worry so as we have got to see each other there is only one thing to do – you must come here in time for Xmas. We might be able to arrange a small trip to a sunny clime after Xmas – and if E could not go I might go with you for a short space. Next year I hope things will be better and I can definitely come home – if worse I think I'll have to for good! I am so disappointed as

I've had a heart set on it and I would come without E if I didn't think it a dirty trick to leave him at this time. The fact of leaving him under ordinary circumstances would not even enter into my returning home as naturally it would be very seldom he could come with me and then it would be for a month only and I should always stay true. Now answer me frankly don't say you'll come just to settle things and then really not tell me the truth about your ideas on the subject and as soon as possible. All my love

WALLIS

PS E says he hates to be selfish and keep me from going so won't you please come here.

But Aunt Bessie was unable to abandon her employer, Miss Adams.

A fact which emerges from the correspondence is that Wallis, though a very energetic woman, was not in fact physically robust. She had begun 1931 with a long, feverish cold. In the spring she had suffered from ulcer attacks - to which she had been prone since the mid-twenties and which would recur, sometimes cripplingly, at moments of nervous crisis. In the autumn she reported to her aunt a serious operation for the removal of inflamed tonsils.

Friday, November 13th   Bryanston Court

Darling

I suppose you were as surprised as I was myself that I decided to part with the tonsils. As you know it was done a week ago and I didn't send a wire about flowers for mother as I thought you would think it odd if I didn't mention the operation - and I didn't want you to know until they were out. The Nursing Home I chose was Lady Carnarvon's supposed to be the best and I must say everything was very nice - 18 gns per week, tiny room. I had the night nurse 6 nights and the day the whole ten days I was there. I just returned yesterday. I think it's a terrific operation. My tonsils were so septic that of course I had rather a bad time because the tissues took so long to heal they found an enormous abcess under one got nearly a spoonful of puss from it and they were both covered with lesions etc. so I think I'll be better off now. At the moment I'm rather weak as I've only been able to take solid food the last 3 days. It was quite a little party costing just over $500 but I'm able to get it on the $1000 I borrowed last summer. I seem to be doing nothing but borrowing and Ernest likewise – the great attempt to hang on until other times. I have only one evening dress this year and 2 day things so I am going shy in that line. I can't tell you how really kind people were while I was in the nursing home so many flowers and yesterday the flat was full on my arrival. I have to stay in bed until 11 a.m. and then go back again at 6 p.m. for a few days and keep away from crowds and dust until I'm thoroughly healed. I am frightfully disappointed about your decision about Xmas. I had so looked forward to having you here. Perhaps you'll change your mind and come anyway just to see the new throat. I never count Corrine as family. She was the least concerned over the last event. She is really very selfish. She and George are odd ducks. Ernest was rather annoyed by their indifference. Tamar came every day. Corrine twice in 10 and stayed about 15 mins. All love

WALLIS

Tuesday, Nov 17th   Bryanston Court

Darling

I am gradually beginning to feel human again but have not been able to go out once since I got home. Nothing but fog. While I was in the nursing home the weather was wonderful. However though not bright today the Dr has told me to go out. It's depressing always sitting around the flat watching everything get dirty with fog. Maud sails for NY tomorrow. She seems to be the only Simpson with money. I suppose more nasty letters from Mr Simpson will arrive as of course she will stir up as much trouble for us as possible. I wish I was on my way home for a visit. I'm fed up with English weather and the dowdy looking British public at the moment. We are going to Knole for the week-end. The change will help but the bridge is awful. We shan't have Thanksgiving – too much effort to lassoe a bird. Do take care of yourself. I'm always thinking of you and wishing we were together.

WALLIS

Sunday, November 29th   Bryanston Court

Darling

A filthy day heavy fog in fact we have hardly seen the sun the entire month but not much rain and so the English say it's been a marvellous

Nov. It makes me miserable to hear about all your sunshine but I must say it's the only bright thing I've heard about home. Everything every- where seems to get worse and worse and you can't help but be de- pressed by it all. We have nothing but a series of unpleasant business or family news – much cutting down in office staff and closing of branch offices, Mr Simpson in a panic and so disagreeable. He would not give a penny as I wrote you. He chopped $3000 off the loan he had agreed to make E and as you remember last year he didn't give us an Xmas cheque so you can see he would let us rot here before helping us home. We appreciate all your generosity but really can't move away from all our debts – they need nursing! I got the food bills down £15 last month – but of course we hardly ever entertain which I miss as I think it's so true that people forget you or don't ask you as much if they don't think you can return the cutlet. I feel much better but am taking things slowly which is easy as everything is quiet. I went out at night for the first time last Thursday to a charity thing at the Café de Paris. Anne Sackville spent 2 nights this week here and has asked us to Knole for Xmas week-end and the New Year's one. I am leaving it open in the hope that you might change your mind and come over. Knole will not be thrilling but better than staying here. I am hit in the candle department as I've bought all the flesh-tinted American candles Harrods had in stock which was only 12 so now will you send me 2 dozen of each size and undervalue the parcel. They are Mastercraft candles conical hand dipped flesh pink sizes 2 and 3. If no sizes marked send longest. Let me know cost etc. Have no more news I'm afraid. All my love

WALLIS

Tuesday, Dec 8th   Bryanston Court

Darling

I am becoming quite a May Adams in bed so much. I now have succeeded in catching a cold in the head. I want to lose it before next week the best full week to get the servants Xmas things they being the only people outside the Sackvilles that I'll be giving away anything to. There is no news. People are really not entertaining at all and we least of all. It's rather slow recovering from the tonsils as they were so septic that I got a good dose of poisoning when they came out. It seems you always absorb quite a bit. My stomach has been all right but the Dr says it will take 6 months for it really to recover and I have a diet. We were asked to dinner with PW [the Prince of Wales] last week but he was ill at the last minute. Tamar is giving herself a birthday party the 17th and he is to be there. I shall miss you terribly as you know and want to see you so badly. I wish I could manage to come over for a month even after Xmas and we return together – but things seem to be worse instead of better. No one is really very cheerful as the men are so worried. However the Americans here have more money than ever. I am enclosing you a tiny check to buy a little something for your dear self. It has to be tiny as Texas Corporation is the only thing I've left that pays a dividend! Ernest's boils were a great success. He has never looked as well though has a scarred neck. Have told the Sackvilles we would come for Xmas as no good news about you has come. We go down Xmas eve and return Monday a.m. then return there for New Year's eve and that week-end. The latter I don't want to do as Thelma invited us on a party but the Xmas invitation I found means the 2 week-ends or none so could not get out of it. I can't tell you how I long to come home. Ernest I don't think can ever return to the USA as he will be arrested on the dock. He's not going to give Dodie[1] any money from Jan on and has told her his mother will take the child and clothe and send to school so it's provided for. She can't do anything as long as he's here but things could pop for him in NY and he simply hasn't got it to give. My food bills were only $150 last month – not bad but hardly a party. Katherine's farewell party is last dinner of 12 I've had. Hope I haven't filled this letter with germs. I'm so stopped up but not on chest or in throat at all. We are not having our plate put on Xmas cards as it's cheaper to buy a few. I hate to think of our not being together. You do see I could not get to you. But you really could have come here. I can't go on much longer without seing you and it does seem foolish to have such long spaces between the times we see each other and you are really much more free than I am. Men I suppose are necessary but certainly tie you down. Please let's try not to have such gaps between visits. I forgot to say the pop-over rings are going to York House. Thelma wants PW to sample pop-overs[2] so I have to lend the rings. Don't tell this as several stories of equally absurd things have come

1. Ernest's previous wife, Dorothea, who lived in America with their daughter, Audrey.
2. An American variety of bread-roll, similar to a doughnut in appearance and to Yorkshire pudding in taste and consistency.

46

out in the American papers about her and she is about to sue one of them. Please take best care of yourself and I hope Xmas will be gay and that you haven't a minute alone. I shall be thinking of you all the time and wishing I was there. All my love and a big kiss

WALLIS

And so 1931 ended as it had begun, with Wallis in the grip of a fever but faced with the prospect of attending a party with the Prince of Wales. It would be their fifth meeting.

CHAPTER TWO

1932: Guest

In a surprisingly brief and offhand manner, Wallis's first letters to her aunt in 1932 reveal two important developments. Having seen the Simpsons at Tamar Thaw's birthday party before Christmas, the Prince had accepted their invitation to dine at Bryanston Court.[1] And he returned their hospitality by inviting them to spend the last weekend of January at his country retreat, Fort Belvedere.

Sunday, January 24th   Bryanston Court

Darling

The candles arrived and are grand. I enclose cheque. I can't accept everything from you. We (meaning Cain and self) loved the butter pats, especially the one with HRH's feathers on it. It was a shame it didn't arrive in time for use the night he dined here which by the way passed off pleasantly the party breaking up at 4 a.m. so I think he enjoyed himself. Cain nearly died of excitement. We have been out a lot lately to small dinners and have another busy week ahead though my hands are tied for the rest of the month having given 2 dinners of 12, one of 8 being all we can really afford. Agnes leaves me Feb 11th getting married so I'm concentrating on a new housemaid which does not seem easy to find. Food is up here on account of the new tariffs, everyone gloomy and practically all my friends off the 'champagne standard', beer being the beverage now. Read with envy of the bargains in NY, also of styles that I didn't dream existed in this frowzy dressed town. Any little tricks cost pounds if you can find them. Do come over very soon. I have had rotten luck at bridge lately. You and I would make a great pair. I never hold higher than a jack. Am writing

---

1. But in her memoirs, the Duchess wrote that she only entertained the Prince for the first time in July 1933 – an indication of how her memory, jogged only by the sight of her old engagement books, was often at fault in matters of detail.

Mary for some stockings as she knows the shade and I think they're better in NY than Washington. All love,

WALLIS

From the Duchess of Windsor's memoirs:
The news [that the Prince had accepted an invitation to dine at Bryanston Court] threw my staff into an acute state of panic. My cook Mrs Ralph and Cain the parlourmaid were beside themselves with excitement. ... I decided to give him a typical American dinner: black bean soup, grilled lobster, fried chicken Maryland, for the sweet a cold raspberry *soufflé*, and, as a concession to my English guests, a savoury of marrow bones. In my excitement I was bursting to tell the fishmonger and greengrocer ... [but] I had acquired too much British restraint. ...

Ten of us sat down to dinner – the Prince at the head of the table and Ernest at the foot. I was sure that if the lights didn't fail, Cain would certainly trip with a soup plate and scald either Thelma or Connie. But everything, I am happy to say, went very well. The Prince seemed to enjoy his American dinner and paid me the compliment of asking for my recipe for the raspberry *soufflé*.

Thursday, Feb 4th   Bryanston Court

Darling
We have been buzzing like bees for the past few weeks, many small dinners followed by bridge losses. We haven't been out at night for 2 weeks. Ernest is dead, I'm tired but seem to have my old pep back again and the 4 pounds in weight have improved my disposition if not my 'behind'. Last week HRH invited us to Sunningdale for the week-end and I enclose you a copy of the poem we sent him for a bread and butter letter instead of the regulation one. Of course you have to begin Sir and sign your obedient servant. I think old E did pretty well and I believe PW was quite pleased with it. Matilda Pell Kohler is just back from America and says people are more depressed acting than here. I think that's because they are used to hard times here more than we are and take giving up things and doing without quite normally. Theaters are full and night clubs also I hear. We never go unless took which is seldom. No one very cheerful about any better times in sight

and if I could bring myself to turn Gowan out of a job would certainly let the car go, as I would rather have the remainder of the money to take a trip with if something amusing turned up.[1] Certainly there is no hope of Ernest producing anything for car or trip. Shipping gloomier and gloomier. I hear even Maud is giving up some things though no one seems able to say what! Mr S writes in glowing terms of her economies. Am having difficulty in getting a housemaid though I heard there were many to be had. I haven't found it so – a flat is still to an English servant a terrible place to be and you have to bait them. Agnes was to leave on the 11th but the young man she is to marry fell down and has done something to his knee so the marriage is to be in August and she is willing to stay until then but she is doing her work so badly I don't know that I can keep her anyway. E says the devil you know is better than the devil you don't but I don't know. Corrine is back full of sunburn had a fine time but says Switzerland empty and I hear Paris is cheaper. I find all the cheaper rumours are the brink – nothing that way here but higher on account of the tariffs. When are you coming over to look the British lion in the face? Am longing to see you. All my love

WALLIS

PS I hear there is a good cook book called The Blue Book. I would like it if possible.

It is strange that Wallis should describe her first visit to 'the Fort' so fleetingly to Aunt Bessie. At that time, of course, she could not know what a large part that place would play in her life; but in her memoirs, she writes at length and with love of what would turn out to be the first of numerous week-ends she would spend there.

> From the Duchess of Windsor's memoirs:
> Then, out of the blue, came an unexpected invitation – a note from the Prince of Wales asking us to spend the week-end of January 30 with him at Fort Belvedere. Ernest was no less delighted than I, and the pleasure of my maid, Mary Burke, when I informed her that she was to go with me, could hardly have been greater if the summons had come directly to her from His Royal Highness. Thelma, I am sure, had suggested that we be

---

1. Wallis had kept on driver and car out of her own small income.

included, for I learned almost immediately from Connie Thaw that she and Benny would be there too.

It is with a lump in my throat that I begin to write about this place that will always be the most romantic house I have ever known – that half-enchanted castle that David has always called the Fort, never Fort Belvedere, just the Fort.... The Fort was singularly David's; it meant more to him, I suspect, than anything else in the world save honour. ...

The Fort was one of the so-called 'Grace and Favour' houses on crown property bordering Windsor Great Park ... at the disposal of the Sovereign for the accommodation of relations and senior courtiers. The Fort's origins go back to the early eighteenth century and William, Duke of Cumberland, third son of George II.... Later, George IV commissioned the famous Sir Jeffrey Wyatville, who had restored Windsor Castle during the early part of the nineteenth century, to finish and enlarge the building.... During Queen Victoria's time the Fort was uninhabited and fell into partial ruin until George V undertook extensive repairs and modifications early in his reign. ...

From the Duke of Windsor's memoirs:
[In 1929, the Fort had fallen vacant.] When I went to my father to ask if I might live there, he was surprised. 'What could you possibly want that queer old place for? Those damn week-ends, I suppose.... Well, if you want it, you can have it.' I thanked him. My real reason for desiring the property lay deeper than a mere wish for a place to spend week-ends at. I was thirty-five years old; the rolling stone was beginning to seek a resting place. ...

By the time I came upon it, it had become a pseudo-Gothic hodge-podge. An intrusion of yew trees kept one side of the house in perpetual shadow, staining the walls with green, acidulous mould. The garden was untended; the surrounding undergrowth was wild and untidy. But the half-buried beauty of the place leapt to my eye.

Northwards the land descends in a gentle slope towards Virginia Water, where as a child I had paddled in rowboats with Mary [his sister] and my brothers. Here the grassy approaches were guarded by a broad arc of stone battlements, with more than a score of handsome, eighteenth-century bronze cannon mounted in embrasures. Windsor Castle was six miles away, on the opposite side of the Great Park; and from the top of the tower on a clear afternoon one could see London and with a spyglass make out the dome of St Paul's nearly twenty-five miles away.

I had a wonderful time fixing up The Fort, both inside and outside.... Inside I introduced, to the extent that space and the old walls allowed, many of the creature conveniences that I had sampled and enjoyed in the New World – a bathroom to nearly every room, showers, a steam bath, built-in cupboards, central heating.... Outside, the changes also went on apace. Down came the gloomy, encroaching yew-trees, to let in light and air. A muddy lily pond below the battlements was transformed into a swimming-pool. I cleared away acres of dark laurel and replaced them with rare rhododendrons. I cut winding paths through the fir- and birch-trees, revealing the true enchantment of the woodland setting.... I was in such a hurry to make the place perfect that I begrudged as lost a daylight hour that did not see the work progressing.... I pressed my week-end guests into arduous physical labour to which some of them were unaccustomed....

The Fort laid hold of me in many ways. Soon I came to love it as I loved no other material thing – perhaps because it was so much my own creation. More and more it became for me a peaceful, almost enchanted anchorage, where I found refuge from the cares and turmoil of my life.

It is not readily apparent from these accounts that the Fort was in fact quite a small house – not so much a fort as a miniature folly, 'a child's idea of a fort', as Diana Cooper put it. Only a limited number of guests could be accommodated, and the bedrooms were tiny. A raised voice – as the officials and advisers who were to congregate there during the Abdication crisis were to discover – could be heard throughout the building.

From the Duchess of Windsor's memoirs:
Sunningdale is about twenty-five miles south-west of London. Ernest and I drove out in the late afternoon, timing our pace to arrive at six. It was dark when we approached the Fort. Our headlights picked out a gravel driveway winding in graceful turns

through a wood; suddenly there materialised a fascinating, sha-
dowy mass, irregular in outline and of different levels, the whole
surmounted by a soaring tower bathed in soft light thrown up by
concealed flood lamps. Even before the car ground to a stop, the
door opened and a servant appeared. An instant later the Prince
himself was at the door to welcome his guests and supervise the
unloading of our luggage, an attention which I was to discover
was a habit with him. The Prince led us through a narrow hallway
into an octagonal hall with white plaster walls in each of the eight
corners of which stood a chair upholstered in bright yellow leather.
The floor was of black and white marble. We then moved into the
drawing room. Thelma, the Thaws, and 'G' Trotter had preceded
us. I was instantly struck by the warmth of the room, which, like
the hallway, was octagonal. Curtains of yellow velvet were drawn
across the tall windows; the walls, which were panelled in natural
pine, were hung with handsome paintings, which I later identified
as Canalettos; the furniture my now quite experienced eye recog-
nised as mostly Chippendale, except for a baby grand piano and
a gramophone; and opposite the fireplace on one wall were shelves
of books in beautiful bindings.

The Prince himself insisted on taking us to our room on the
second floor, and I could not help noticing that before he left he
swiftly appraised the condition of the room with the practised eye
of a careful host, a side of his character which was totally unexpected. Having assured himself that all was as it should be, he left
us, saying he would expect us down shortly for cocktails.

Another small surprise came as we returned to the drawing
room. The Prince was sitting on a sofa, his head bent over a large,
flat screen, his right hand rapidly plying a needle from which
trailed a long coloured thread. I could scarcely believe my eyes –
the Prince of Wales doing needle point [an accomplishment he had
learnt from his mother].... Two Cairn terriers, Cora and Jaggs,
tussled at the Prince's feet....

Compared to the stately routine of Knole the Princely existence
at the Fort was amazingly informal, even though everyone dressed
for dinner – Thelma, Connie and I in our simplest evening dresses.
The Prince was wearing a kilt ... and a silver-mounted sporran
from which I was amused to see him presently produce a small
cigarette case. There were cocktails, and then we went in to dinner.

The dining room was by no means as large as the drawing room. It likewise had walls of natural pine and contained a walnut table and two Georgian mahogany sideboards. The dining room chairs were of mahogany and ten in number – all the walnut table would seat. On the walls were paintings of horses by George Stubbs, the famous British equestrian painter. The food was simple but delicious – oysters, which the Prince explained came directly from his own oyster beds in the Duchy of Cornwall, an excellent roast of beef, salad, a sweet and a savoury.

Thelma and 'G' Trotter kept up a running conversation in which the rest of us joined. I knew from the newspapers that the Prince during the preceding months had travelled extensively through the depressed areas of England, but never once did he mention anything about himself or his work. He seemed tired, in fact, and the impression formed in my mind that there must be a tacit understanding in this place and in this company that he would deliberately put aside his official concerns. . . .

After dinner there was coffee in the drawing room. There were cards for those who wanted to play. Otherwise, the Prince suggested, those who preferred a more rigorous test of mental skill might try to put together an extremely complicated jigsaw puzzle of which the pieces were scattered on a long table in front of the main window. The Prince invited the rest of us to play 'Red Dog' with him, a game which I had not played in years. He offered to coach me. . . .

Thelma was standing beside the gramophone, going through some records. 'I feel like dancing', she said.

A look of pleasure came into the Prince's face. 'Perhaps we all do', he suggested. The gramophone started; and as Thelma turned, the Prince was moving towards her, with outstretched arms, to dance her into the octagonal hallway off the drawing room. I have a poignant memory of the melody. It was *Tea for Two*. . . .

The Prince danced briefly with Connie and me in turn. I found him a good dancer, deft, light on his feet, and with a true sense of rhythm. Then, all of a sudden, he seemed tired. 'This being your first visit to the Fort', he said, 'perhaps I should tell you about the rules. There are none. Stay up as late as you want. Get up when you want. For me this is a place of rest and change. I go to bed early and get up early so that I can work in the garden.'

Well before midnight he said good night. The rest of us lingered only a moment of two, then departed for our rooms. That was my introduction to the private life of the Prince of Wales – a model of sedateness. . . .

The next day was of a piece with the evening before. The maid who brought breakfast told us that His Royal Highness had finished his an hour before and had gone into the garden. Shortly after Ernest and I had wandered into the drawing room, I observed advancing up the terrace slope an incongruous figure in baggy plus-fours, a thick sweater, hair tousled, and carrying in one hand a billhook, a machete-like tool for cutting brush. It was the Prince, with Cora and Jaggs yapping happily at his heels.

. . . 'Ah,' said Thelma, with mock consternation, 'I take it your guests are to be ordered to cut the laurels.'

'Yes,' said the Prince cheerfully, 'I'm always happy for recruits.'

'You'll find', muttered 'G' Trotter, 'that the harder you work, the more popular you'll be.' . . . Ernest glanced at Benny Thaw, who, having previously skirmished with the Prince on the briar-enmeshed slopes beneath the Fort, made a wry grimace. 'It's not exactly a command', interjected 'G' Trotter, 'but I've never known anyone to refuse.' Exercise was a pursuit that Ernest only favoured in the role of a spectator. . . .

Ernest went upstairs for a sweater. While he was gone, the Prince took me out on the terrace to show me the grounds. . . . He tried to sound casually matter-of-fact as he described what he had done; but his inner pleasure . . . burst through the guise of nonchalance. . . .

Following the laurel-cutting expedition and a buffet lunch, the Prince took the Simpsons on a tour of the house.

He was especially proud of the little library, which contained some good pieces of Queen Anne furniture. His own bedroom, off the hall on the ground floor, was a charming room, with tall windows hung with red chintz curtains looking out upon the garden. The bed and other furniture, like that in the drawing room and the library, were Chippendale. The walls were painted white; and all about were photographs of his family. The upstairs bedrooms, of which there were six, all had names. One was called 'Prince George's room', for his younger brother, who often spent his

week-ends there. Another was called 'The Blue Room', because
the predominant shade of the decorations was blue. There was a
'Yellow Room' and a 'Pink Room', a 'Green Room' and even 'The
Queen's Room', so named for some reason lost in the mists of
time. In view of the relative shortage of bathrooms in British
houses, the Prince was rightly proud that he had managed to provide, despite the handicap of the ancient walls, a bathroom for
practically every room. But what fascinated me was the architec-
tural wizardry that had been exercised in imparting to the interior
of this sprawling fort such an atmosphere of warmth and infor-
mality. For a bachelor's country house, the whole effect was aston-
ishingly warm and attractive.

*While mentioning none of these details, Wallis's letter to Aunt Bessie
of 4 February did enclose the text of the poem which Wallis and Ernest
had sent the Prince by way of a thank-you letter:*

Sir: —
Bear with me and do not curse
This poor attempt at thanks in verse.
Our week-end at 'Fort Belvedere'
Has left us both with memories dear
Of what in every sense must be
Princely hospitality.
Too soon the hours stole away,
And we, who would have had them stay,
Regretful o'er that fleeting slyness,
Do warmly thank Your Royal Highness.
But with your time I make too free –
I have the honour, Sir, to be
(Ere too long my poetic pencil limps on)
Your obedient servant

WALLIS SIMPSON

*Such was Wallis's first visit to the Fort. She had loved it; but she could
not possibly have imagined that it was destined merely to be the first
of many dozens of such visits, that it would become perhaps the most
important place in her life, and that one day she would supplant
Thelma as mistress of the house. All that was far in the future. Indeed,*

Sir: _____

Bear with me and do not curse
This poor attempt at thanks in verse.
Our week-end at "Fort Belvedere"
Has left us both with memories dear
Of what in every sense must be
Princely hospitality.
Too soon the hours stole away,
And we, who would have had them stay
Regretful o'er that fleeting slyness,
Do warmly thank your Royal Highness.
But with your time I make too free —
I have the honor Sir to be
(Ere too long my poetic pencil limps on)
Yours ~~or other~~ obedient Servant
            Wallis Simpson —

*following their week-end at Sunningdale in January 1932 the Simpsons
do not seem to have seen the Prince again until October of that year.*

*After this touch of fairy tale, Wallis returned to the real world. Her
subsequent letters to Aunt Bessie that winter reflect her usual concerns
– mounting money worries, problems with the Simpson family, her
longing for a holiday.*

Sunday, Feb 14th   Bryanston Court

Darling

I had a hunch you were sick and have been worried about you. I
hope you're really all right now. We have had snow and sun for two
days – a great treat to have it clear and dry. Nothing of interest to tell
you except that Mrs Simpson arrives in London about the 25 of this
month: We don't know why exactly. The length of the visit not
announced. I am hoping Mellon's arrival will not change the embassy
staff.[1] I should be lost without Tamar. We have had such good times
together. I have an old admirer Lord Decies always asking me to
lunch.[2] Ernest says it's sure to mean 'pinch and tickle' so have steadily
refused. People from home say England has a much more cheerful air
than the US but I notice a great difference in people's houses, restaurants etc. We hope to pay the last $1000 on the decorators' bill
within the next 3 months which will help to have the flat payed for at
last! Maud telephoned Ernest about Mrs S's arrival and said Mr S had
stopped her allowance. I hope we're not to meet the same fate. I am
counting on your remaining over all summer and then I hope to come
home with you for about 6 weeks but wouldn't want to land before
Octo so do make your plans that way. London won't be bad from the
first part of April on so you would come direct here. I am going over
to play bridge with Bristol[3] who is ill this afternoon and then we go
to a Sunday night theater club with Tamar. Please take care of yourself
and come here soon. All love

WALLIS

1. The Republican aluminium tycoon and former Treasury Secretary Andrew W. Mellon was
appointed Ambassador to London early in 1932 in succession to General Dawes, but recalled a
year later after President Roosevelt's election.
2. Colonel John Beresford, 5th Baron Decies (1866–1944), a roguish Irish peer.
3. Captain Arthur L. Bristol USN, who had succeeded Galbraith as principal Naval Attaché at
the US Embassy.

Sunday, Feb 21st   Knole, Sevenoaks, Kent

Darling

Have been worried about you as I had no letter on the last boat. Do hope you have lost your cold and are all right but have a hunch you're not feeling up to the mark or would have written. It's time you got away and came over to us. Don't delay much longer. We have just had a divine invitation from Ernest's Romanian friend Georges Sebastian[1] who has a house near Tunis. He is in London for a week and his wife in America. He is joining her towards the end of March there but in the meantime has to return to Tunis to attend to some electrical work in his house. He wants us to go with him. It's 2 days from London and our only expense railway, which is about $120 round trip each but E says the trip would cost $500 and we aint got it. I should have loved the sun and warmth and he was going to motor us to the edge of the Sahara. However can't be helped. Also Mike Scanlon is driving to Paris Tuesday and I could have gone for only boat fare on the cargo boat with him & car. Tamar and self were dying to go but again no financial backing! Benny is back and says Washington most cheerful place in the US, parties same as ever and whisky $1 a bottle.[2] Some shipping firm in the US just gone bust owing SS&Y[3] much money and Ernest has to find 13 thousand dollars to put back into firm – that being his share of losses last year. Naturally don't mention this but isn't it all depressing and we only wonder how much longer we can hang onto flat. I'm rather tired of being lashed to the place and never able to move. Perhaps one room better and more circulation. Very cold here and Cranmer's room our bed room like a frigidaire.[4] Anne in nursing home having had thyroid goitre removed. She got on well. We're here with a Mr Ramsay to keep Charlie [Lord Sackville] company. Not too exciting but a change from sooty London. Write me soon and tell me how you really are.

WALLIS

1. A fashionable international aesthete, whose house near Tunis with its collection is now a museum. A curious friend for Ernest to have.
2. Prohibition was still in force at this time.
3. Ernest's firm of shipping brokers, Simpson, Spence & Young.
4. Built in the fourteenth century, Knole had once been the residence of the Archbishops of Canterbury. Cranmer had been the last archbishop to live there before the estate was confiscated by the Tudors and granted by them to the Sackvilles.

Feb 26th   Bryanston Court

Darling

I was glad to have your cable as I felt quite worried about you as you're generally pretty good to me about writing. We are in gala mood at the moment in spite of the fact that E's ma arrived this a.m. In my last letter I wrote you that E's friend Georges Sebastian had invited us to Tunis and that we couldn't go as the journey was too much money. We refused and lo and behold he has sent us tickets for there and back again! We simply could not resist accepting such a gesture (as you know having made a much larger one to the family) and so we leave Tues March 8th by Golden Arrow – then the 8 o'clock train to Marseilles that night – boat from there at 10 next a.m. and Tunis next day the 10th. We will stay in Tunis a few days and then go by car to the edge of the desert. All sounds grand. We will be gone 2 weeks in all. I am only getting one light colored flannel suit for the trip which can be used here in the country afterwards. I hear one needs wool – it's a little warmer than Cannes in the winter. Maud has invited me to Sunday lunch with all the family but Ernest thinks life has been so peaceful without her that he is going to accept for himself but says he thinks it better if I don't come thus taking the blame and still letting us remain on estranged terms because if I went I must then have them here and then all the mess would surely start again. I believe even the old girl says too much Maud impossible. I have invested my Xmas present from you in a glass clock for dining room and a table for pictures for my room. This is the time to buy. Even Yamanaka accepted my offer for the table and I got £8 off the clock getting it for £19. Times are no better in business though people say they are better but that it doesn't show as yet. Anxious to hear just when you're sailing. Am impatient for your arrival. Come before the furniture is seized please! All love,

WALLIS

The holiday in Tunisia duly took place; and in the spring of 1932 Aunt Bessie finally joined the Simpsons in England. In July the three of them set out on a tour of France and Austria; but Wallis experienced a severe recurrence of her stomach trouble, and they had to return to London where she was under a doctor's care for some weeks. She appears to have recovered, however, by the time the letters to Aunt Bessie resume in the autumn.

Monday [postmarked 30 September]   Bryanston Court
Darling

We came back from another Knole week-end this a.m. Mrs Diercks
was there – you remember when my evening wrap was stolen at her
dance. We are out every night and I am so tired by now. Nothing
large in the way of parties but simply seeing the people who are
returning. Then two nights per week for those damn Simpsons. If they
were only together we could save a night. Benny keeps shooting birds
and bringing them here to be cooked. They are now at Grosvenor
House [Hotel] while fixing a flat they have taken in Park Street. I
dismissed Williamson and now have a new [housemaid] who has already smashed my Venetian glass vase on the tray table in the drawing
room. I payed £3 for it. Can you bear it? Have seen more of Thelma
than Tamar as she is *so* intimate with Mala Brand[1] and the gossip is
pretty bad so I don't want to be connected with them. Thelma is
furious about it all. I hope Tamar will gradually see the mistake she
is making and also realise she is losing her decent friends and not see
so much of Mala.

I started this to you Monday and now it is Thursday. I am really so
ashamed but it again has been every night. The mornings asleep and
as the weather has been good I have been golfing with Berta [Grant].
We played 36 holes yesterday. The sad news is that the Grants depart
for NY on Jan 22nd for good. The Guggenheims are closing London
office on Lester's advice. I shall really miss them. However have already engaged Berta's 2nd housemaid to replace my last effort. Enclose
snapshots taken by Mike [Scanlon] at Hove and sent with love &
kisses by him to you. Feel quite depressed as today is the last of Gowan
and car. We have both been brave until the end. I enclose you stupid
piece written in Tatler about your niece. Still no word from Corrine.
All love

WALLIS

*That autumn, Ernest and Wallis were twice more asked to the Fort
by Thelma and the Prince – once for tea, once for the week-end.
Apart from these visits, and a few week-ends at Knole, their social life
was restricted by their financial problems and Wallis's health. At
the beginning of December she was confined to bed by another ulcer*

---

1. A Bohemian of the period, the daughter of a South African Jewish millionaire.

attack. She was, however, cheered by the prospect of going to America in the New Year.

Sunday the 11th [December]   Knole, Sevenoaks, Kent.

Dearest Aunt Bessie,

I am staggered by the size of the cheque and have a sensation of being a millionairess. You know you should not have sent it and I shall be killed by generosity! I have sworn I shall not pay a bill with it or buy anything for the flat as I have done with your other presents. This I shall invest in myself. My few days in bed did me a world of good and I look ten years younger. I certainly must have a certain amount of rest and leave rich food alone. Also I am only allowed whiskey and plain water for the next 6 months, can this be supplied at 1911?[1] I should adore coming in February for about 6 weeks but whether we can swing it remains to be seen. Perhaps March would be better about the middle so that I really could take advantage of the clothes for the spring. The Grants and ourselves are here keeping Anne from being alone. Charles S is getting along marvellously and will I think be home with a nurse by next week-end. We are having a grand restful time. We were invited to the Prince's so I feel a bit bored thinking of the whoopee there but console myself with the fact this is healthier! Pa Simpson left on the 3rd and is at Monte Carlo, we still have Ma but she leaves on the 28th hurrah. We are having her for midday dinner Xmas and I have asked Thelma, Mr Morgan,[2] Gladys,[3] Mike, Thaws to help shout the old lady down. George [Murray] has the same thing I have wrong with his stomach and is taking just what I am namely bismuth and belladonna[4] and is also only allowed whiskey and water, plain food and plenty of rest. We are comparing notes tomorrow when he comes for a family dinner. I haven't met the Frazers yet,[5] I should have done so at the reception but I never thought of them, but after Xmas I'll make the Thaws have me for a KT with them. I am enclosing this funny little cheque which you'll have to have a magnifying glass to see the amount with. I want you to take out for

1. Aunt Bessie's address in Washington was 1911 R Street.
2. Harry Hays Morgan (1860–1933), late of the US Consular Service, father of Consuelo, Thelma and Gloria.
3. 'Mike' Scanlon's girlfriend Gladys Kemp, whom he was shortly to marry.
4. An extract of deadly nightshade, then used in medicine as a sedative.
5. Robert Frazer, whose sister was Aunt Bessie's friend, was appointed US Consul-General in London in November 1932.

the flowers for mother and then darling just let yourself go on the rest. Perhaps it will buy a bottle of booze.[1] Anyway all my love goes with it and all sorts of hopes of being with you in the spring. A big hug and kiss from

WALLIS

1. Still prohibited, though F. D. Roosevelt, who had just been elected to the presidency, was pledged to repeal the Eighteenth Amendment.

CHAPTER THREE

1933: Friend

1932 had not been a good year for Wallis. She had suffered a near-breakdown in her health; her husband's business affairs had gone from bad to worse; the longed-for trip to America had failed to materialize; and her spirits were affected by the continuing general atmosphere of gloom in England. After the excitement of meeting the Prince in 1931, she and Ernest had in fact seen little of him in 1932: in her memoirs, Wallis could remember no encounters with him that year apart from their visits to the Fort in January and in the autumn. Now her best American friends in London were leaving – the Grants, Mike Scanlon and the Thaws. In the meantime, however, Wallis's friendship with Thelma had grown much closer.

The 1933 correspondence opens with a letter written at the Fort. Ernest is abroad on business. (The fortunes of his shipping firm are very slowly starting to pick up, and his frequent absences will be a significant factor in the events of the next three years.) For the second week-end in succession, Wallis has been taken down to the Fort by Thelma. (For Thelma's hold on the Prince's affections is beginning to slip; her aim is to distract him by surrounding him with amusing new acquaintances.) The only other guest is the Prince's old boon companion 'Fruity' Metcalfe.[1] In these circumstances, Wallis is able to get to know the Prince rather better.

Sunday, 29th January   The Fort, Sunningdale, Ascot

Darling

I have been so gay since the 16th when the first party was given for the Grants. They sailed on the 25th and there wasn't a night without a party. Ernest had to go to Italy on the 19th, the day after our dinner

---

1. A handsome Irish cavalry officer whom the Prince had met in India in 1922 and taken an enormous liking to, and who had served for a time as his equerry. He had married a daughter of Lord Curzon.

for them, so I became the merry widow assisted by George [Murray] who is still a widower. Last week-end I came here with Thelma and commuted to London for parties but this week-end I am remaining until Tues having arrived Fri night. E is still away. The bathroom in the flat above has leaked through and ruined my ceiling of course they must fix it but not pleasant. I have had my numerology (spelling doubtful) done and it seems I am in a bad year nothing terrible but lots of little upsets and I seem to be having them. It is cold for England now and since arriving here we have been skating out on the water with the Duke and Duchess of York.[1] Isn't it a scream! Also you can imagine me on the ice but due to having roller skated I have not been too bad. The Prince presented T and self with skates etc. I have almost decided to come in spite of money. We can't be much worse than the present and I want to come to the USA before I grow a long grey beard. Now please be frank about what you think it right for you to contribute because you must keep something for yourself. You have given all your inheritance away I'm afraid so just say and then I can make more definite plans. I think I can only manage to be away about 6 weeks in all. I am having farewell dinner for the Thaws on the 1st but Ernest will not have returned by then. I am writing under rather trying conditions – in the drawing room, Thelma & Prince doing *needle work* and 'Pops' [Thelma] reading aloud, my boy (or that is the one asked for me), 'Fruity' Metcalfe, having developed flu this a.m. I can't stand the Morgan voice so asked permission to write you during the reading. I am losing a lot of my good friends and shall have to look about in hopes of replacing them. My foxes are really lovely – you better have them when I come to see you. All love,

WALLIS

Further week-ends at the Fort followed: Wallis's engagement book records that she was there with Ernest twice in February 1933 and once in March. 'If the Prince was in any way drawn to me', she wrote, 'I was unaware of his interest.' Thelma was always there, and often the Prince of Wales's younger brother Prince George. Around this time, as the letters show, the Prince accepted further invitations to Bryanston Court.

1. The Prince of Wales's brother 'Bertie' (the future King George VI) and his wife Elizabeth (the present Queen Mother).

Saturday, Feb 18th

Dearest Aunt B

I am really worried about your having such a long siege of pain. Isn't there something or some place you could go that would cure it? We have been having a fairly gay time. The Prince came again to the flat Tuesday and I had Gladys and Mike [Scanlon] as he likes Mike. The Sackvilles are away on a cruise for 6 weeks. I went to a charity bridge with Mrs Mullins and won a brace of pheasants! I am just waiting to hear whether you will come over and be presented and we all hope you will decide as of course it's an opportunity and $500 would do it. If however you don't want to do that, I am coming to Washington on condition you still feel like parting with $500. I have had a talk at last today with Ernest and we think if I came around March 14th and returned before May 5th (his birthday) and also if you sent me your cheque in dollars I can have the advantage of the exchange in buying tickets and could return any excess to you. I would buy a round trip as there is a great saving ($100 dollars or more) on any line by doing this. Ernest will see where he can do the best and the most convenient sailings etc. It would certainly be nice to see America under pleasant circumstances. My two trips home since I've lived in England were so dreadful.[1] I would wait to get clothes in USA. However though it sounds silly I can't remember whether March is cold enough for fur-trimmed coat or not and when do you put on straw hats? Poor Katherine – though I really feel sorrier for the Hanrahans than anyone. Imagine having it happen in your own house! All love,

                                                            WALLIS

Just as Aunt Bessie was about to send off the cheque for $500 which would enable Wallis to sail for America, the deepening financial crisis there – caused by nervousness of businessmen at the programme of President F. D. Roosevelt who was about to take office – led to a bank holiday throughout the United States. Wallis's next letter was written on the day of Roosevelt's inauguration, just after she had listened to his famous broadcast address.

1. In 1929, in connection with her mother's illness and death.

Saturday, March 4th

Dearest Aunt B

After being in a state of excitement, having got E into the mood of sending me home, today does not look hopeful for the trip. We must now await the developments of this banking mess and you can cable me how you feel about still giving me the trip. If this situation clears up I shall have to cable you about the best way to get me the money. It may be best to send a draft in sterling for the amount of my round trip. I find due to the exchange I can get a round trip on the White Star–Olympic sailing March 22 and return on the Majestic sailing May 5 for $300. Ernest thinks the faster boats are worth the difference in that I have more time with you. I could sail on the Bremen with Thelma and Gloria March 24 and return Europa May 3 for $50 more including tips as on those boats I must tip in dollars. We have worked everything out by the exchange and of course one can tip in pounds on the White Star in these days. I think there is more use for $50 than a day and a half difference in time and the Morgan twins' company. I have thought of coming straight through to Washington asking Mary to meet me possibly lunch with her and then to the train. Naturally a lot depends on docking time. I thought of spending the last week in NY to get some clothes etc and if I went over a day or two ahead of you and got the worst over you could then come over for my last 4 or 5 days. If this doesn't suit you anything you arrange will be OK by me. On talking over the time situation with E I see that actually the White Star gives me $1\frac{1}{2}$ days longer than the German in America so there is really no choice as to the wisest to come on. I will have the parents of Frances Rickatson-Hatt for company – not exciting but better than nothing. I have just been to Mike's to hear Roosevelt's address on the radio. I don't think it very encouraging and am afraid it looks as though there would be inflation and America off the Gold Standard.[1] Bad news all round. We are living in exciting times and shall more than likely all be looking around for jobs. Well here's hoping that banks permitting I will be with you this time next month. All love –

WALLIS

1. Two accurate predictions.

Having seen nothing of her native land since her mother's death in the autumn of 1929, Wallis finally sailed for New York at the end of March 1933. In her memoirs she writes that Ernest travelled with her, but this was not the case. Her memory was playing her false. But there is no reason to doubt another story in the memoirs. She tells us that, as England dropped out of sight, a breathless messenger brought her a 'bon voyage' telegram from the Prince, looking forward to her speedy return. Thereafter she was treated with extraordinary respect by the ship's company. 'Let me be candid,' she writes, 'the attention was flattering. I enjoyed every minute of it.'

Wallis's sojourn in Washington coincided with the famous 'hundred first days' of F.D. Roosevelt – a momentous time, which saw the abandonment of the Gold Standard, the creation of the Civilian Conservation Corps, the introduction of new taxes and the announcement of a massive programme of relief and public works. None of this seems to have made much of an impression on Wallis: she was not a political animal. She did, however, have a wonderful time in America, where she saw many old friends.

Wednesday [17 May]   On board RMS OLYMPIC

Darling

What can I ever say to make you know how much I appreciate your giving me this marvellous trip and then a dress and coat besides? Maybe you realise that I am enough like my mother to be completely inadequate at expressing my feelings when I feel the most. I'm afraid I then generally joke the most. I really never knew such an unselfish and beautiful character as you are and I don't deserve one bit of your goodness except for the fact that you know I love you better than anyone in the world and will always be on hand when you need me. I have had very little sleep since Sunday as I have collected 4 men who never leave me be. Certainly I have something this trip that I'll never have again. The night of sailing I went on deck to have a last glimpse at my native shore and I ran into the Purser such a nice man and he took me to his cabin for a drink where we were joined by A.E. Matthews[1] the English actor and an artist named Walter Tittle[2] whom

1. Alfred Edward Matthews (1869–1960), English character actor known for his gentlemanly roles in popular plays and films.
2. Walter E. Tittle (1883–1966), the fashionable portrait artist from Springfield, Ohio.

Frances Hill once brought to my house to dinner in London. Later the Purser changed my room to an *enormous* one on aft deck (not to be told). The price of all this was that I had to sit at his table which you know I hate and still do, though I'm the only woman. Have played bridge every night and only 4 shillings down so far. We have had an awful roll all the way but I've felt fine. It is going to take a bit of discipline to settle down into the domestic type again especially as I know it really was my swan song unless I can hang onto my figure and take a trip before I'm 40 which is only 3 years off. I hope I didn't worry you too much rushing around so. I thought you showed signs of strain but maybe it did your neuritis good. Please write me honestly how you get on and don't neglect yourself again please. Jack's[1] cacti are too grand and gramophone records and pecans beside. Can you bear it and what is it about? Kiss Wiley[2] for me if you see that mug again. Ethel sent me a nice wire. All my love and it really was all too grand and exciting for words and if I never move again I'll be content with this one. A big hug

WALLIS

The captain has been very nice. I went for a KT but found him inclined to pinch so never again.

After her return from America, Wallis's letters to her aunt indicate the beginning of a new phase in her relations with the Prince of Wales. While there is no hint as yet of real intimacy, she and Ernest are clearly becoming accepted into the inner circle of the Prince's friends. They are regular week-end guests at the Fort. They accompany him to night clubs in London. He dines quite often at Bryanston Court. Wallis sees much of Thelma, both with and without the Prince. Meanwhile the financial difficulties which press upon the Simpson household continue; while the holding of an international economic conference in London[3] brings many of Wallis's friends over from the United States – including John Wiley, her recent escort in Washington.

1. Probably her old friend Jack Warner, the movie mogul.
2. John Cooper Wiley (1893-1967) of the US Foreign Service, subsequently US Ambassador to Portugal, Iran, etc.
3. The London Conference – the brainchild of the late President Hoover – lasted from early June to mid-July and was to discuss the stabilization of exchange rates. There was a huge American delegation, accompanied by numerous lobbyists and journalists.

Tuesday, May 30th   Bryanston Court

Darling

This is my first letter to you since arriving. Everything has been so upside down and confused and I'm still dazed from Washington. I must admit to a terrible feeling of being let down and also to feeling a little reluctant about taking up the domestic life once again. I miss the attention of the boys! We have been out a lot at night and spent the week-end at the Prince's and then have been to the Embassy Club Monday and Tuesday with him. Thelma is still the Princess of Wales and I think the trip did a lot of good. Ernest met me at Cherbourg. I had rather a late night and didn't wake up until 12 noon when the stewardess rapped on the door and said there was a gentleman to see me and presented me with Ernest's card. It was a great surprise.

As I told you I knew bad news would be at this end. With the exchange almost normal again and the insurance companies only lending certain amounts it practically leaves no money for us so we really can't do but the very minimum entertaining – one dinner per month – and of course can't go to any of the shows that are on such as Ascot, Aldershot etc. And of course, with blue dress perfect for Ascot and Posy Guinness[1] saying she would take me any day I must refuse as the tickets are 4 guineas and lunch one guinea a day. I went to the Derby with the Scanlons. No one had arranged a bus party – Ernest didn't want to go – so we 3 went. Took our lunch, parked the car and strolled about – very tiring. Yesterday the Warren Robbins[2] arrived and I saw them at cocktails at Rolland's[3] after the Derby, and am trying to get the Prince for next week for dinner to say goodbye to Mike [Scanlon] and have the Robbins at the same time. Mike sails the 8th, Gladys remaining until July and then to America.

I have been writing this letter since Tuesday and today is Friday. The Robbins tell me that [John] Wiley may come over for the Conference and that they planned that I must come to Paris for a trip with all of them. I can't afford it unless I sell the Allegeheny [sic] which might be just as well to get something out of it. I have let the kitchen

1. Wife of the inventor Kenelm Guinness, of the famous brewing family. In her memoirs, Wallis describes her as 'an old friend, young, blond, vivacious and pretty'.
2. Warren Delano Robbins (1885–1935), a well-born American diplomatist. Minister to El Salvador, 1928–30; Chief of Protocol at State Department, 1931–3; Minister to Canada from 1933 until his early death.
3. Bernardo Rolland, Counsellor at the Spanish Embassy.

maid go. Mrs Ralph is always nice about helping out in a tight place. Cain was simply thrilled with your stockings and the dress. The butter moulds are a huge success except that everyone wants to steal them. I have secured the Prince for Tues night. Robbins and Scanlons. I see the funny moulds going – I am sure he will ask for them for Thelma she is so mad for them and I have refused her. I miss you so much and so hope you are taking care of yourself. I wish you would come over here for the summer. As you know it would mean London and no car but still it's not too hot. I have never seen anything so divine as the weather, nothing but sunshine and warm enough for dresses without coats. My clothes are really a huge success. PW calls the picquet [sic] one my white tie dress. E is well but worried. I think he is on the point of asking Ma for money which will be nice after my performance. The Grants arrived Wed. We dined with them last night. They are here for 5 years and she told Ernest they had about 20 thousand dollars per year so not exactly poor in my mind and looking at large houses. I hear from Lester that things are brighter in the US but we will be sunk until the currencies are fixed. All my love

WALLIS

Sunday [11 June]

Darling can you beat this – Wiley arriving in London! He got here Thursday night and we lunched together Friday. We are dining with him tonight – the first meeting between the boys. There are many dinner parties every night and I suppose the season is gay. Julie Shipman[1] produced the Atwater Kents[2] father and son and they gave Thelma and self some parties especially as she produced the Prince. One was so tall and the other so short that I called them the long and short wave lengths. Gladys and myself gave a joint KT party, about 50 in all. Mike got us the gin through the Embassy. My party for Mike and the Robbins came off beautifully lasting until 4 a.m. I haven't seen the Dunns as yet. Tamar arrives tomorrow and is staying here until Thelma comes back from Ascot the end of the week. I am having the Grants to dinner tomorrow, the first time I've been able to have them for a meal since their arrival. We have been out all the time. Last

1. A Chicago heiress.
2. A. Atwater Kent (1873–1949), the famous wireless inventor and manufacturer, and his son of the same name.

week-end was Whitsun and we spent it at the Prince's again. Prince George, Grand Duke Dmitri [of Russia] and wife were the party. It was fun but a touch too royal. We have had very hot weather but nothing compared to what your weather has been. I wonder what you're going to do and if you shouldn't get away quickly from the heat. Remember we would love to have you over here. Tuesday Mr S is taking us to the [Aldershot] Tattoo. I supply the supper and he the wine and car. Mrs Ralph departs July 20th. I haven't started looking as yet for another. I believe I can never replace her for this household because she is economical and good. The Coxes[1] after never asking us into their house all this time have finally asked us to drinks next Saturday. Love and a big kiss,

WALLIS

On 19 June Wallis celebrated her thirty-seventh birthday. Four days later, the Prince celebrated his thirty-ninth – the occasion of the first letter he received from Wallis to be preserved among his papers. Accompanying her presents to him, it is short and correct.

Friday, June 23rd   5, Bryanston Court, Bryanston Square, W1

Sir –

Many Happy Returns of the day. This small 'presy' is to conceal Bryant & May's [match] books on your dining table at the Fort. I am also enclosing your own spoon which I borrowed from Osborne[2] for the marking.

Your obedient servant
WALLIS

[25 June]

Darling

Many thanks for the cable. I did have a grand birthday. Lunched with Wiley, then everybody met here at 7.30 for drinks and then drove to the restaurant on the river where the Prince met us after a very gay dinner. We went back to his house where we made whoopee until 4.30 a.m. so you can judge by that the party went well. Also I'm sure the

1. Raymond E. Cox (born 1893), First Secretary at the US Embassy.
2. Butler at the Fort.

own spoon which I
borrowed from Osborne
for the marking.
Your obedient servant
Wallis

Friday, June 23rd
5, Bryanston Court,
Bryanston Square.
W.1.
Ambassador 2215

Sir —

Many Happy Returns
of the day. The small
"pussy" is to conceal
Bryant & May's boxes
on your dining table
at the Fort. I am
also enclosing your —

Dunns and Wiley appreciate having been included. The night of the
charity show I gave a dinner before and had Willmott [Lewis] afterwards. We went to Thelma's and Willmott had a long chat with HRH
so I have done well by Washington. I had note from Corrine telling
me in confidence that Henry had been sent away from the school for
insubordination. Don't mention it though I'm sure she has probably
told you. I don't find it as much fun having Wiley here as in Washington as I never see him alone. Gloria V[anderbilt] has arrived and is
staying with Thelma. Tamar still here but never home. She leaves July
first. I imagine you would have cabled me if you had decided on a
summer plan. I am still homesick for Washington and am certainly
treated like an older woman here by the men. That was my swan song
all right. All my love and a big kiss

WALLIS

PS Even Wiley treats me like a happily married woman.

*Wallis saw much more of the Prince that summer. On the Fourth of
July she gave an 'American dinner' for him at Bryanston Court. (In*

her memoirs, she says that this was the first time he was a guest there: but we know from the letters this was not so. He had dined with the Simpsons as early as January 1932, and on several occasions since.)

Ernest having to go to Norway on business in late August, the Simpsons decided to extend their trip there into a holiday. They stayed with their friends the Thaws, Benjamin Thaw having become Counsellor at the American Legation in Oslo.

Wed, August 30th   1 Halvdan Stratesgatan, Oslo

Darling

We got here Thursday. Tamar has a very nice house on the outskirts with a garden and 3 excellent servants. We go every afternoon to the golf links. They are lovely as to scenery being surrounded by mountains and running along the shores of a lake. The course itself not too good as it is very new. Not many people on it and we play 18 holes in peace. Excellent for E, who may have to go to Hamburg on the way home. We expect to leave here about the 15th or 16th but hope to be able to arrange to return a different way if not more expensive. I will have no cook on arrival and am wondering if you will have. I too would like to think we could again motor on the continent but the outlook isn't bright and here in the home of shipping they are all poor and depressed. Danke has a very attractive nephew. We are golfing with him today. Oslo itself just a village and no clothes needed. How is the neuritis? All love,

WALLIS

Sept 9th   Oslo

Darling

We are still enjoying the Thaws' hospitality which consists of 18 holes of golf per day and a quiet evening. We have had 2 drinks parties here. We (E and self) have been to 2 Norwegian dinner parties being the only foreigners present. Very interesting – and how the natives drink! E has had a lot of business to try and do each morning and as a result had to give a dinner to Norwegian shippers last night at the firm's expense. The Thaws attended and it all went very well to the tune of £12, ending at 3 a.m. and hopes of business! Benny is acting extremely well considering his father's death and his make-up combined and really made an effort for E last night. He has gone off shooting again today for 10 days and really insisted upon our remaining until his return. Our plans still indefinite as we haven't heard from NY whether E has to go to Hamburg but we have tentative bookings on 20th via Bergen arriving London 22nd. If however we go to Germany we would leave on the 23rd arriving Hamburg the night of the 24th and England about 4 days later via our old friend the Hook of Holland–Harwich. I am more than thrilled to know that you haven't spent *all* of the Coleman legacy[1] on *relations* and that your trip to London next spring is assured. All my love and a big hug & kiss

WALLIS

Returning to England after Ernest's brief business trip to Nazi Germany, the Simpsons immediately found themselves invited to the Fort – the first of many week-ends they were to spend there that autumn. Meanwhile their financial problems were such that they were faced with the prospect of having to sell the flat at Bryanston Court.

Saturday, Oct 14th

Darling

Very tricky new stationery you have produced. I am so sorry about the corsets but as I wrote I must have waist measure. We have been out every night but 2 since our return from Hamburg. E had the flu for a few days but I still went on. I have a new cook and new k maid arriving Monday. Had to go back to having the KM, simply could not find a cook that sounded possible who would come without one. This is the first dark English weather we have had and I am spending the day in bed as I really got awfully tired and nervous with the rush here and trying to have something to wear. At which thought I have ordered 2 evening dresses as US ones are falling apart. I have put blue moire where the white piquet [*sic*] was. You must not think of helping me. I want everything put on cures for your arm. I can't get over the fantastic situation of Newbold and the sisters. I can't think the winter in W for either of them will be pleasant. E says he will know in January whether we must try and rent the flat as unless the firm gives him something in the way of income we can't afford to run it. Food

1. Rose Coleman, a friend of Aunt Bessie, had died in March 1929, leaving her a legacy of $10,000.

is so expensive, 4/6 for 6 ears of corn making one vegetable come to $1. The papers over here don't print any encouraging news about America coming out of the depression. The stockbrokers seem to be the only people who have made something to tide them over. Hotels and restaurants are full here also the theaters. Lots of love

WALLIS

Wallis's allusion to 'the fantastic situation of Newbold and the sisters' refers to a scandal which had broken out in the Montague family. Her comments are interesting and tell us something about her moral attitudes.

Aunt Bessie's rich and beautiful first cousin in Virginia, Lelia Montague Barnett – 'Cousin Lelia' – had two daughters, another Lelia[1] and Anne. Anne was in love with the journalist Newbold Noyes, son of the head of Associated Press and brother of Wallis's great friend Ethel, who was married to Sir Willmott Lewis.[2] Noyes, however, had conceived a passion for Anne's sister Lelia. All three were already married; all three marriages collapsed, with unhappy consequences. Anne took to drink. Lelia now turned up in London with her friend Madge Larrabee, where she gave Wallis a first-hand account of the affair.

Sunday, Oct 29th

Dearest Aunt Bessie

I have really neglected you these past two weeks but we have been on the go every night and my days have been fittings and trying to lunch and play bridge which is a great mistake. But I have been lucky at the latter. Then I have been to the estate agents about renting the flat. They say we won't get more than 12 guineas, and as we pay 15 unfurnished it's hard to know what to do. The advantage of letting it go at 15 would be to get rid of the expenses of running it. They say maybe at the beginning of the season we can get more. In the meantime E is getting grey and trying to get up the courage to ask his father to restore the allowance. He really is the most selfish old pig never gives a cent or does a thing for us unless he gets something out of it. Imagine giving E £10 at Xmas and £10 at his birthday. I really detest the old

1. 'Cousin Lelia' always refers to the mother; 'Lelia' on its own to the daughter.
2. A further association was that Newbold Noyes (1892–1942) was editor of the *Washington Evening Star*, the principal shareholder in which was Aunt Bessie's employer Miss M. B. Adams.

boy and have to make such a fuss over him and see him the nights we should have off to rest between parties. Besides hopping in and out of taxis when he never offers the car to me during the day – and the 'Tart' riding in state. E is perfectly resigned to it all however and I suppose there is really nothing he can do about his father's make-up. I got the corsets and have sent them by Lelia. She and Madge arrived a week ago today but I didn't see them until the Monday night when they came to dinner just with E and self. After dinner we had the Noyes affair. I so agree with you that the Noyes divorce is a long way off. It seems that Lelia could have had her divorce in Paris about 2 weeks but that Newbold cabled her not to that it would look better if Alix[1] got her's first and the latter it seems is too nervous to go to Reno until January. Of course she is simply stalling for time and for New-bold to get over this new idea. She has seen him in so many situations of this sort and always plays the time game. It seems she and Lelia have had plenty of talks together about the whole situation. It's really pretty awful and I shall think Newbold an utter cad if he does not marry Lelia. She has given up her home and packed and shipped her things at great expense. Madge tells me that Bob[2] really behaved beautifully and Newbold should realise that she never would have come to the point of leaving Bob except for him – and to leave her flat with 4 children would be too low. However I for one believe him capable of it. The situation between the 2 sisters will be impossible. Do write it all to me. We always have some form of scandal it seems in the family. I didn't tell Lelia where I had heard of the thing from, as it happens it was from Anne and she asked me if Anne had said anything to me and I said that we had no chance for a talk as we had been always on a party. Tuesday the Prince and Thelma came for dinner and we went to a cinema and as Lelia and Madge were going to the theater I asked them back here for a sandwich and beer. They came and I think were thrilled at meeting him. He stayed until 3 a.m. and played the bag pipes for them stood on his head and gave Madge a book of war pictures that he had intended for E but decided they would be a good thing to have seen in America. Madge and Lelia looked like 2 frightened rabbits when they came in. My new cook has turned out to be not only a bad cook but very impudent and Saturday

1. Newbold's wife Alexandra Ewing, whom he had married in 1915 and by whom he had three children.
2. Lelia's husband Bob Dickey.

gave me notice she was leaving tomorrow Monday. They are not entitled to do that in England. One must give a month's notice. I went at once to the agency yesterday and found out I do not have to pay her for the time she has been here – 2 weeks. As a matter of fact I was going to give her notice myself tomorrow but counted on a month to look for another. I am certainly having a time this fall gathering together and probably when I do find the right one some one will rent the place. I think you better let your flat go and come to us as 'paying guest'. How about it? Cousin Lelia wrote a note saying she might come to London. I simply can't ask her to stay. Do you think she would expect us to have her? E has banned all guests except *you*. Perhaps you can drop hints or come with her and move into your room. I do think though that in a couple of months the requests for our society will lessen as we will not be able to entertain in return and people that you don't know very well don't keep on asking you. Before the flat had a reputation for good food etc and I think people liked to come and not going or entertaining does simplify the clothes question and Thelma takes us to so many night clubs & that means new evening dresses. Now that the family has the Noyes affair to chew over it must be very amusing when the clans gather. Do write it all. And when Anne shoots them both cable!

It will soon be the anniversary of mother's death. Will you attend to flowers for me and let me know the cost? She would have suffered terribly in these hard times coupled with the loss of a 3rd husband. Poor darling, perhaps she is better off even if we aren't and are left to always miss her. All love,

WALLIS

Tuesday, November 7th

Dearest Aunt B

We went to the Osbornes Friday and they don't give one much chance for writing. I sent love & kisses by Lelia but suppose they will be lost in the Noyes concentration camp. I hope the corsets are OK. Isn't the dollar too awful. I think R must be going mad. The papers here print alarming things about the US. One can't believe it all. Do more people seem to be losing their money? Or is it as gay as when I was there and has the cost of living and clothes gone up? I took a deaf cook and now Florence and Cain are complaining. She can't hear over the telephone even so I have another change to make. I am beginning to wish someone would come along and rent this place. Not a nibble so far. Someone told me you could get an unfurnished flat in this building like mine for £450 and we pay £750 and they refuse to reduce our rent. More and more apt houses are being built in London and rents are bound to come down. We of course took ours when modern flats were scarce. Nothing in the way of parties on the books this week as we haven't had a dinner party this autumn. I suppose people are now waiting for the returns. The rest is welcome and we will be able to see Pa who gets cross if not payed a lot of attention and who really devils E to death. I am going to miss Thelma terribly when she goes to NY after Xmas. Tamar is going from Oslo to France and sails from there so I shan't see her. Sorry this letter is so dull but can think of nothing interesting. All the excitement is on your side of the Atlantic. All love

WALLIS

Saturday, November 18th

Darling

Such an influx of cheques. You are too good to me as you know. However I am not going to cash them but will wait a month to see what happens. Surely Roosevelt can't be allowed to go on this way. The papers here think he has gone too far but maybe that is the English idea. Anyway it's alarming. Never have I heard of such a mess as Lelia. The Noyes have the most convenient nervous breakdowns and I imagine the family are punishing Newbold and not giving him any money. Aileen Winslow[1] is here. Berta [Grant] is having a dinner for her Monday. I had her for tea also Grants yesterday and PW came. Aileen knew him in Chile and Washington. Tamar is not going to NY – financial trouble – but is coming here to spend Xmas with the Milford Havens. She goes there instead of here so as to be able to have the girl friend which we wouldn't have in the house last spring. Mr S is still here getting more grouchy each day and more difficult and deaf. My deaf cook I have given notice to but have arranged for her to stay until after Xmas. Then there is a chance of Mrs Ralph returning for the 2 months as her husband's ship is on a cruise. That would give me

---

1. A friend of Wallis who was pseudonymously to write a book about her just before the Abdication under the title *Her Name was Wallis Warfield*.

time to really look around or maybe the flat will be gone – one Frenchwoman came to see it but I heard no more. We are still fairly dated up which is a surprise as we have yet to have a dinner. I blame it on rotten cooks. I have however had people for KTs quite often. Thelma is giving a dinner for Noël Coward next Fri. I think it will be very amusing to meet him. Miss Frazer is coming to lunch on Tuesday and the following week I lunch and go to a matinee with her. She sails Dec 29. The dollar is sending a lot of us home. Julia Diercks goes the 7th due to exchange. Betty Lawson Johnston is sailing the 29th of this month but just for a trip. She is coming to Wash. Do let me hear of her activities. Please come to see me early in the spring. Even if the flat is gone we will be in such a cheap hotel it would be OK. I don't blame you for not wanting the winter, the lights have been on the cars since 10 this a.m. It is as dark as night. Please take care of yourself and write me of your Xmas plans. All my love and thanks a million times

WALLIS

On the whole, 1933 had been a jolly year for Wallis – marred, however, by the chronic financial problems of the Simpson household. These had reached a critical point, and one could but hope that things would improve in the year ahead.

Sunday, Dec 10th   Sludge Hall, Billesdon

Darling

I am not going to take the $30 as it is to come out of the $300 but as I don't want to touch the cheque yet due to exchange I am going to cash the one for $30 so as to pay something on the F&M bill which is a certain size and then I am going to send you the difference in one of my cheques. Mr S got off Monday on the same boat with Betty L.J. and also Mrs Mullins. We had quite a week of him. Friday I dined with Maud and then she invited herself and that swine Peterkins[1] to supper with us on Sunday night. I had asked the old boy and the Hunters and at 7 Sunday she rang up and asked if they could come. Not surprising as I wrote she would start. However I am going to put a tactful or if necessary tactless stop to it all. Even Pa S was annoyed at her forcing herself on us. This is a very nice hunting box so-called

1. Maud's dissipated son, Peter Kerr-Smiley.

but with every possible comfort and it's like being in Warrenton again hearing nothing but horses discussed. We return tomorrow. Wednesday is the gay 90's party. My costume not bad. And the red wig fairly becoming. Total rent £4/4. Xmas week-end has developed in a large way. Sat dinner at my house, Sunday the Grants, Monday the Cartwrights and Tuesday we always feel depressed. I do think you could arrange to spend an Xmas with me. I've never been with my family since I married. I know the Hunters very well. They are a grand couple. I am enclosing when I get home tomorrow one of my usual large cheques for you to purchase your sweet self a 'something' for your stocking. The Prince gave me a nice photograph in a leather frame. We go there next week-end. Cain is having most of her teeth pulled out. My deaf cook most disturbing element in this house. We are all living at high tension waiting for Mrs Ralph's return. Mr S loosened up to the extent of six pounds and a Virginia Ham for my present and £15 to E. The latter has told him (Pa) that he can't remain over here with a depreciated dollar unless he restores some of his allowance. I made E take this tack and let's hope it works. We are going to return your money. I know that you have given up a lot to send it to me and I feel the pig I am. A big hug and kiss for Xmas and may it be a merry one and soon after the New Year please come to us. You have grown reticent of late about your date of arrival here. Please start to make plans. All love

WALLIS

CHAPTER FOUR

1934: Favourite

After 'a lovely and gay Christmas', Wallis lamented the usual winter exodus of her American friends from England. This year, the departing contingent included Thelma Furness. 'I am going to miss Thelma terribly', Wallis had written to her aunt in November, 'when she goes to NY after Xmas.'

January first

Darling

Happy New Year and everything you want in 1934. You should not have sent me a thing as from the looks of the Simpson fortune you'll have a long grey beard before the return of the $300. No allowance from Pa as yet. I shall paint the kitchen with $20 out your cheque. We had a lovely and gay Christmas. Xmas eve at Berta's, then lunch here for seven on Pa's Virginia ham, then a few more came in for cocktails and later Beatrice had a dinner and dance which went on until 4. Boxing Day we lunched with a man named Wheeler and played bridge all afternoon and then to Thelma's for dinner and a movie. We then took 3 days off except for a luncheon with Maurice Chevalier and went last night to Thelma's, a dinner of 16. With PW afterwards to a restaurant then back to the Spaniard's flat[1] ending up at 5.30 this a.m. Tonight I have 8 for dinner including PW and then we go to the Chelsea Arts Club Ball as his guests, so you see I've had quite a festive season. We had lots of cards but sent very few. Thelma gave me 3 rings, one of sapphire, then ruby and one of diamonds. Very nice. She bought them in a second-hand shop. The Prince gave me a table for the drawing room. Very pretty. (I picked it!) Julia Diercks had an automobile accident with Rolly [Bernardo Rolland] and the glass for the door broke and cut two fingers off the right hand. Isn't it too

1. Probably the flat of their friend Javier 'Tiger' Bermejillo, Second Secretary at the Spanish Embassy.

awful? She is sailing on the 11th and is also in same mess you were with Geoffrey Dodge. Minerva brought the corsets. Thelma is sailing around 25th, she can bring them and post on to you. Tamar is here. She and Thelma on the outs making it very awkward for me. Tamar stopping with Mrs George.[1] Have not written for some time due to all the goings on – please forgive me. Jack Warner here, very difficult to entertain, really such a bore but so nice. He spent Xmas at Knole and also New Year's so I didn't have to do anything about that. I took the girl named Russell that Miss Frazer introduced me to to Thelma's last night and am having her here tonight. She made quite a hit, seems full of fun. Today is the worst fog I've seen for 3 years, can't see your hand in front of your face and traffic being conducted by flares. Do plan to come over soon. The fogs are over by March. All love

WALLIS

From the Duchess of Windsor's memoirs:
I had, of course, been seeing a good deal of Thelma. We often lunched at the Ritz or Claridge's, sometimes alone, more often with other women. Our relationship was friendly and easy but scarcely intimate; neither of us, I suppose, was given to exchanging confidences. Around the turn of the year she announced that she was planning a trip to the United States. The day before she sailed she asked me for cocktails. We rattled along in our fashion; as we said good-bye she said laughingly, 'I'm afraid the Prince is going to be lonely. Wallis, won't you look after him?' I promised that I would, but privately doubted that he would be in need of solace.

From the memoirs of Thelma, Viscountess Furness:[2]
Three or four days before I was to sail, I had lunch with Wallis at the Ritz. I told her of my plans, and in my exuberance I offered myself for all the usual yeoman's services. Was there anything I could do for her in America? Were there any messages I could deliver? Did she want me to bring anything back for her? She thanked me and said suddenly: 'Oh, Thelma, the little man is going to be so lonely.'

1. A friend Tamar had made in South America, famous for her needlework.
2. *Double Exposure, a Twin Autobiography by Gloria Vanderbilt and Thelma Lady Furness* (Frederick Muller, London, 1959).

'Well, dear,' I answered, 'you look after him for me while I'm away.'

Thelma sailed for the United States on Thursday 25 January.

Friday, Jan 26th

Darling

I am feeling rather lost again with Thelma, Diana, Julia in America and Tamar back in Oslo. We have gone over the budget again and have now reduced dinner parties to one of 8 every 6 weeks and no girls' lunches over one of 4 once a month. Last week we spent at the Fort. We were six in all and PW. I tried my best to cheer him up. He will miss Thelma terribly but leaves himself in a couple of weeks.[1] He came and dined here Wed. I had the Pat Andersons and he took us to Quaglino's afterwards. Tonight Ernest (his firm paying) has 2 shippers with wives to dinner and we are going to a Vaudeville afterwards. I'm not looking forward to it much. Jack Warner is still about and really seems more of a bore than ever. Berta's sister is over here, Helen's mother staying with Helen and will go to Berta in Feb. Helen is much better but I don't think looks awfully well. Minerva couldn't look better and they have got a house in Hyde Park Square which they hope to get in in about 6 weeks. These next 2 months will be ones of rest, nearly everyone is going away. I love your new note paper, it is so thin. Have discovered that Miss Frazer's friend Mrs Russell was a Miss Hoover and that her father is the USA consul in Amsterdam. We are dining with Mrs R Sat night. Please take care of yourself and I do hope you have found the cure for the pain. All love

WALLIS

From the Duchess of Windsor's memoirs:
I was happy that in spite of Thelma's absence our association with the Prince continued much as before. The week-end after she left we were back at the Fort, and in the middle of the week the Prince came to Bryanston Court for dinner. A few days later Cain came hurrying into my room. 'Madam, the Prince of Wales

1. Probably a reference to the Prince's forthcoming tours of distressed areas to further the work of the Social Service Council.

Honeymooning in Spain
with Ernest Simpson, 1928

Navy wife in California, 1919

The Prince of Wales: a portrait by H. Ludlow completed in January 1931,
the month in which Edward first met Wallis

Dressed as a debutante for presentation at Court, June 1931

The Fort and its master   Skiing at Kitzbuhel, February 1935

At the Derby, May 1933.
Left to right: Prince George, the Prince of Wales, the Duke of Gloucester

With Aunt Bessie at Biarritz, August 1934

An infra-red photograph taken at a film première in 1934.
Left to right: Lady Queensberry, the Prince, Lady Portarlington, Wallis, Ernest Simpson

At Cannes, August 1935: above, Wallis and Edward; below, Wallis and 'Slipper'

At the Fort: lunch on the terrace;
with Katherine Rogers

WE are two, 1935

wishes to speak to you on the telephone.' It was the first time he had ever called in person. He wished to ask us to a dinner party that he was giving at the Dorchester for two old American friends, Fred and 'Gebe' Bate. Fred was the Western European representative of the National Broadcasting Company, and I had met them at the Fort.

That dinner [which took place on 30 January] was memorable for a special reason. Before, the Prince had never dwelt upon his duties and the particular function that he fulfilled in the imperial scheme of things. In fact, I deliberately kept the conversation from these topics, as if the subject of his working hours was something to be thrust aside in hours of relaxation. But on this particular evening some chance remark of mine broke through his barrier, and suddenly, while the others, as I recall, were away from the table dancing, he began to talk about his work, the things he hoped to do, and the creative role he thought the Monarchy could play in this new age, and also dropped a hint of the frustrations he was experiencing.

I was fascinated. It was as if a door had opened on the inner fastnesses of his character. What I now saw in his keenness for his job, in his ambition to make a success of it, was not dissimilar to the attitude of many American businessmen I had known. I cannot claim that I instantly understood him but I sensed in him something that few around him could have been aware of – a deep loneliness, an overtone of spiritual isolation.

From the Duke of Windsor's memoirs:
One evening I invited a few friends, Wallis among them, to dinner at the Dorchester Hotel. The conversation turned to my interest in the new social service schemes for the unemployed. It so happened that only that afternoon I had returned from Yorkshire, where I had been visiting working men's clubs in towns and villages. In the company to which I was accustomed the disclosure of such a chore would usually have brought some such sympathetic responses as, 'Oh! Sir, how boring for you. Aren't you terribly tired?'

Wallis had read in the newspapers about the Council for Social Service. She wanted to know more about it. I told her what it was and what it was trying to do. And, being an American, she was curious to learn just what a Prince's working day consisted of.

Although the orchestra was making a good deal of noise, I did my best to explain that, too.

From the Duchess of Windsor's memoirs:
'But I am boring you,' he said, as if ashamed of revealing so much about himself.

'On the contrary,' I answered, 'I couldn't be more interested. Please, please go on.'

While he was still looking at me questioningly, as if gauging my sincerity, the music stopped and the others began converging on the table. Then he said a surprising thing. 'Wallis, you're the only woman who's ever been interested in my job.' A little later on, as we were dancing, he asked if I would mind his dropping in at Bryanston Court for a cocktail now and then when his other engagements permitted.

He seemed to find stimulation in the changing company in front of my little cocktail table. In the beginning he stayed briefly. Then one evening he stayed on and on. The other guests, one by one, had to excuse themselves. Finally, only the three of us were left – Ernest, the Prince and I. By now it was long after dinner time, and finally in desperation I suggested, 'Sir, would you like to take pot-luck with us?'

The upshot was that in a few minutes the Prince was seated at the table between Ernest and me. This was the beginning of many such pot-luck dinners. We never knew when he was coming or how long he would stay. Sometimes he came once in a fortnight to stay only for a few moments; other times he was back twice in a week and would remain all evening. It always seemed to happen that he picked an evening when Ernest had brought home some work from the office or the evening we had set aside for going over the household accounts. After a succession of these disruptions of Ernest's routine, he developed the art of tactfully excusing himself and retiring to his room with his papers. The Prince seemed to have a new enthusiasm every visit, whether it was a new housing project that he was sponsoring or a design for a new planting at the Fort or a scheme for promoting a British trade drive in some part of the world, or even the latest American jazz record. During week-ends he increasingly singled me out as his partner during the dancing.

Thelma's absence stretched into weeks. Finally he asked me whether Ernest and I would like to bring some of our friends to the Fort....

Monday, Feb. 12th   The Fort, Sunningdale, Ascot

Darling

I have been very slow with letters these past 2 weeks. We have inherited the 'young man' from Thelma. He misses her so that he is always calling us up and the result is one late night after another – and by late I mean 4 a.m. Ernest has cried off a few but I have had to go on. I am sure the gossip will now be that I am the latest. However he is very sweet and we have been able to have some of our friends invited here – the Pat Andersons last week-end and the Hunters this one. I had a book in the form of a letter from Corrine telling all the heavy news. She is very upset by the Noyes affair as are the Howards here. There is no secret concerning the family movements any longer. We always have a slight scandal it seems. Mary writes me that her mother is in the hospital and can never get well as it is now definitely pronounced cancer. Isn't it awful? We are waiting to hear from Mr Simpson. E has written that he can't carry on without some help. Personally I don't think he will give any. Benny [Thaw] was here 2 days last week on his way to NY, dined with us twice – just as gay as ever! I think you better send me the dress as soon as possible as I'm really naked. I imagine in USA the styles are already launched for the spring. Mrs Jordan I think will know about my type. I am still wearing her little number. I want something sophisticated either red blue black or combination of colours but no pictures or greens and not over $59.50 and to be valued much lower. I hope you are not freezing – the papers here have alarming accounts of the cold in the USA. E's partner's death will increase our large income at about the rate of $100 per month but as E is so indebted to the firm we can't see it at all. Gladys writes that she and Mike parted for good Jan 7th but as the letter was slightly incoherent having been written at 3 a.m. after upset I can't see what it is all about. Forgive me for not writing but this man is exhausting. All love,

WALLIS

Monday, Feb 12th,

THE FORT,
SUNNINGDALE,
ASCOT.

Darling – I have been very slow with a letter these past 2 weeks. [...] Lane invited the "young man" from Thelma – the music less so that he is always calling us up and the result is one late night after another

Sunday, Feb. 18th

Dearest Aunt B

Enjoyed your letter and the clippings. Am also behind on my letters to you on account of the Prince who is here most of the time or telephoning 2 and 3 times a day being completely at a loose end. However Thelma will be back very shortly and it has occurred to me if you send the dress to her she could bring it in for me. I believe she is sailing about the middle of March so if you sent it to Thelma, Viscountess Furness, c/o Mrs R. Vanderbilt, 49 East 72nd St, NY enclosing a note to say it is for me. Did many people entertain Betty [Lawson Johnston] in Washington? I hope not. She is so full of herself but is not going as big here since PW doesn't pay much attention any more and never went there this winter. Am delighted the corsets are OK. We are in town this week-end for a change and dined with the Steens last night and tonight go to see Garbo and to supper with the Hunters afterwards. The embassy is filling up with new secretaries and wives. Walter P[rendergast] tells me they are attractive. We have never had so many bad fogs as a result the flat is filthy – curtains, lamp-shades, furniture covers all black, to say nothing of the walls. Mrs Ralph not so good as before I think – knowing it is only temporary she doesn't care quite so much. I can't believe the Lelia–Newbold marriage will ever come off with Lelia still without divorce. I am afraid the icing will be off the cake before everything is arranged. Wish Miss A had taken you to Florida for your arm. She's a pig. All my love

WALLIS

PS It's all gossip about the Prince. I'm not in the habit of taking my girlfriends' beaux. We are around together a lot and of course people are going to say it. I think I do amuse him. I'm the comedy relief and we like to dance together – but I always have Ernest hanging around my neck so all is safe.

Thursday, 22nd [February]

Dearest Aunt B

I understand from PW that Thelma is sailing between 15th and 25th of March so you may find me something very chic by then. I have no news. It is really quiet here, so many people away. We are going to the Prince's for the week-end. Rolly and Posy Guinness are the others. The Hunger Marchers[1] arrive in London tomorrow so we are going to the country in time for dinner. However there is never much mob excitement in this country. We are also faced with a *water shortage*. There hasn't been rain for weeks – if not oceans in 3 weeks the papers say we will be rationed. Awful with the dirt of so many fogs upon us. I am feeling very well but am quite thin not in the face but in the figure. Naturally worry over finances is not fat-making. I weigh 8 stone undressed but eat and drink as usual. Your side of the world has more news than here at the moment. Take care of yourself and all love.

WALLIS

One month later, on 22 March, Thelma returned from America. In New York, and on the sea voyage back to England, she had seen much of the young and rakish Prince Aly Khan;[2] and the Prince of Wales had got to hear of this association.

From the memoirs of Thelma Furness:
The Prince arrived at my house in Regent's Park that night. He seemed a little distrait, as if something were bothering him. Suddenly he said, 'I hear Aly Khan has been very attentive to you.'

I thought he was joking. 'Are you jealous, darling?' I asked. But the Prince did not answer me.

At the Fort, the Prince, although formally cordial, was personally distant. He seemed to want to avoid me. I knew that something was wrong. ...

When I got back to London I told Wallis about my talk with the Prince, the odd reference he had made to Aly Khan. What had happened? Did she know? ... But the only answer I got was a saccharine assurance, 'Darling, you know the little man loves you very much. The little man was just lost without you.'

After a while I said, 'Wallis, the Prince has asked me to come

1. A form of social protest whereby columns of unemployed workmen made their way on foot across the country amidst widespread publicity, relying for food and shelter upon wayside charity. A large march – the first since 1931 – was organized in January 1934 and arrived in London the following month. The Prime Minister, Ramsay MacDonald, refused to see the marchers, but they were allowed to demonstrate throughout the capital.
2. Son – and for a time heir – of the Aga Khan, the fabulously rich Ismaeli Muslim leader. He was twenty-three at this time and known as a lady-killer. He died in a car crash in 1960.

to the Fort next week-end. It's Easter week-end you know. Would you and Ernest care to come down? It might help.'

'Of course,' Wallis replied warmly, 'we'd love to.'

... That week-end was negatively memorable. I do not remember who was there, other than the Simpsons; there were about eight of us in all. I had a bad cold when we arrived.... Most of Saturday [1st April] passed without incident. At dinner, however, I noticed that the Prince and Wallis seemed to have little private jokes. Once he picked up a piece of salad with his fingers; Wallis playfully slapped his hand. ...

Wallis looked straight at me. And then and there I knew the 'reason' was Wallis.... I knew then that she had looked after him exceedingly well. That one cold, defiant glance had told me the entire story.

I went to bed early that night, without saying goodnight to anyone.... A little later the Prince came up to my bedroom. Was there anything he could have sent up for my cold? ... 'Darling,' I asked bluntly, 'is it Wallis?' The Prince's features froze. 'Don't be silly!' he said crisply. Then he walked out of the room, closing the door quietly behind him.

I knew better. I left the Fort the next morning.

In her own autobiography, Wallis gives a briefer and somewhat different account of the same episode.

From the Duchess of Windsor's memoirs:
Thelma returned early in the spring. Something had happened between her and the Prince. She was back at the Fort once, but the former warmth and easiness of their relationship was plainly gone. One afternoon she came to Bryanston Court. It was an unhappy call. She told me that the Prince had obviously been avoiding her – she couldn't understand why. He would not speak to her himself on the telephone. No more invitations to the Fort were forthcoming. Finally, she asked me point-blank if the Prince was interested in me – 'keen' was the word she used.

This was a question I had expected. 'Thelma,' I said, 'I think he likes me. He may be fond of me. But if you mean by keen that he is in love with me, the answer is definitely no.'

Sunday, April 15th   The Fort, Sunningdale, Ascot

Darling

I have the dress and it's grand. I wore it here last night for the first time. It was too big so had to have it fixed – an easy alteration. We are still coming here I suppose too much but of course it's tempting as one is comfortable and has such fun. Thelma is still in Paris. I'm afraid her rule is over and I'm trying to keep an even keel with my relations with him by avoiding seeing him alone as he is very attentive at the moment. And of course I'm flattered. Cousin Lelia wrote a long drool from Florida and told me you were motoring with Katherine [Galbraith]. I am delighted you have given yourself something. It's really alarming about Anne. She may do anything. Is she still drinking? And does Henry[1] know the cause of all this? Does Anne see Newbold and do Lelia and Anne speak? We haven't had a party for so long. Am saving up for the influx of Americans. We are having the most divine weather and I am writing to you in the garden with just a wool jumper on. Cousin L spoke of coming over to England this summer. I hope at the same time you do so that I will not have to put her up. She is not an easy guest and I don't think very restful. Have been hopeless about writing but actually am kept on the run by HRH and also try to keep up with my friends at the same time. All my love and do take care of yourself and the dress is divine.

                                                        WALLIS

Friday night [postmarked 21 April]

Darling

I'm so sorry you have had to cable. It is simply that I never have a night to write in. The Prince is here unless official things and there is Ernest and my friends the other nights. You can well imagine I'm a bit worn – never a restful moment as it requires great tact to manage both. Thelma still in Paris and we leave for the week-end tonight. Mr Simpson sailed for *Japan* today with girlfriend leaving us well in debt and no help. Isn't he a beast. Just 80 and still seeing the world. We are cookless but the place is used as a hotel these days. We never eat here and of course since I've produced PW several places we are filled with invitations from many sources who have been quiet up to now.

---

1. Anne's husband Henry Suydam.

Wouldn't mother have loved it all? When you come I shall have Mary send you some shoes for me and any cheap pale blue summer dress for country wear you see about $20 get for me. The royalty stuff very demanding on clothes. All love and please come soon. Getting fatter.

WALLIS

Wednesday, April 25th

Darling

I am so anxious to know whether I have the right dress as I have not seen Gloria as she went to Paris with Thelma. The latter has still not returned – which is very sensible as I think the royal affair is very much on the wane. I shall doubtless be blamed as for the moment he is rather attentive though sees equally as much of Mrs Dudley Ward[1] his old flame. I am much sought after and am trying to meet English people through him and he has had different ones every week-end lately. I am afraid I'll have to give up soon as it naturally takes more money to play around with him. More clothes, week-ends etc – then the tips there and all his friends are so rich – I think I'm the only poor one he has ever had. Am dying to be asked for Ascot week even if I have to steal and also still hopeful about the continent in August. All this of course if he doesn't find another girl or return to Thelma and I can find the cash and also keep Ernest in good humour. At the moment he's flattered with it all and lets me dine once or twice a week with him *alone*. I see John Wiley has married his Polish friend. The new man at the Embassy named Johnson[2] who came from Washington is not too hot. In fact there are not many attractive extra men here or women. I haven't had a party here for over a month. Have a lousy temporary cook and still the curtains are away. Can't get PW to ask the Grants – not his type. Still eating but can't gain too much – worry combined with excitement and never a chance to relax. It all takes a certain amount of tact handling another swan song before 40. Let me know when to expect you. I would like one or two country dresses – 1 linen, 1 wool – and Mary will have two pairs of shoes for you. Both

1. Freda Dudley Ward, the sensitive and vivacious wife of a Member of Parliament, with whom the Prince had had a love affair lasting from 1918 to 1924. Since then he had continued to pay her regular friendly visits, but in the late spring of 1934 – only a few weeks after Wallis wrote these words – he suddenly ceased to do so.
2. H. V. Johnson, the new First Secretary.

dresses blue I think on printed linen for that one or white trimmed blue. If asked to Ascot I haven't an idea what I could wear there and then the rest of the time I have the pale blue and brown from last year for one day, and I suppose a print for the other. He demands one to look chic. I know you'll be tired of hearing all this but it is rather thrilling for me. Write me soon and all love

WALLIS

Ernest is saving money or lacking it to such an extent that I had a masseuse for 15/- and we didn't speak for a while it made him so furious. I thought it cheaper than a Dr and very good to remove acidity. It is this expensive flat we can't get rid of.

Monday, May 7th

Darling

After writing you from the Fort [not found] I have had an invitation to the Prince's Ascot house party which starts on the 19th and ends on the 25th. He is giving me the ticket and the party doesn't go until after lunch and you need only go the 2 big days so my best number from last year and the other thing will do. I can't resist going so it would be better to come way before Ascot or just after as I wouldn't want to rush off just as you arrived unless you wouldn't mind being here those days without me. Ernest can't go – (1) the ticket, (2) the time from the city, (3) clothes. Trying to get this on the boat tonight. All love

WALLIS

Tuesday, May 22nd   The Fort

Darling

You did give me a lecture and I quite agree with all you say regarding H.R.H and if Ernest raises any objections to the situation I shall give the Prince up at once. So far things are going along beautifully and the 3 of us are always together in the little spare time PW has at this time of year. Don't pay any attention to gossip – anyone he looks at always creates jealousy and naturally Thelma doesn't like our seeing him so much in spite of the fact she has the Prince Aly Khan as a heavy suitor and has been off to Spain with him. I'm not taking her place in any respect anyway. Ernest is leaving next week for the con-

Tuesday, May 22nd

THE FORT,
SUNNINGDALE,
ASCOT.

Darling — you did give
me a lecture and I quite
agree with all you say
regarding H.R.H and
if there raises any
objections to the
situation I shall give
the Prince up at once

tinent for 2 weeks, will not be back until the 22nd so I have the Ascot week here as a free lance. I am feeling fine and have gained weight at last. I think playing golf and being here in the country has been a great help. I have cashed the cheque and paid for my massage which I continued in spite of poor E as they did do me loads of good. He is frightfully upset over my taking so much from you and does hope for better times but seems to think they will not come in shipping for another 2 years. We are waiting for a letter from you saying when you will sail. As you know Gladys [Kemp] and Mike [Scanlon] were married a week ago today. I hear she couldn't bring herself to marry the rich Jew. Give me enough notice before you leave to have Mary give you some shoes and stockings. It is still cold here but no rain. We had lunch out of doors but were nearly blown away. We have been here for the Whitsun holidays and leave tonight. Please don't think I'm completely in the ether. Mentally I'm quite sane about it all but I am not given much time to do things. Also I am doing over some of his 2 houses for him which fills up my days so much. Hurry over to see me and then you'll realise everything is OK. The fact Thelma is annoyed doesn't worry me as she is so wrong in London anyway. I have met some nice English people and they have been sweet to me. I have gone out of my way to make him see his old friends again as that was one of the criticisms of her that she surrounded him with awful people. All my love and a big kiss

WALLIS

From the Duchess of Windsor's memoirs:
Not long afterwards he [the Prince] mentioned casually that he was planning to return to Biarritz in August and take a house for his summer holiday. 'Won't you and Ernest come and stay with me?' he asked. Delighted as I was, I had to decline, explaining that Ernest had to go to the United States on business and Aunt Bessie had already arranged to stay with me during his absence. Though regretting Ernest couldn't join the party, he nevertheless brushed aside my other reservation, namely that a lady in her seventies would be a damper on the Prince and the young friends he had around him. 'Nonsense,' he said. 'I'd love to have your Aunt Bessie. From what you've told me about her I'm sure she'll be the life and soul of the party.' And so it was arranged. In early July Aunt Bessie arrived, and a week later Ernest sailed.

The first of August found us on our way with the Prince and the rest of his guests. It was a small party, initially composed of his Assistant Private Secretary, Hugh Lloyd Thomas;[1] 'G' Trotter and John Aird, his equerries;[2] Lieutenant-Commander and Mrs Colin Buist;[3] in addition to the Prince, Aunt Bessie and me. The Prince had rented a commodious villa called Meretmont, over-looking the ocean. As at the Fort, life was simple – swimming and sunbathing, golf, sometimes a little bridge. Soon the Prince and I fell into the habit of leaving the others once a week and dining alone at one or another of the little bistros whose special-ities he had come to know and appreciate on previous visits.

Later in the month we were joined by Mrs Kenelm Guinness. 'Posy', as we called her, was an old friend.... She was a cousin by marriage of Lord Moyne, a son of Lord Iveagh of the famous Guinness brewing family ... [who] was cruising nearby in his yacht *Rosaura*. Posy suggested that it might be fun to take a cruise with him, and she was sure that he would be delighted to have us. Having by now had enough of Biarritz, the Prince jumped at the idea, and very soon a formal invitation was extended by Lord Moyne. Aunt Bessie had planned to take a motor trip into Italy and – wisely, as it soon turned out – refused to be diverted.

The memoirs describe how they encountered a terrible storm in the Bay of Biscay, followed, however, by a delightful cruise along the Spanish and Portuguese coasts. The recital of events continues:

Only eleven days after leaving Biarritz we reached Cannes.... One evening, after we had been with Herman and Katherine Rogers for dinner, the Prince took from his pocket a tiny velvet case and put it into my hand. It contained a little diamond and emerald charm for my bracelet....

The original idea had been for our party to disband at Cannes, and I was going to rejoin my Aunt Bessie at Lake Como in the

1. Hugh Lloyd Thomas (1888-1938), a diplomat by profession who had been the Prince's Assistant Private Secretary since 1929.
2. Major (later Sir) John Aird (1898-1973), who had been the Prince's equerry since 1929. Wallis wrote of him: 'Jack, as we called him, was a Grenadier Guardsman; being then a bachelor, he lived at York House; he was tall and lean and had an amusing but biting wit.'
3. Commander Colin Buist (1896-1981) and his wife Gladys, old friends of the Prince.

north of Italy and return to Paris with her. At the last moment, however, the Prince suddenly decided that we were all having such a good time it would be a pity to end it so abruptly. He therefore invited Herman and Katherine Rogers to join us and to go on to Lake Como. As Lord Moyne had offered to let us continue in the *Rosaura* as far as Genoa, we sailed there the next day; then we motored up to the lake....

September was nearly over, and the Prince had a long-standing engagement to join his father and mother, who were going to perform the ceremony of launching the *Queen Mary* on the Clyde. We stayed at Lake Como for a week; and then we went to Arona to board the Orient Express for Paris. There the Prince and Jack Aird left us to fly back to London, leaving the rest of us to do a little shopping in Paris.

On the night of September 26, 1934, Aunt Bessie and I boarded the *Manhattan* at Le Havre, she to return to the United States while I would get off at Southampton.... As we were having dinner, and while I was telling her about the cruise, she asked in what she hoped would appear to be an off-hand way: 'Wallis, isn't the Prince rather taken with you?'

'Whatever makes you think that?' I asked.

'These old eyes aren't so old that they can't see what's in his every glance.'

'Aunt Bessie,' I finally answered, 'I would like to think that he is truly fond of me.'

My aunt looked hard at me. 'Isn't all this very dangerous for you? If you let yourself enjoy this kind of life, it will make you very restless and dissatisfied with everything you've ever known before.'

'You don't know what you're talking about,' I said. With true Montague arrogance I added: 'I'm having a marvellous time. It's all great fun. You don't have to worry about me – I know what I'm doing.'

My aunt sighed. 'Very well, have it your own way. But I tell you that wiser people than you have been carried away, and I can see no happy outcome to such a situation.'

On this foreboding note we finished our dinner, leaving me with much unsaid and still more unresolved in my own mind....

In one of the most frank and revealing passages of her memoirs, the Duchess goes on to describe how she had felt about her affair with the Prince at that time. Her common sense told her that it was no more than an adventure; but her 'not-so-common sense' made her aware that he was in love with her, though she found it hard to understand why.

Searching my mind I could find no good reason why this most glamorous of men should be seriously attracted to me. I certainly was no beauty, and he had the pick of the beautiful women of the world. I was certainly no longer very young. In fact, in my own country I would have been considered securely on the shelf.

The only reason to which I could ascribe his interest in me, such as it was, was perhaps my American independence of spirit, my directness, what I would like to think is a sense of humour and of fun, and, well, my breezy curiosity about him and everything concerning him.... Then, too, he was lonely, and perhaps I had been one of the first to penetrate his inner loneliness. Beyond this point my speculations could not carry me; there was nothing else real or tangible to nourish them.

I had no difficulty in explaining to myself the nature of the Prince's appeal to me. Over and beyond the charm of his personality and the warmth of his manner, he was the open sesame to a new and glittering world that excited me as nothing in my life had ever done before. For all his natural simplicity, his genuine abhorrence of ostentation, there was nevertheless about him – even in his most Robinson Crusoe clothes – an unmistakable aura of power and authority. His slightest wish seemed always to be translated instantly into the most impressive kind of reality. Trains were held; yachts materialised; the best suites in the finest hotels were flung open; aeroplanes stood waiting. What impressed me most of all was how this could all be brought about without apparent effort: the calm assumption that this was the natural order of things, that nothing could ever go awry. That evening, turning these assumptions over in my mind, it seemed unbelievable that I, Wallis Warfield of Baltimore, Maryland, could be part of this enchanted world. It seemed so incredible that it produced in me a happy and unheeding acceptance.

Ernest was at Southampton to meet me. In reply to his questions about my trip I said: 'I can't describe it. All I can say is that it was like being Wallis in Wonderland.'

Ernest looked at me quizzically. 'It sounds to me', he said thoughtfully, 'indeed like a trip behind the "Looking Glass". Or better yet, into the realm of Peter Pan's Never-Never-Land.'

From then on the Prince was always 'Peter Pan' to Ernest. He meant no disrespect; in fact, Ernest genuinely liked the Prince, and revered him as the man who would one day be his King. I laughed, but even so, I felt a slight annoyance.

Our life resumed its now familiar pattern. The Prince had gone on to Balmoral to spend a few days with his parents after attending the launching of the great Cunard liner named after his mother. Soon after his return he came to Bryanston Court for dinner and invited Ernest and me to the Fort for the week-end....

The letters to Aunt Bessie resume at the end of October.

Friday [27 October]   Bryanston Court

Darling

A month tomorrow that we said goodbye and I haven't written a line. I offer no excuses but it certainly isn't because I haven't been thinking of you and missing you. I have had an upset household – no cook upon arrival – notice from Florence and the kitchen maid. I bribed the latter by offering her £5 more to stay. Florence goes next Thursday and I have a new one coming, also Mrs Ralph returns. Ernest is looking much better. He has been a week in Paris and returns tonight from a week in Norway to leave again on Tuesday for Italy. There have been lots of shippers with wives here which we have had to entertain – very trying. Corrine stopped with us for a week and then went to the Holts. I took her to the Fort for a week-end. She sailed on the ghastly boat Tuesday. Have many clippings of the Vanderbilt case.[1] It's pretty bad. The papers here are very full of it all. I

1. The sensational case of 'The Matter of Vanderbilt' – in which Gloria Vanderbilt sought to recover custody of her daughter from her sister-in-law Gertrude Whitney – took place in New York from 28 September to 21 November 1934. Both of Gloria's sisters, Consuelo Thaw and Thelma Furness, gave evidence; and Consuelo (testifying on 13 November) mentioned Wallis's name in connection with the holiday at Cannes in 1931, in the course of which Gloria was alleged to have taken part in homosexual acts.

also have plenty of clippings about myself from the USA. The blue-eyed charmer is still the best beau and keeps me pretty busy but I haven't been out much in public. Minerva's house is very nice. John Aird's father died and he is now Sir John Aird. Hugh Thomas said to remember him to you. The Prince speaks in glowing terms of you always. I have ordered a set of Posy's pictures for you. She is still enjoying abdominal merriment. The Grants spent a night at the Fort. I arranged it at last. I bought a coat and dress with the $200 the Prince gave me and some leopard skins which I think will make a lovely sports coat. I had a note from Mrs Franklin and she is coming to tea Monday. The Perrins came to a cocktail party. The [Georges] Sebastians have been here, Merritt Swift and Buzzy Hewes – always some out-of-the-country talent. I feel grand as a result of a summer without responsibilities and many luxuries. Ernest saw the Rogers in Paris. I think I could have them as guests if I could urge them. It's a shame you didn't know of Miss A's plans before. You need not have sailed so soon. There is much excitement over the Royal Wedding.[1] I am going with Bertha Baron to see the procession. The seats are £1 each! The Prince offered a seat in the Abbey but I couldn't take it alone! Forgive my not writing – it isn't because I don't love you. Keeping up with 2 men is making me move all the time.

WALLIS

Monday, Nov 5   The Fort

Darling

I hope you took flowers to mother's grave for me on the 2nd and let me hear my share. You have been very patient with me about letters and I will try to do better. Don't listen to such ridiculous gossip. E and myself are far from being divorced and have had a long talk about PW and myself and also one with the latter and everything will go on just the same as before, namely the 3 of us being the best of friends which will probably prove upsetting to the world as they would love to see my home broken up I suppose. I shall try and be clever enough to keep them both. E is away. He went last Tuesday and leaves Paris tomorrow for Rome and Trieste. I expect him back the end of the week. I saw Mrs O'Malley at the Embassy Club the other night. I was with PW, Prince George, Lady Louis Mountbatten, Foxy

---

1. The forthcoming marriage of Prince George to Princess Marina of Greece.

Gwynne[1] and Hugh Thomas. She spoke quite nicely about you. Lady Jean Mackintosh[2] – you remember, from Biarritz – has asked me to several things and on the whole I could be stepping about every minute. Gladys Buist I have seen a lot. I am going to Melton [Mowbray] for a week-end with her. The new maid arrived Thursday and I am afraid is going to prove a dumb bunny as she laid the drawing room fire practically on the rug nearly burning us all up and smoking the now dirty green walls a little more. It is so cold here now and the fogs have started. My carpet in my bedroom is threadbare but I am going to wait until the spring. Ernest hopes to make expenses at least this year which is more encouraging than the partners putting money back each year. Mr S just as kind as ever. E asked him for the loan of a thousand dollars. Nothing doing flat refusal and yet he has the entire responsibility on this side of the water and no extra salary. I am having the same trouble adjusting myself to normal conditions as you. It really was fun this summer. The Prince speaks of going for winter sports after Xmas. Maybe I'll be asked! I am going to the theater with Prince George Tues night the Prince being away. Posy is also coming bringing a boy friend. Also I am shopping with him tomorrow. I do well with the Windsor lads. All my love and everything is absolutely grand between E and self.

WALLIS

The reason Wallis was then seeing so much of Prince George (who had now been created Duke of Kent) was that he was living at the Fort while preparing for his marriage at the end of November to Princess Marina of Greece. This was a spectacular event, and the Prince of Wales ensured that both Wallis and Ernest were included in the festivities.

From the Duchess of Windsor's memoirs:
Many brilliant dinners and soirées were held for the young and popular couple, culminating in a state reception given by the King and Queen at Buckingham Palace a day or two before the wedding. Ernest and I were invited. We took our places in the line of guests that by custom forms on either side of the reception rooms

1. Mrs Erskine Gwynne, a lively friend of Wallis from Washington days. She had once been a fashion model, and owed her nickname to her red hair.
2. Best friend of Posy Guinness, a daughter of the Duke of Hamilton.

on the approach of the Sovereign and his Consort. As they proceeded with great dignity down the room, members of the Royal
party followed in their wake, stopping now and then to speak
with friends. The Prince of Wales brought Prince Paul, Regent of
Yugoslavia and also brother-in-law of the bride, over to talk with
us. 'Mrs Simpson,' said Prince Paul, 'there is no question about
it – you are wearing the most striking gown in the room.' It was
a simple dress, designed by Eva Lutyens, daughter-in-law of the
famous architect, but the violet *lamé* material with a vivid green
sash made it outstanding.

The reception was rendered truly memorable to me for the
reason that it was the only time I ever met David's[1] father and
mother. After Prince Paul had left us, David led me over to where
they were standing and introduced me. It was the briefest of
encounters – a few words of perfunctory greeting, an exchange of
meaningless pleasantries, and we moved away. But I was impressed by Their Majesties great gift for making everyone they
met, however casually, feel at ease in their presence.

The wedding took place at 11 a.m. on November 29, and the
Abbey was crowded with foreign royalty, members of the British
and Dominion Governments, the diplomatic corps, and many other
dignitaries. The ceremony was solemn and moving. The Prince
had provided Ernest and me with very good places on a side
aisle, from which we had an uninterrupted view of the altar....

Monday [3 December]   The Fort

Darling

I simply never have a moment to do what I want to myself and I
have been too awful about writing but sleeping until 12 a.m. and then
the dash for lunch and shopping for the Prince afterwards. I am buying
his Xmas presents 250 of them for servants to be wrapped besides my
poor flat and things are quite neglected. The wedding was a marvellous
sight and we were asked to the reception at Buckingham Palace which
was something to see. I borrowed a tiara from Cartier. Ernest had to
go in knee breeches. We looked all right and the Prince brought the
Queen up to me [*sic*] also the King. We had marvellous seats in the

---

1. The last of the Prince's seven Christian names, by which he was known among his family
and by which the Duchess of Windsor calls him in her memoirs from this point.

Abbey and saw the whole ceremony. I am sending you some pictures from the papers here. E looked handsome in his scarlet uniform for the wedding. I sent the pair 2 lamps – quite smart ones as the ones they had received were rather awful. Betty L. Johnston gave me £50 for Xmas but in time to spend on the two royal parties. A great help but in return I got her asked to the reception and she had the thrill of her life. Ernest is grand in spite of having slight row with his father and one with the NY partners. However we pay no attention to all the gossip and all remain friends going out every night last week together. I can't believe Xmas is so near. Too near. We will have one meal with Maud and probably have some people to the flat. I have no housemaid. They seem impossible to find. I had a terror for the past month who left Sat. E has finished his trips at last. I am sending you a cheque for $35 for Xmas. Please buy something for yourself like bag. It's all I think that you can get for such a tiny amount. However next year things may be better as E says they will break even this year in business which is a load off his mind. I am feeling fine and there is no doubt that the summer in the air and with the sun did me worlds of good. I have a cairn puppy – adorable and aged 4½ months. You will love him. I have 2 more bracelets and a small diamond that sticks into my hair. Smart. Ernest says the insurance is getting steep! A big kiss and all love

WALLIS

The Cairn puppy that was Wallis's Christmas present from the Prince was called Slipper; for fairly obvious reasons, they nicknamed him 'Mr Loo'. He was to play an important part in their relationship.

1934 had been a thrilling year for Wallis. Nevertheless she was relieved when the Prince went off to spend Christmas with his family at Sandringham, giving her a respite from her breathless career as a royal favourite.

Sunday, Dec. 30th   Bryanston Court

Darling

Isn't it great the dreary thing is over. I always hate Xmas out of America. We spent Xmas eve with the Grants & then had 11 for lunch Xmas day. Boxing day (Wed) we lunched with the Hunters & then Ernest and self had a snack here and we two went to the theater and since then we have been home at night *resting* until last night when I had Tiger [Bermejillo] (who appeared just before Xmas much to our joy) and we went to a cinema. Today is being spent in writing thanking letters – and speaking of letters you must have had more than one since Sept for I have given 3 to Osborne at the Fort to post. Didn't you get one saying how ridiculous all the divorce talk was etc.? The US press certainly has a knack for getting details wrong. Nada [Milford Haven] had nothing to do with P[rince] G[eorge]'s romance. Do send me any clippings you get and I would like to have some of the V[anderbilt] Case when it comes up again – the papers here don't say much. I wrote you all about the wedding and the excitement of the Prince bringing the Queen up to Ernest and self [*sic*] in front of all the cold jealous English eyes. I have told him you want to give him something but he wants to wait a bit until the Xmas things are sorted out. They are mostly for the Fort and then see what he still needs. Posy also left me a cheque and he wants to hold that over also. So will let you hear when the great mind decides! The Prince has thank God been at Sandringham since last Monday which has been a lovely rest for us and especially me. He returns tomorrow in time to have a snack with 8 of us here then takes us to the nigger show which is a huge success in London and then we go on to see the NY in at Quaglino. My k-maid leaves next week and the housemaid I took in haste just before Xmas. I am not repenting at leisure but sending her off also others so you see what I shall be doing for the next few weeks. Cain's face is very long over so much changing but was lifted slightly due to the fact the Prince invited her and Mrs Ralph and Mary to the servants tree at York House. I would like some of those butter moulds of the animals. Mine have worn down and I can't use them any more. Send 2 of each kind. We had a small tree entirely trimmed with white things. It looked pretty in the drawing room and I really had lovely flowers. Happy New Year darling and my resolution is to write more. I return the picture and will get more from Posy somehow. Thank you again in which Ernest most gratefully joins. He is writing. I forgot to say I am sending a few more of the pictures which P[osy] produced. Will you keep safely in case I never get the films as some day they will be fun to have. All my love

WALLIS

Among the Duke of Windsor's papers, there is a small blue deckle envelope covered with the handwriting of Wallis, probably dating from this moment. As to what it originally contained, or to what it was attached, one can but guess. It reads, quite simply:

With my love and all my childish dreams having come true through you and I do believe perhaps it's the best part of the New Year.

CHAPTER FIVE
1935: Beloved

1935 was to be Wallis's annus mirabilis, *the most thrilling year of her life. She now had a recognized status in Society as the Prince's favourite. Suddenly, everyone wanted to know her. She was the talk of London. She found herself hotly pursued with flattery and invitations – by the most prominent hostesses, by politicians and ambassadors, by the grandest Americans visiting England. The names quoted in these letters make an impressive catalogue.*

Wallis was immensely excited by these unfamiliar social attentions; there is something touchingly naïve about her delight in them. At the same time she was sufficiently realistic to recognize that they had come about solely because of the Prince, and would continue only for so long as he remained interested in her. And she could not imagine that his interest would endure indefinitely. In her letters to her aunt that year, she writes of her life with the Prince – and the brilliant social life it brings in its wake – as a fairy tale which is bound to come to an end sooner or later, but which she is determined to enjoy while it lasts. 'It's fun for once in one's life', she writes in June; and again in September: 'I never had so much fun before or things so easy and I might as well finish up what youth is left to me with a flourish.'

However, the Prince's infatuation for her did not cool that year. On the contrary, it grew ever more intense, until his feelings for her amounted to nothing less than worship of her, and he could not bear to be apart from her even for a single day. By the autumn he no longer had the slightest doubt that here was someone who meant more to him than anyone he had ever known and with whom he wished to spend the rest of his earthly existence – not as lover and mistress, but as man and wife.

What did he see in her? What was the nature of their relationship? These questions have given rise to endless speculation. It was widely believed, both at the time and afterwards, that Wallis had made all the running in the affair, bewitching the Prince with some kind of

*sexual sorcery. But one may well wonder, having observed the person-
ality of Wallis in the preceding chapters of this book, whether she
really had the make-up of a Cleopatra. And many who were close to
the Prince have testified that his attachment to her was more psychological than physical. As Winston Churchill has written:*

> He delighted in her company, and found in her qualities as neces-
> sary to his happiness as the air he breathed. Those who knew him
> well and watched him closely noticed that many little tricks and
> fidgetings of nervousness fell away from him. He was a completed
> being instead of a sick and harassed soul. This experience which
> happens to a great many people in the flower of their youth came
> late in life to him, and was all the more precious and compulsive
> for that fact; the association was psychical rather than sexual,
> and certainly not sensual except incidentally.[1]

*And Walter Monckton, the Prince's old friend from university days
who was to be his closest adviser in the Abdication crisis, has similarly
written:*

> No one will every really understand the story of the King's life
> ... who does not appreciate ... the intensity and depth of his
> devotion to Mrs Simpson. To him she was the perfect woman.
> She insisted that he should be at his best and do his best at all
> times, and he regarded her as his inspiration. It is a great mistake
> to assume that he was merely in love with her in the ordinary
> physical sense of the term. There was an intellectual companion-
> ship, and there is no doubt that his lonely nature found in her a
> spiritual comradeship.... He felt that he and Mrs Simpson were
> made for each other and there was no other honest way of meet-
> ing the situation than marrying her.[2]

*Such were the views of two good friends of the Prince who had
known him since his youth and were in touch with him throughout
this time. But we are now able to look at the relationship of Wallis
and Edward with an understanding denied even to these contempor-*

1. Martin Gilbert, *Winston Churchill*, Vol. v (Heinemann, London, 1976), p. 810.
2. Lord Birkenhead, *Walter Monckton* (Weidenfeld & Nicolson, London, 1969),
pp. 125–6.

aries – an understanding given by their own intimate correspondence, hitherto secret and unpublished. To begin with it consists of little more than an exchange of romantic notes and messages, interspersed with the occasional substantial letter; as time passes there are longer and more frequent and more urgent letters, some of which are of real historical importance; eventually, in the crisis-ridden months leading up to their marriage, there is a whole series of passionate love letters which, alike from the historical, literary and psychological points of view, must be regarded as unique of their kind. But all the items of this material – even the shortest billets doux *– give a picture of their feelings for one another which it would be impossible to imagine before reading them. For the first time, it is possible to see clearly of what the relationship consisted.*

As to whether the Prince had sexual relations with the woman he loved, and, if so, of what sort, the reader of these letters must decide for himself. All that will be said here is that a judicial enquiry in the winter of 1936–7 uncovered no evidence that they had been guilty of an adulterous relationship;[1] and that, in subsequent years, the Duke of Windsor always reacted violently against the suggestion that she had been his mistress before their marriage.[2] What the correspondence reveals, however, is that theirs was no adult love affair of an ordinary sort. It was, overwhelmingly, a mother–son relationship. His letters to her are infantile, adoring, trusting, full of baby talk; they plead for affection and protection. Hers to him are sensible, affectionate, admonishing, possessive; as Monckton says, they radiate an insistence 'that he should be at his best and do his best at all times'. The correspondence resembles nothing so much as the letters exchanged between a fond but wise parent and a lonely, hypersensitive child at boarding-school.

It is impossible to understand the nature of the feelings they developed for one another unless one bears two things in mind.

The first is the Prince's upbringing. This had been strictly Victorian: he had seen little of his parents as a child, being reared by tutors and governesses; and at the earliest opportunity he had been removed from

---

1. See Chapters 11 to 14 below.
2. In 1937 the Duke successfully sued the author Geoffrey Dennis for suggesting that Mrs Simpson had been his 'mistress'. And in 1958 he went so far as to threaten a libel action against Sir John Wheeler-Bennett because, in the first version of his official life of King George VI, he had described the former Prince of Wales as having been the 'lover' of Mrs Simpson.

home and packed off to a tough educational institution, in his case a naval training-college. Many children who undergo these classic emotional rigours later achieve a warm understanding with their parents; but this was not the case with the eldest son of King George V and Queen Mary. The King was a brusque and intensely conservative ex-naval officer, with little intelligence and even less imagination; he regarded his glamorous heir with fear and jealousy and in a spirit of perpetual criticism. The Queen had once been a sensitive and outgoing woman, but the paralysing routine of royal life had taught her to repress her feelings and had made her cold and reserved. Placed on a lonely pinnacle and adored by the masses, condemned to an official life of empty pageantry, the Prince yearned for a happy home life and especially for a mother's sympathetic attentions; and he was starved of these. Throughout his first forty years he sought, in a succession of amours with older married women, an ideal mother figure; and this he at last found in Wallis.

The second thing to remember is that Wallis was a woman of the American South, which was then an intensely matriarchal society. In the Southern tradition, she had been taught to cherish and look after her man. The brand of affection which she naturally offered was the same as that which the Prince wanted and needed.

What meanwhile of Wallis's relations with her own husband? In almost every letter she sends Aunt Bessie in 1935, there is an emphatic – almost suspiciously emphatic – assurance that all is well with Ernest. He approves of her friendship with the Prince; he shares and enjoys her brilliant new social life; there is no question of any separation.... There is, indeed, nothing to show that Wallis wished to put an end to her marriage at this period; on the contrary, Ernest still represented material and emotional security, while the Prince seemed to represent just a transient, if thrilling, episode in her life. As she writes to the Prince with remarkable candour, she does not want to lose 'something noble' for the sake of 'Peter Pan'. And judging from Ernest's letters to her – sentimental letters of a somewhat old-fashioned sort, full of high-flown compliments and literary quotations – he remained in love with her at least up to the summer of 1935: on 25 June he assures her, writing from Norway, that he adores her 'as much as ever' and that she will 'always be the only girl in the world' for him. However, the truth was that Ernest – for all his reverence for royalty, and undoubted initial complaisance at a situation which brought him into the princely orbit – was finding his wife's ever-growing association with another man increasingly hard to bear. It was a fact which Wallis understandably sought to hide from her aunt; but, throughout 1935, her marriage gradually deteriorated.

There is one other important developing theme in the Aunt Bessie correspondence for 1935: the growing and unwelcome interest in Wallis of the American press.

Monday, Jan 14th   The Fort

Darling

Life goes on the same here quite peacefully with Ernest in spite of HRH on doorstep. I got a lovely pin with 2 large square emeralds for Xmas and some photographs of himself and he had the plate destroyed. I shall arrange about a picture for you but must await the right moment. I got for your Xmas present to him two red leather books for here – one for the card accounts and one a guest book.[1] He is delighted. They came to 3 pounds. I wrote ages ago how much the ham was loved but you know one never gets thanked for anything by him. The Prince is thinking of going to Kitzbuhel in February and has invited Foxy Gwynne, Lord Dudley,[2] Captain and Mrs Bruce Ogilvy (Lord Airlie's younger brother who used to be one of his equerries). To be gone 2 weeks – if it comes off. It depends on the King. I shall only have the skiing suit to get which can be had for 4 pounds. I would love getting away. I had such a servant problem in the way of housemaids – a new one tomorrow again – and Ernest entertaining business people for dinner. We have had only 3 days of winter weather the rest warm and rainy and makes one feel so listless. Mary Kirk is living apart from Jackie [Raffray] – paying a series of visits to friends. Maud is the same. We must dine with her Thur night. She is more jealous than ever, but pleasant. The Prince is making the 2 small bedrooms into one large room and I am being allowed to select everything for it. I am thrilled. Mr Simpson sends some fantastic accounts

1. All who stayed as the Prince's guests at the Fort – or wherever else he happened to be – henceforth signed this book. The entries for the period January 1935 to December 1936 are reproduced in Appendix 2.
2. Eric Ward, 3rd Earl of Dudley (1894–1969), a landowner and industrialist who was an old friend of the Prince and had accompanied him on his trip to South America in 1931.

of the Prince and self from the US papers. Do send anything you happen to see. Take care of yourself and all love

WALLIS

From the Duchess of Windsor's memoirs:
Until now I had taken for granted that Ernest's interest in the Prince was keeping pace with mine [*sic*], but about this time I began to sense a change in his attitude. His work seemed to make more and more demands on his time in the evening. Often he would not return in time for dinner, or when the Prince suggested afterwards dropping in at Sartori's or the Dorchester for an hour or so of amusement, Ernest would ask to be excused on the plea that he had an early appointment or that papers from the office needed his attention. He also seemed less and less interested in what I had to say about the Prince's latest news and interests.

I first realized how far Ernest and I had grown apart when the Prince invited us to Kitzbuhel in February for the winter sports. . . . When Ernest returned home that evening, I told him excitedly about the trip to Austria. He was unresponsive and cut me off with an announcement that he had no interest in skiing and moreover had urgent business which would require his presence in New York at that time.[1]

Later that evening, after a rather silent dinner, he asked me whether my mind was definitely made up to go. I remember answering: 'Of course. Why not? I wouldn't dream of missing it.'

He got up from his chair and said: 'I rather thought that we might have gone to New York together. I now see that I was wrong.' I asked if he couldn't come out for at least some of the time. He answered that it was quite out of the question.

With that he went to his bedroom, and for the first time I heard his door bang.

Friday [9 February]   Grand Hotel, Kitzbuhel, Tirol

Dearest Aunt B
We arrived here Tuesday amidst rain once again. However since then we have had sunshine & snow. I had my first ski lesson Wed and

---

1. But according to the letter which follows, Ernest's trip to New York was only planned for the spring, and Wallis did hope to accompany him then.

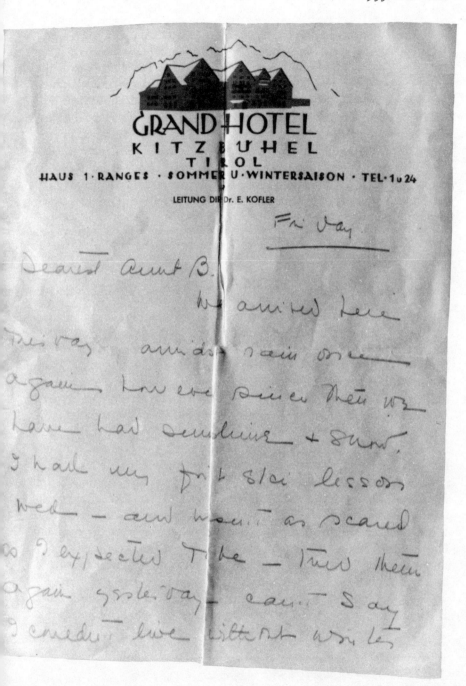

GRAND·HOTEL
KITZBÜHEL
TIROL
HAUS 1·RANGES · SOMMER U·WINTERSAISON · TEL·1·24
LEITUNG DIR Dr. E. KOFLER

Friday

Dearest Aunt B.

We arrived here
Tuesday amidst rain once
again however since then we
have had sunshine + snow.
I had my first ski lessons
Wed — and wasn't as scared
as I expected to be — tried them
again yesterday — can't say
I couldn't live without winter

wasn't as scared as I expected to be. Tried them again yesterday. Can't say I couldn't live without winter sports. It is quite cold here when the sun goes down. The hotel fairly primitive rather like Marienbad, the village absolutely charming and 4 amusing 'pubs' to go to which pleases our host. How long the skiing will last I don't know. It is dull for the women as there is no other form of excitement except the skis. The plan is ten days here, 3 days Vienna, 3 days Budapest, Paris, home. You can well imagine whether the schedule will remain. My flat is a mess while I'm away. Ernest moving about from room to room but very gay with invitations so I shan't be missed. Ernest may have to come to NY in April for about 6 weeks. I shall try to get the cash to accompany him. All love

WALLIS

Tuesday [13 March]   [York House] St James's Palace

Darling

I can't remember whether I have written since I returned two days ago or not. Naturally there was a lot to do at home as I had all the walls washed and carpets cleaned while away. The trip was a great success and Budapest the best part, such a gay amusing place. 2 days in Paris where I bought a couple of hats and then the entire party returned en masse. I was very interested in the clippings. What the US papers don't put on to this poor Prince. Imagine him ever saying such a thing. I wish you had sent me clippings about the diamond and my glass coat. I have a small diamond that clips into my hair which HRH gave me and the coat is cellophane. Don't send me any clippings. I am enclosing a photo of us at Kitzbuhel. The Prince in his Tyrolean number and I look like a Russian immigrant but everyone wears those things around the head there. They are taking ages to do the face cloths. However there is no hurry. Ernest doesn't expect to go to NY after all. I don't think I can manage to leave here for many reasons – and I could not borrow any more money from you darling. However we'll see what E's state is re the bank if he does have to come. I think I better remain here and look after the Jubilee Boy![1] I don't see how

---

1. Having reigned for twenty-five years, King George V and Queen Mary were celebrating their Silver Jubilee that spring.

England can afford another royal gala after the Kent Wedding. I hope you are well and happy. Both E and self send much love.

WALLIS

Monday [9 April]   The Fort

Darling

Katherine [Galbraith] got here Tues and we have been on the run ever since to say nothing of my having been out to both lunch and dinner for the past 2 weeks with decorating this place and York House between times. I am really tired so do forgive my not having written. This week I am trying to arrange to take it quieter but with Katherine still remaining on I imagine it won't turn out to be as you know what a demon for doing things she is. The Prince gave a lovely party for her at York House the day she arrived showing the film of the [Grand] National after dinner. We had a divine time at the race lunching in Lord Sefton's box[1] with many swells but best of all I put a pound each way on the winner and won twenty-seven pounds 10 shillings. I nearly died of joy. It was only because I had lunched with the owners once at Melton [Mowbray]. We got home about 8.30 and then E and the Prince and self went to Quaglino's and celebrated, the Prince having followed me but putting £5 on was much richer. The Buists who went to the race with us both sent love to you, likewise Jackie [Aird] who is here this week-end. I am enclosing the picture of me which appeared in the Sketch. I didn't know it was to appear so had nothing to do with the caption but it isn't bad. I am sending you the photographs as soon as I can get them properly done up. Cousin Lelia wrote me a very sweet letter, said she might come over and spoke of going to Carlsbad and also thinks it would be good for your liver. Why don't you do that coming to London first? Ernest has to remain here as a man is arriving to see him but will probably go to the US in the fall as he has to go to the West Coast. Mr Simpson arrives in May some time. I expect to have to borrow the tiara again as the Prince has to give a reception May 7 for the silly Jubilee. I was sad to hear of Warren Robbins' death, Gladys and Mike will be very upset. I have

---

1. Hugh Molyneaux, 7th and last Earl of Sefton (1898-1972), a dashing figure prominent in the racing world who was a good friend of the Prince. He later married 'Foxy' Gwynne.

never seen anything like the Morgan twins' publicity. I am sorry about my face and only wish if it must appear it could be a newer picture. Mrs Loel Guinness[1] a very smart society woman here. Has left her husband and gone off with *Aly Khan* and is supposed to be going to marry him. Bill Guinness, Posy's husband, has had a serious operation and all last week was not expected to live but is better today. I am sorry about Willy. He has always had the worst breaks in the world almost as bad as my poor little mother only she did have more fun out of of life than Willy has. It's alarming to think what bad luck we have. I wonder what will happen to me – it isn't meant for us to have things go on easily. Take care of yourself and all love

WALLIS

PS As bad taste as the clippings are do keep sending them. We have no plans for Easter.

Accompanied by their friends the Hunters, Wallis and Ernest spent Easter motoring with the Prince around his estates in Cornwall.

It was during this trip that the Prince wrote the first of his letters to Wallis which appears to have survived. It is no more than a billet doux *accompanying a present to her; but it suggests that there had already been much correspondence between them, for they had already developed a private language. The meaning of most of their intimate expressions must be left to the imagination of the reader, but the two most important may be identified here: their device WE, standing for their joint first names Wallis Edward and symbolizing their union in love; and the adjective* eanum, *meaning tiny, poor, affecting, pathetic.*

Edward to Wallis

St Austell Bay Hotel, Par, Cornwall

My [twice underlined] Eanum – My [thrice underlined] Wallis

This is not the kind of Easter WE want but it will be all right next year. The Easter Bunny has brought this from Us All [twice underlined] & Slipper says he likes it too but it has to be fitted & christened later. I love you more & more & more each & every minute & miss you so

---

1. Joan, daughter of Lord Churston, wife of the then Member of Parliament for Bath. She married Prince Aly Khan in the spring of 1936.

[thrice underlined] terribly here. You do too dont you my sweetheart. God bless WE. Always your [2 words twice underlined]

DAVID

With much excitement, Wallis now began to prepare for the London Season of that year, which would include the celebrations for the Silver Jubilee of King George V and Queen Mary.

Monday, April 29th   The Fort

Well darling,

I hope you had better Easter weather than we did in Cornwall. It was cold and terrific showers all day. However we had a lovely trip between the showers. I have never seen such lovely gardens and having tea with their owners was an experience. The air was wonderful and I've slept so well. It did us all good and the Prince enjoyed it. Of course the Hunters were in the 7th heaven. We got home Tuesday and naturally the sun came out and it was warm! Sara Elkin now with her 4th husband Knight Woolley has arrived and they were here for the week-end and that ball of fire Jack Warner also is in London all very difficult and Mr Simpson here about the 8th. We are not going to the [Jubilee] service in St Paul's May 6th as we could not see the procession if we did so we chose the latter and the Prince is getting us some seats to view it from. Then the night of the 7th is the Prince's reception for 1200 at the palace and I should think that would finish the Jubilee for us. Naturally we will not be asked to the State Balls. The crowds in London are awful and it takes hours to get places. Jack tells me America is in a bad way but all I hear about is parties. I lunched with Rowley the other day and also took him to a party with PW. He is living in London and is separated from his wife. He is only 29. Now think what a baby he was 8 years ago. He has asked me to go out dancing but E won't let me – evidently thinks him more dangerous than the Prince. I have some lovely jewellery to show when we meet. Not many things but awfully nice stones. One of my face cloths is ripping away from the initials the first time used. You might just mention it to them if in there. It's too complicated to return. All my love

WALLIS

Haven't forgotten the photos.

The first serious letter from Wallis to the Prince which we have was probably written around this time. It is undated, but the ballet mentioned at the end may refer to the Russian Ballet, which came to London at the time of the Jubilee and was one of the great artistic sensations of that year.

The letter – written after a quarrel between Wallis and Ernest provoked by the Prince's thoughtless behaviour – reveals much about all three of them.

Wallis to Edward
Tuesday a.m.

David dear

I was and still am most terribly upset. You see my dear one can't go through life stepping on other people. I know that you aren't *really* selfish or thoughtless at heart but your life has been such that you have been the one considered so that quite naturally you only think of what you want and take it too without the slightest thought of others. One can arrive at the same result in a kinder way. I had a long quiet talk with E last night and I felt very eanum at the end. Everything he said was so true. The evening was difficult as you did stay much too late. Doesn't your love for me reach to the heights of wanting to make things a little easier for me. The lovely things you say to me aren't of much value unless they are backed up by equal actions. I should have come back Sat and I didn't. Then last night you should have left by 8. Then you telephone the second time – which just did finish the evening and made a row. You must have understood from my conversation the first time that I was upset and also very disappointed in a boy and that nothing you could say could help in the least – because David what are all those words if what they say isn't enough for a little sacrifice on our part to do what is really the right thing for all concerned. So far you have always come first in my actions if there had to be a choice (like Sat.). It isn't fair and cannot always be that way. Sometimes I think you haven't grown up where love is concerned and perhaps it's only a boyish passion for surely it lacks the thought of me that a man's love is capable of. Please understand I am not writing a lecture only your behaviour last night made me realise how very alone I shall be some day – and because I love you I don't seem to have the strength to protect myself from your youthfulness. I ask you not to come in

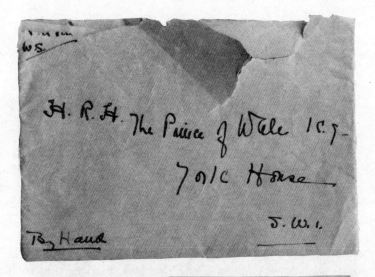

Wed. night after the ballet but will try to see you Thurs afternoon some time. God bless WE and be kind to me in the years to come for I have lost something noble for a boy who may always remain Peter Pan.

PS 'All of us' would like you to tear this very inadequate letter up as of course 'all of us' realize we can't write as well as we talk and act.

From the Duchess of Windsor's memoirs:
This was the year of the Silver Jubilee.... Never have I witnessed such outpouring of public respect, admiration and love. Dominion Prime Ministers, Indian princes, African potentates, sheiks, tribal chieftains, and other lords and masters of the Empire assembled from the far corners of the earth to pay homage to a greatly beloved sovereign. By day there were drives in an open landau through the streets, the King and Queen each time taking a different route and not ignoring the shabbier districts; and in the evenings there were state dinners, balls and celebrations of every sort.

Because of David, Ernest and I were invited to the State Ball at Buckingham Palace on May 14. After the King and Queen had made their entrance and taken their seats on the dais at the end of the room, the dancing began. As David and I danced past, I thought I felt the King's eyes rest searchingly on me. Something in his look made me feel that all this graciousness and pageantry were but the glittering tip of an iceberg ... filled with an icy menace for such as me. Also through the panoply of pomp I discerned that here was a frail old man. The King was then only a few days away from his seventieth birthday, and David had told me more than once of his concern over his father's failing strength. A premonitory shiver ran through me....

The letters to Aunt Bessie resume.
June 8th   The Fort

Oh darling,

I am so sorry about not having written for a month but I can't begin to tell you what my life has been. The telephone goes so much that the company made me have another one installed which only makes matters worse both ringing by my bed at once. They said they had too many complaints about the line being busy. You see since I've met more of the natives I am besieged by people asking me to things not for myself but in hopes the PW will want to come also which has happened so many times that they think that in asking me they'll get him. Then the charity shows etc. Anyway I try to be polite and answer all notes. Actually I should have a secretary. It will be lovely when something happens to break it up – which brings me to the Carrick story[1] which is as fantastic as the divorce. As you know they met us in Vienna and I don't think we ever looked in Marion's direction and since our return in Feb the PW has seen them once when he dined with them at my house and we went to the Savoy. However I have enjoyed the clippings because of Mr S who can now see how one only has to be seen with him once to have notice taken by the press. I showed the things to Bernard Rickatson-Hatt and he knows the head of Hearsts' Universal Service and has cabled him to NY not to distribute any more about us and also the Reuter man in Paris is going to see that Jane Eads who Bernard also knows and put her wise so perhaps we'll have some peace. On the other hand I am enclosing some nice clippings from the London papers. I saw the Jubilee procession from St James's where the Prince had a breakfast party before starting. His reception was the next night and afterwards he had a supper party of most distinguished people at York House. I borrowed tiara etc and also we were asked to the Court Ball, a thrilling thing. The Prince danced with me after the opening one with the Queen so you see I am not neglected on the right things. After that we went to a lovely party at Lord Stanley's, Lord Derby's son.[2] I really know them all now and must say they are grand to me. Naturally only for the duration of my length of service. I imagine anyway I am doing far far better than Thelma on far far less. The place is filled with Americans – Diercks, Aileen W[inslow], Garnetts, Mixsells, Yuilles with husbands. Everybody lets me know of their arrival. Isn't it a scream? The blue-eyed one remains the same, also Ernest, and both object to anyone else I fancy. Life is funny. I have lovely diamond clips as a Jubilee present. I am afraid I had taken the whole letter up with WWS but I do want you to realise it isn't from lack of love and thought of you that I have been silent. I

1. The 8th Earl of Carrick, a young Irish peer, had been an occasional visitor at the Fort. His American wife Marion, from Philadelphia, had evidently been linked in the newspapers with the Prince of Wales.
2. Edward Stanley, Lord Stanley (1894-1938), eldest son of the 17th Earl of Derby, a junior minister in the Government and prominent as a Conservative political host.

come here for Ascot on the 17th for a week. Ernest leaves that day with Mr Waters for a month on the continent. To add to the complications in between I have given dinners for shipping – Germans, Norwegians and Americans out of the bottom drawer, hard to take. The pictures are coming and please don't be cross and come over here this summer. All love and big kiss

WALLIS

At the end of this letter to Aunt Bessie, there is a postscript in the handwriting of the Prince.

Please Mrs. Merryman not to be cross with Wallis for writing you [*sic*] in so long! It really has been quite a busy time with the Jubilee and various ceremonies and social functions connected with it. I wish you could have seen one or two of them. Mr Hearst seems to have been quite busy but who cares! Do come over and see us again soon.

EDWARD P

Aunt Bessie replied to the Prince from Washington on 27 June.
Sir

I thank you so much for your little note added to Wallis' letter. I will not be cross with that very busy young woman as cables have kept me in touch but her letters are always of intense interest and I miss them when they do not come. I hope Sir that you have kept well through all the arduous duties of the Jubilee which must also have been most interesting and thrilling. I note Sir that in the past few days you have passed another milestone along the road of life[1] and I would like to add my felicitation and congratulations to the many you have received and send you all good wishes for the years to come. I am Sir your obedient servant

BESSIE L. MERRYMAN

1. The Prince's forty-first birthday.

Please Mrs Merryman
not to be cross with
Wallis for writing you
in so long! — It really
has been quite a busy
time with the Jubilee
      ceremonies and —
and various / social
functions connected with it —
I wish you could have
seen one or two of them —
Mrs Hearst seems to have been
quite busy but who cares! — Do
come over and see us again soon — Edward P

the money you have
received and send you all
good wishes for the
years to come -
New Year
Your obedient servant
Bessie L. Merryman

1911 R STREET   June 27

Sir. I thank you so much
for your little note
added to Wallis letter.
I will not be cross with
that very dear young
woman as Cater here

Wallis's letters to Aunt Bessie continue.

June 15th   Bryanston Court

Darling

I ran into Buzzy the bore Hewes at Claridges yesterday and he tells me that you really are upset by Hearst's reporters' lies. You know I am not going to get a divorce. Ernest and myself are perfectly happy and understand each other so please put it all out of your head and tell people they can't believe the press. I have been in a rush getting rags together for Ascot. I go Monday for a whole week. The Buists, Hugh [Lloyd] Thomas and wife, G. Trotter is the party and Emerald Cunard[1] for Wednesday night. The Doellers arrived last night and the Prince has asked them for the following week-end. They are going to Ascot. Mary Dunn is also returning. I hope Ruth will let me know of her arrival a bit in advance as I am pretty well filled up day and night to the middle of July. I shan't see the Doellers until a week from today. The post has just come and I find in it a lovely cheque from you. An Ascot bonnet. Many thanks but you should not have done it as you know. I know I have been a beast about writing but I have cabled a bit. Do you ever get them as I give them to Osborne at the Fort to send? I am very tired but feel well though I know I must arrange a few days off and not see people. Besides one gets tired of having people make a fuss over you because they want to see HRH. I have got some pretty jewellery and it's clever of the US papers to know who gave it to me. Ernest is off tomorrow. Last night we went to the Aldershot Tattoo with Pa. Maud and [her daughter] Betty sailed for NY today to see the old girl who has been ill. Maud in lousy mood and sick from jealousy. Pa has been nice but not generous. All my love and many thanks for my lovely present.

WALLIS

The 19th of June was Wallis's thirty-ninth birthday, and the occasion of the Prince's next surviving note to her.

1. Emerald, Lady Cunard (1872–1948), one of London's most brilliant hostesses, known for her scintillating conversation and her waspish manner. American by birth, she had married the British shipping tycoon, Sir Bache Cunard.

Edward to Wallis   The Fort

Wallis

Of course the old gold fish bowl can remove your beauty parlour when you are thru. I'm sorry I forgot the Lanson[1] '15 but I was so drowsy. Oh! so many happy returns my sweetheart and God bless WE for ever. More and more and more we all of us say. HE is terribly excited about new hair pin and HE hopes SHE is too (I'm hiding my face). Please call hello from window later to your

DAVID

The letters to Aunt Bessie continue.

Saturday, June 29th   The Fort

Darling

It is so lovely today just like the Riviera and we are doing the day by the pool which will remind you of last year. Ruth has been to cocktails with me but unfortunately the Prince couldn't come in. I am having her and Miss Hickey to lunch Tuesday and I will try for the PW another day. I have been so gay – a dance nearly every night – and I dined at the *Londonderrys*[2] Wednesday a dinner of 50. It really was an experience. Then on to the Dudley dance. The Prince gave a dinner last night for the Kents. Next week there are 3 more dances, Mrs Corrigan,[3] Lady Weymouth[4] and Lord Moyne's.[5] That ends the dance list and only a dinner at the German Embassy left. My evening clothes will just make it. It is very amusing what one is invited to in hopes of PW. All the very best titles come across whereas no one noticed Mrs Simpson before. It's fun for once in one's life but it isn't disturbing Ernest and myself so don't worry please. Ernest left Sunday for Norway, won't be back until the middle of July. The Sims[6] are here and I have seen Henry Dickson lots. He met PW etc and seems very nice but I suspect he's a pansy judging from his boy friend. The

1. The brand of champagne.
2. The 7th Marquess of Londonderry (1878–1949), a Cabinet Minister in the National Government, and his wife Edith. Their great house in Park Lane was famous for its political receptions.
3. Laura Corrigan (1879–1948), a hostess from Colorado who sought to storm London Society.
4. Daphne, Countess of Weymouth, a prominent London hostess.
5. Walter Guinness, 1st Baron Moyne (1880–1944), a Conservative politician. It was he who had lent the yacht *Rosaura* to the Prince and his party in the summer of 1934.
6. Harold Sims, formerly of the British Embassy in Washington.

Prince talks of taking a house either in Austria on a lake or the Riviera provided he can get the Chateau de la Garoupe which has its own sand beach and also rock bathing and he would not have to see the awful people that haunt those shores and of course guaranteed climate. You can imagine my difficulty in writing you as I have Kitty [Hunter] sitting with me who hasn't stopped once, talking about everything that goes on. I am not going to the naval review which is the 15-16. I am taking advantage of a rest in bed for those 2 days. Something very novel. I need it. I hope the Hearst papers cease now but if they don't, push the dirt along. All my love

WALLIS

I have sent you the photographs.

July 16th

Darling

Again a whirl and no letters – really there has never been such a time and the joke of the people from home who have looked me up would make you laugh. I feel I have Mr Hearst to thank for much telephoning, notes etc. I had Ruth Ceno & Miss Hickey to cocktails with the Prince & all passed off well. I had Saunders Wright from Norfolk[1] the same day. Imagine him suddenly coming to life! Ernest still on tour. I have tried awfully hard this year to be nice to the natives, answering thousands of notes, going to boring parties. I thought they might as well see who the Prince was supposed to like. The Prince has taken a villa at Cannes from August – has his own rocks and will rent a boat. The Buists, Lord Sefton, Mrs Fitzgerald[2] and perhaps the Andersons in sections as last year, also Jackie [Aird]. No Posy [Guinness] however and I'm sure she'll be distressed. No one knows this as yet. He can get golf and the villa belongs to Lord Chomondley (spelt wrong).[3] I couldn't take Biarritz. Ernest may have to go to spend a week or so with his mother in Conn. and then go to

1. The naval base in Virginia; Wright doubtless having been a sometime colleague of Winfield Spencer.
2. Mrs Evelyn Fitzgerald, a pretty and lively London hostess who had become a friend of Wallis. She was the sister-in-law of the press tycoon Lord Beaverbrook.
3. The 5th Marquess of Cholmondeley (1883-1968), who was to become Lord Chamberlain at the Court of Edward VIII. He had married the sister of Sir Philip Sassoon, a rich and exotic politician who was prominent in royal circles.

San Francisco and New Orleans. If that was the case I would try to come over the end of Sept to meet him. It is so difficult to leave things here at the moment you understand besides I rather hope for a trip to *Nassau* [sic] next winter where we could meet each other. I hear it's lovely there from the Kents. I have had a series of domestic mishaps – bugs in the housemaid's room which have had to be eliminated and I have had to board her out, a flood in my bathroom above ruining everything but the building must pay, and the housemaid who is ex-cellent leaving this Sept to be married. I see Hearst admits to E and self being together so Bernard [Rickatson-Hatt] did do some good. I do think it sad about Anne. Do you think Newbold the cause of it or would it have been that way anyhow? I hope you have not suffered from the awful heat I read about. Do be careful. Love to Katherine & Billy and a big hug for yourself.

WALLIS

Hope the pictures came OK

That July, the Prince took part in a naval review in the English Chan-nel. In the middle of the night he wrote to Wallis from on board his ship.

Edward to Wallis

Tuesday [23 July], one o'clock a.m.   HMS Faulknor

Wallis – A boy is holding a girl so very tight in his arms tonight. He will miss her more tomorrow because he will have been away from her some hours longer and cannot see her till Wed-y night. A girl knows that not anybody or anything can separate WE – not even the stars – and that WE belong to each other for ever. WE love [twice underlined] each other more than life so God bless WE. Your [twice underlined]

DAVID

The idea of being out of communication with Wallis for as much as two days, however, had become unbearable to the Prince; and later that morning he could not resist the indiscretion of sending her a telegram from the ship's radio, addressed to Bryanston Court and no doubt destined to meet the curious eyes of Post Office telegraph operators. It read:

GOOD MORNING WE ALL SAY MORE AND MORE AND MORE = D

The next day (Wednesday the 24th), he sent another:

I FEEL SO EANUM NOT HAVING TALKED TO YOU TODAY ARE YOU
MISSING ME AS MUCH AS I AM YOU MORE AND MORE = D

The letters to Aunt Bessie resume at the end of July.

Wednesday, July 31st

Darling

It's better now my countrymen are scattering and the Jubilee spirit dying. It all ended last week and we have been most peaceful for 3 days. I am leaving Sunday for Cannes for the Prince's villa which he doesn't know the name of (typical) but he will by Friday when he sees the owner so will write you. Unfortunately E is not going as his mother arrives tomorrow and he is off to America in ten days as he has to return with a businessman first of Oct. He will be in NY a few days then flies to New Orleans then from there to San Francisco back to NY for 10 days and then home. He expects to try and spend one night in Wash with you if there end of Sept/1st of Oct. His office address is Simpson, Spence and Young, 8-10 Bridge Street and he expects to stay at the Gladstone. My party consists of Lord & Lady Brownlow,[1] Buists – Colin only remaining a week but Gladie forever – Mrs Fitzgerald and Lord Sefton. Très chic. E is quite content for me to go as he can do nothing for me in the way of a holiday. What happens in Sept is a mystery as usual. A yacht was considered but also considered too expensive when the price turned out to be twenty five thousand dollars for a month! I should think a return to Budapest or some place outside or maybe join Emerald Cunard in Venice. Anyway you know it will be fun and comfortable. All the guests taking cars this year. I would like to come home some time this winter but must wait to see if any cash is forthcoming from these business trips. We are closing the flat entirely so that saves a bit. I had a cable from Gladys Scanlon saying she was coming over but no date. Tamar will be in her house in Wash, Bennie at State Department. Don't think her very friendly to me between Mala [Brand] and Thelma. Take care of yourself please and try

1. Peregrine Cust, 6th Lord Brownlow (1899-1978), a Lincolnshire landowner and friend of the Prince.

to have a look at Ernest who is still the man of my dreams. Mr S sneaked away yesterday – what a one! All my love

WALLIS

And so Wallis departed on her second summer holiday with the Prince. This time we have a record of the vacation in the form of letters to Aunt Bessie as well as the WE correspondence. As was now usual, Ernest did not accompany his wife; and he chose this moment for his long-planned visit to the United States.

Saturday [10 August]   Le Roc, Golfe Juan, A[lpes] M[aritimes]

Darling

We got here Monday to find a lovely villa *in the water* – our own rocks and all the privacy in the world and *sun* but very hot so I don't think you would have liked it as well as Meremont.[1] The servants are not quite up to those either but the chef is good. The Prince is very happy and likes it much better. We have only seen the [Herman] Rogers, Elsie Mendl[2] and Lord and Lady Portarlington,[3] the usual game of keeping to ourselves being played. The Duke of Westminster[4] has offered his yacht Cutty Sark to the Prince from August 26th for a month. He may accept and I think go to the Dalmatian Coast and the Greek Islands avoiding however the stormy part. Ernest is having much trouble with Ma who if possible is more difficult than before her illness and much deafer. She was in London 3 days before I left. It is a problem as she needs someone to look after her. Maud is hopeless and fussing with everybody. Ernest expects to sail on the Berengaria Aug 28th and will only be in NY 3 days but you might be in touch with him. He is most anxious to see you. His date of return is Oct 5.

I started this on Sat and now it's Monday. There is very little to write as the days only consist of swimming, boating, *late* dinner and the people the house party. I shall get your things in Paris. I thought I might stay a few days if I can manage it after the Prince goes to Balmoral and may be able to get some clothes as Foxy Gwynne thinks

1. The villa the Prince had taken at Biarritz the preceding year.
2. The famous American decorator and society figure, the former Elsie de Wolfe who had married Sir Charles Mendl of the British Embassy in Paris.
3. The 6th Earl of Portarlington (1883–1969) and his wife Winnifreda.
4. Hugh Grosvenor, 2nd Duke of Westminster (1879–1953), known as 'Bendor', the fabulously rich landlord of some of the smartest districts of London.

she can get me good prices at Mainbocher if they do as well as Scha-parelli. I think the Prince could get them in to England for me. We never heard a word from Willmott [Lewis] so don't know if in London. Where is Henry and child living? What a frightful situation. I hear Lelia very popular with people in Wash. All except Ethel [Lewis] who I believe doesn't like her. It's too hot to write longer. Everything sticks. All my love

WALLIS

PS What prices were the last corsets you ordered?

A number of undated notes survive, written from Wallis to the Prince during their stay at Cannes. They illustrate the extent to which she had taken charge of his domestic life.

Wallis to Edward

Le Roc, Golfe Juan, A.M.

David

Have the table moved back as far as possible and if the V[ansittart]s[1] are coming there would be far more room for 10 if the Finn could produce chairs without arms. Here is a suggestion for seating. I would also have two sorts of cocktails and white wine offered as well as the vin rosé, the servants to serve the wine. Also I didn't see a green vegetable on the menu. Sorry to bother you but I like everyone to think you do things well. Perhaps I'm quite fond of you. Do take V off after lunch and get the information we want. Don't forget to tell chef 10. Hello!

Wallis to Edward

Le Roc

I think it would be nice to have the [Winston] Churchill drinks on the porch outside the drawing-room. I think also that you are a very nice boy.

1. Sir Robert Vansittart (1881–1957), Permanent Under-Secretary at the Foreign Office and a friend of the Prince. Presumably they wanted to consult him about the trips they hoped to make in view of the unsettled international situation.

LE ROC
GOLFE JUAN
A.M.

I think it would be
nice to have the
Churchill drinks on
the porch outside the
drawing-room
I think also that you
are a very nice Boy.

The letters to Aunt Bessie resume.

Saturday, 17th August   Le Roc

Darling

Many happy returns for Monday. I wonder if you will be as secretive as you were at Baden-Baden or whether Katherine & Billy will give you a small bottle of wine. We are all having a lovely quiet time here still basking in sunshine and much heat. Too much for you. I went to Nice yesterday on my way to Cap Ferrat where Walter Prendergast is staying with Lady Hadfield and I passed by the Ruhl and thought of Walter I can't think of his last name now giving you a kiss on the porch. This morning I had a letter from Mr Simpson saying he is at the Grand Hotel Cannes having just completed a motor tour of the Chateau country. Can you beat that old boy and the rest of the family struggling with the old lady in London who now says she will return with Ernest but so far can't get a cabin. Ernest will communicate with you upon his arrival. What are your September plans? My Biarritz numbers look quite well here and no one has the short skirts. Tomorrow we go off on Mrs Fellowes'[1] boat for two days to see some islands near Hyeres, arriving back Tuesday in time to greet Mrs Fitzgerald and Lord Sefton (the best-looking man I've ever seen) upon their arrival. The offer of the Duke of Westminster has been accepted and we will probably leave about the first week in Sept, maybe train to Venice and then Dalmatian coast – Greek Islands – Istanbul train to Budapest for a day or two – Paris – home. Sounds divine but may not come off. Think of having such a gift, no expense except food and wine. You also can think how spoiled I am getting with so much luxury and Miss Burke unbearable.[2] Do keep an eye on the US papers re this trip because Jackie has tried to handle the reporters more kindly than last year as the result of a few words of wisdom from Bernard R-Hatt. However one can't count on either Jackie or Mr Hearst. I hope you are well and happy and that we are going to meet soon.

WALLIS

Owing to the Anglo–Italian tensions caused by Mussolini's designs on Abyssinia, the Prince had to cancel his proposed cruise in the eastern Mediterranean.

1. The Hon. Mrs Reginald Fellowes, a chic figure socially prominent in England, France and America. She was Daisy, daughter of the French Duc Decazes and one of the Singer sewing-machine heiresses.
2. Wallis's maid Mary Burke.

Wallis to Edward
[undated]   Le Roc

I think it does look fairly hopeless. You could of course mention it as a possible trip before going to Austria should the September 4th meeting[1] end in 'love and kisses'. You know the King and the way to handle him, it is hard for me to advise. I think you should write [the Duke of] Westminster a very nice note and tell him what goes on. I shall go into Cannes about 4.45 and meet you at the station 6.15. We can all decide where to dine. I must write 2 letters today also. I love your eyes.

Wallis to Aunt Bessie
Wednesday, Aug 28th

Darling

I am so worried about your fall and are you really sure you haven't hurt anything? Please look where you are going as you are the top of careless walkers on those tiny feet. I talked to E on the telephone last night and he sailed today leaving a confused flat behind. Cain is ill, something the matter with her leg and the Dr says a month before she can return which is uncertain, housemaid getting married Sept 22nd and I was planning to remain away until Oct 1st. However there it is – to say nothing of the plans of PW which are most upset. We can't take the trip in the Cutty Sark as there is no safe place in the Mediterranean at the moment and if GB declares sanctions the Prince will have to go home as I suppose it means war eventually so we are waiting the King's wishes and the Council on Sept 4th before proceeding to a place outside of Budapest called Kiki where we hear there is a charming hotel on a lake. Your blue eyed charmer is the most disappointed small boy you can imagine. You would think Mussolini had planned this mess just to break up the yachting trip. There is too much wind here but no rain. Dickie Mountbatten[2] is here on his destroyer and the youngest of the King of Spain's sons[3] who is known as the Prince of the Asturias now and who is charming and normal.

---

1. The proposed meeting of the Council of the League of Nations to discuss the Abyssinia crisis.
2. Lord Louis Mountbatten, then thirty-five and commanding a destroyer in the Mediterranean.
3. Don Juan, now Count of Barcelona and, father of King Juan Carlos of Spain.

We went to Monte last Sat on the yacht and had great fun and the week-end here we are going to Corsica and then I imagine we will be off somewhere. It will be the best plan to send letters to the flat. Ernest is thinking of bringing Audrey[3] back to live with us if her mother will agree. You can imagine the discomfort it will cause in my flat to say nothing of added expense with 4 regular meals a day for two extra people as of course she will have to have a daily governess to look after her. However there is nothing I can do about it but face the situation and its complications. I have not sunburned this year and it's so awful in October. Ernest had Emma Jason and Governor Richie for lunch at the flat. Don't know how it went with no Cain for the silver etc. You will probably see Ernest around the end of September. The Rogers will come to Austria with us anyway which is a help after the enormous doses of Englishwomen I had all the season and here in the house also. Gladie Buist is also doing a Posy this year and sticking along with about the same results at popularity as the latter. All love and a big kiss.

WALLIS

Saturday 7th [September]   Carlton Hotel, Cannes

Darling

We still go on with the bathing, golfing, eating. We went to Corsica on the Westminster yacht staying 4 days. We had ideal weather and increased our company by the Rogers. It is the only time the yacht will be used as it is definitely impossible for HRH to go cruising about. We leave Monday for Budapest, 1 day on the train and 2 nights. We shall stay in Budapest until the week-end and then go to some place on a lake for the week-end and then I think motor to Vienna perhaps a touch of the Austrian Tyrol and Paris about the 25th. The party consists of Rogers, Gladie, Jackie and Helen Fitzgerald, though her boy friend Sefton has to go back to London tomorrow so you see we have that great crime an extra woman. PW did not bargain for her coming if the boy friend couldn't but Helen may be like Posy in that respect. Anyway she's very nice and quite an addition. I have loved my holiday and really have had some rest, getting to bed at 1.30 occasionally which very early for me. I think perhaps Bernard has done some good as the papers don't make *quite* such a fool of me as

1. Ernest's daughter by his first wife Dorothy, then about ten years of age.

when that Jane Eads was going at one. The man Leeds who wrote about the voice took her place. I have my dog here with me & you can imagine what that will be on the train. He is to be smuggled back into England in the Prince's plane.[1] Ernest will give you an outline of our life in London since royalty arrived. He thinks it all a great joke. And so it is but I never had so much fun before or things so easy and I might as well finish up any youth that is left to me with a flourish. It is time we saw each other. If war between Italy and Abyssinia occurs perhaps shipping will take a leap and I'll be able to come over. All my love

WALLIS

Wallis to Edward

[written as their train passed through Switzerland]

Hello. I didn't sleep though Slipper slept with me. You bought clocks of course because this is their home. I can't think what you are going to do with them all except Xmas – or you might give one to the Duke of G[loucester][2] so he can see what a good time he is having. I shan't get up for ages, not until the danger of the lunch hour has passed. I ate pounds of wonderful cherry jam. I miss you and long to see you and your clocks.

WALLIS

Isn't the country pretty and the train dirty.

Wallis to Edward
[September]   Hotel Dunapalota, Budapest

Please darling let me off the boat trip as I am a mess after so many tears but will have recovered by the time you return. Don't for our sakes say anything to Gladie in front of any of the furniture [*sic*]. If she doesn't go on the boat trip it is the end after so many apologies and would be a fair way of spoiling your entire trip to make a second scene of not appearing. I have an idea she won't appear – which I do think will be too much. I feel most upset to have started something that can cast a gloom over our lovely holiday.

WALLIS

1. In defiance of the strict British quarantine regulations for animals.
2. The forthcoming marriage of the Prince of Wales's brother Prince Henry, Duke of Gloucester, had been announced on 30 August.

136

Edward to Wallis

Hotel Dunapalota, Budapest

Goodbye my sweetheart. I'm sad not to have seen you before I go but am glad you are making such long drowsy. I hope to be back by six o'clock and to find a girl and her eanum dog waiting for a boy here. I have left the ford WE always use for you to drive in this afternoon but please [twice underlined] be back by six. I have also left a new Time and a letter from Selby re motoring in Austria, but the latter may be too much detail and not your type of thing and a boy will explain it. Oh! I miss you so my sweetheart and hate this afternoon without you. God bless WE Wallis.

DAVID

Edward to Wallis

Hotel Dunapalota, Budapest

Good morning my sweetheart. As you and your dog have not been called yet I am leaving Storrier[1] behind in case you like to send Slipper to the golf later for some exercise with me. I'm so drowsy and weak that the golf will not be good. Will you please wait here for a boy as he'll hurry back to you and we'll do something alone this afternoon. I'll miss you so till then. Yes more and more and more.

DAVID

By the time the Prince returned from his long summer holiday with Wallis at the beginning of October 1935, the idea of marriage to her had become a fixed and passionate desire. He had not yet begun to work out how he might realize this desire; but henceforth its realization was to be his principal aim in life. 'It was all quite vague but nonetheless vivid,' he later wrote in his memoirs, 'this dream of being able to bring into my life what for so long had been lacking, without which my service to the state would seem an empty thing.'

The Prince had no illusions about the difficulties in the way of his marriage to a twice-divorced woman. He had already contemplated the possibility of giving up his rights to the throne. It was his intention to discuss the whole matter with his father that autumn, but the old King was in declining health, and a suitable opportunity for the discussion never arose.

The love letters and billets doux which he wrote to Wallis in the course of that autumn illustrate the intensity of his feelings for her.

1. The Prince's detective.

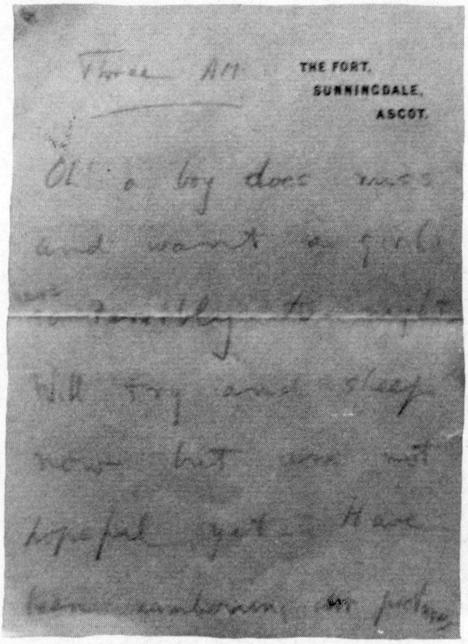

Three AM

THE FORT,
SUNNINGDALE,
ASCOT.

Oh a boy does miss and want a girl here so terribly tonight. Will try and sleep now but am not hopeful yet – Have been [illegible] on pillow

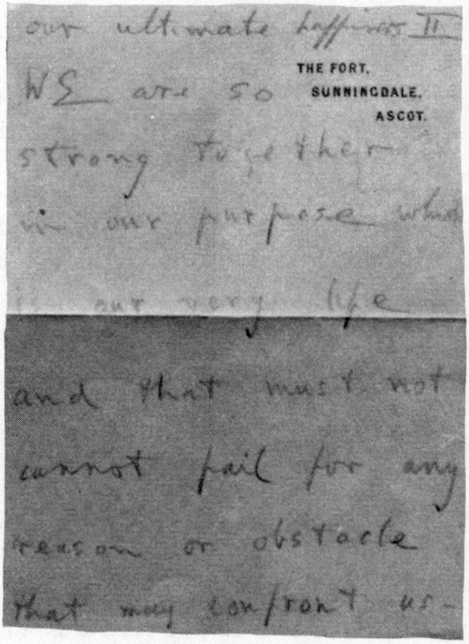

our ultimate happiness II

THE FORT,
SUNNINGDALE,
ASCOT.

WE are so strong together in our purpose which is our very life and that must not cannot fail for any reason or obstacle that may confront us –

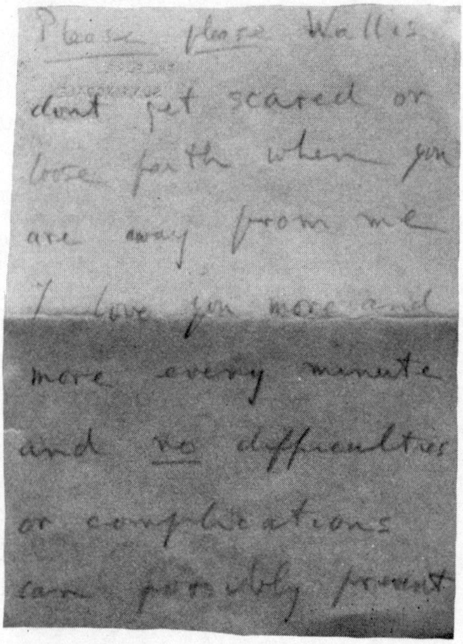

Please please Wallis dont get scared or loose faith when you are away from me I love you more and more every minute and no difficulties or complications can possibly prevent

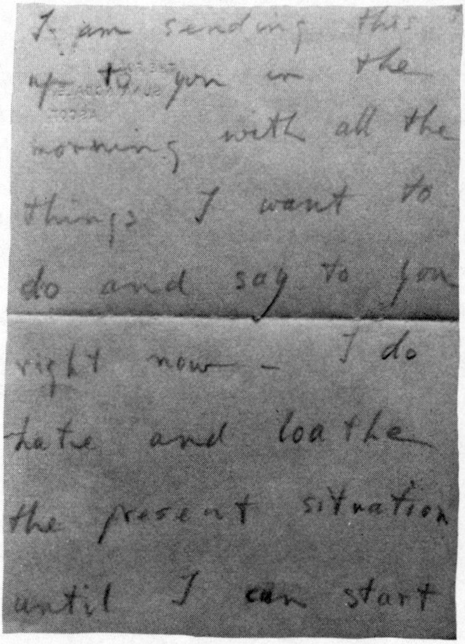

I am sending this up to you in the morning with all the things I want to do and say to you right now – I do hate and loathe the present situation until I can start

THE FORT.
SUNNINGDALE,
ASCOT.

Edward to Wallis
3 a.m.   The Fort

Oh! a boy does miss and want a girl here so terribly tonight. Will try and sleep now but am not hopeful yet. Have been numbering our pictures. *Please, please* Wallis don't get scared or loose [sic] faith when you are away from me. I love you more and more every minute and *no* difficulties or complications can possibly prevent our ultimate happiness. WE are so strong together in our purpose which is our very life and that must not, cannot fail for any reason or obstacle that may confront us. I am sending this up to you in the morning with all the things I want to do and say to you right now. I do hate and loathe the present situation until I can start in to talk more than you do my sweetheart and am just going mad at the mere thought (let alone knowing) that you are alone there with Ernest. God bless WE for ever my Wallis. You know your David will love you and look after you so long as he has breath in this eanum body.

Edward to Wallis
Sat-y   The Fort

Good morning my sweetheart in case I haven't been able to telephone. It's very sad we wont be here this week-end and Slipper is sad too. I've not told him about his cake yet. Take care of yourself until we meet at 'the Castle' this evening. More and more [twice underlined] and more [thrice underlined] sweetheart and please miss me. God bless WE.

DAVID

Edward to Wallis
Sunday   Sutton Place, Guildford[1]

Good morning we all say. I've been awake for hours because that ass Fletcher[2] called me around nine and when asked the reason he replied that 'His Grace'[3] had been called!! I was mad but it's a lovely day so please hurry up and down to a boy my sweetheart and let him take some pictures of you. I was scared alone in this huge room which felt spooky and was missing you terribly. And you? The enclosed was mailed to the Fort – but don't try to decypher it or you'll never be down. And I do wish WE were at the FORT dont you? More and more and more

DAVID

Edward to Wallis

The Fort

My own beloved Wallis I love you more & more & please come down to say goodnight to David. I haven't seen you once today & I can't take it. I love you.

1. The Duke of Sutherland's country seat in Surrey.
2. Piper Alistair Fletcher, the Prince's military servant.
3. The Duke of Sutherland.

The letters to Aunt Bessie resume in the middle of October. Ernest had not yet returned from America.

Monday, Oct 14th   The Fort

Darling

It makes me quite unhappy to think how neglectful I have been as usual about writing but I live such an abnormal life these days never having a second to myself that writing is impossible except Monday morning here when the Prince is out cutting down everything in sight and as I have been on the move since August 5 please try and understand. I see the US papers won't leave me alone but I can't believe anyone can believe what they say especially the one where I am supposed to have spoken about my hat and called him 'Davy'. Can you bear it all? However I am glad they now know who I am and I am no longer the mysterious Mrs S. The Rogers returned here with the party and spent a week out here which I was grateful for as I have nobody in the flat except Mrs Ralph and kitchen maid. Cain still in Scotland with phlebitis and housemaid impossible to get. I am working hard to try and get the place going before Ernest returns on Friday. Cain is expected to be well enough to return on the 21st. However I'm afraid she will never be quite well as the thing returns. Servants are getting as difficult as the ones at home and everybody is struggling to find them here. There is much war talk but I do hope this country won't be silly enough to become involved. It all seems to be a political game. We had a week in Paris. I went with Foxy Gwynne to Mainbocher and she got me everything at half price and the Prince brought them over in his airplane. We lunched at the British Embassy with M. Laval[1] and all the French ministers. Dined with Elsie Mendl and the Prince lunched with the President, a most successful and popular visit for him as he had never been in Paris so long and the King was most pleased with his efforts. Our trip was lovely and the Austrian lakes so beautiful. We had a whirl both in Buda and Vienna and saw Merritt [Swift] and [Georges] Sebastian in the latter place. Motoring from Vienna to Munich we lunched in Salzburg. I think you would like Austria in the summer. There are walks and music. We happened to have beautiful weather. I believe it is a bit tricky however. I shall send you some snaps taken this summer and you will have an idea of our trip. I have sent you 2 pairs of corsets and two bustbodices. I wonder if you will

1. Pierre Laval, President of the French Council of Ministers.

141

see Tamar. As you know Benny [Thaw] was retired on account of the Vanderbilt case. Also Merritt Swift because he was rather rude to people who called at embassies and they went home and said so! Gerry Greene got it too.[1] Tamar has never been very friendly with me since she accused me of taking Thelma's side in their row so if I came home I imagine she will not make an effort to see me. I shall be glad to see that angelic Ernest again and also to hear of you from him. Mrs Simpson is still here and Pa returns next week and she sails! Corrine wrote me from Pensacola, didn't seem too cheerful, spoke about Anne. I hope the case won't come out in the papers it really is a scandal. Corrine says she blames *Newbold* for everything. Willmott never telephoned when he was in London. Everything the same here and too many invitations appear. What a bump I'll get when a young beauty appears and plucks the Prince from me. Anyway I am prepared. This Royal wedding[2] isn't making any excitement. The people are about spent with the foreign princess and the jubilee, so it is hard on the couple coming at just this time making too many cheers for sore throats in a year's time. The Kent baby[3] is a success being a boy. I am having cocktails with Berta [Grant] Wed who has now moved into a much grander house but is just as sweet as ever. Most of your old friends have left London. Tonight I dine with Lord Sefton, tomorrow Diana Cooper,[4] Wed Lady Cunard then Elsie Mendl. Can you beat it? I hope E is all right but he had a very thin time with Dorothy and did not succeed in getting Audrey. Write me soon and all love and a big hug

WALLIS

Ernest returned from America on 18 October. While in New York he had had a whirlwind affair with Wallis's old friend Mary Kirk Raffray. Whether or not Wallis knew of this, she now noticed a further change in his attitude. 'We were going our separate ways', she wrote in her memoirs; 'the core of our marriage had dissolved; only the shell remained – a façade to show the outer world.' Little hint of this, of

---

1. An American diplomat Wallis had known in China.
2. The marriage of the Duke of Gloucester to Lady Alice Scott took place in the private chapel of Buckingham Palace on 5 November.
3. Prince Edward, the present Duke of Kent, had been born in London on 9 October.
4. An actress of aristocratic birth and a famous hostess, one of the greatest beauties of her day. She was married to the then Secretary of State for War, Duff Cooper.

course, appears in her letters to her aunt; though in December she writes to her cherished relative: 'You're all I've got.'

Monday, November 18th   The Fort

Dearest Aunt Bessie

I am so sorry about the corsets. Ernest says they take ages sometimes. However I have written to them and Ernest went to Paris yesterday for 3 days and will go into the shop if can possibly find the time. I am really distressed about Anne and thought the Shepherd Pratt was only for insane people. Cousin Lelia must be very sad over it all. I am dining with the Kents and though I have been there for cocktails several times this will be the first meal not in a restaurant with them. It is too bad Ernest will miss it. I am still trying to find a housemaid that is a housemaid. The one I now have isn't too bad but doesn't like the flat so leaves Dec 4th. The past two weeks I have been entertaining, 2 women's luncheons and 2 dinners, one of ten for Elsie and Charles Mendl and one of 12 for Sir Robert and Lady Vansittart. He is the Permanent Undersecretary for Foreign Affairs and Wednesday I am having a KT party for the Austrian Minister who is forever calling upon me and is such a bore that I have to have help from outside. I enjoy meeting and seeing all these people and some times it seems strange to think of those days of struggle in Earl's Court[1] and the other flat where mother had the café and was forever working herself to death to give me things. I wonder if in any way I'll ever be able to reward her efforts? Or if my insatiable ambitions will land me back in such a flat as the one room on Conn Hill, the Woburn.[2] Only time will show. All love

WALLIS

Monday, Dec 9th   The Fort

Dearest Aunt Bessie

I am so glad the corsets arrived and fitted, for what with exchange and duty it makes them rather expensive. We have no Xmas plans,

1. An apartment building in Baltimore where Wallis's mother had taken a flat after the death of her second husband in 1913.
2. The Woburn Apartments in Washington where Wallis's mother lived in the 1920s, nicknamed by her 'the Woebegone'.

will of course be in London and have Ma Simpson for lunch. I wish you were going to be here. I think Xmas an awful beating, everyone trying to be gay and eating too much and wondering how they'll pay for the presents they have given. I have just completed the shopping for HRH, 165 presents for staff and this week end have been busy wrapping them up. I am still struggling with housemaid trouble and sent one flying on Wed having broken everything so now have a char until after Xmas. Am in a slight flurry over the Kents coming to dinner on Thursday in such an upset household. I lunched with Lady Oxford[1] the other day. She is terrifying. Ernest has put off his business trip to Germany until after Xmas. We are all thrilled over the Scanlons' arrival. Any cooking gadgets you know of or new cocktail food you might give to her and also evening shoes in white from sales. I am going to try my best to come over soon. Ernest having been away so much he is not keen to have me go away at the moment however. We shall see. I am sending you a small cheque. Let me know what you get. Take care of yourself – you're all I've got. Love

WALLIS

From the Duke of Windsor's memoirs:
A few days later I was at Sandringham for the family Christmas gathering. My brothers and their wives were already there. My father had grown thin and bent.... I felt detached and lonely. My brothers were secure in their private lives; whereas I was caught up in an inner conflict and would have no peace of mind until I had resolved it. But this again was hardly the time or place [to raise with his father the matter of his desire to marry Wallis]....

Edward to Wallis
Boxing Day!   Sandringham, Norfolk
(Button does not box as well as Slipper yet)

Good night and good morning my sweetheart – as I won't be able to say either by 'phone. It's helped so much getting a few minutes talk alone at last this evening. I couldn't believe it was possible to miss this way but its so lovely although hell while it lasts. It really is terrible

---

1. Margot, Countess of Oxford and Asquith, widow of the Liberal Prime Minister Herbert Asquith. A great figure in the social and intellectual life of London.

here and so much the worst Xmas I've ever had to spend with the family, far worse than last year and that was bad enough. I just can't wait till seeing you Monday [30 December] and to know that boat has sailed for Canada. I'm longing for an eanum letter Wallis. This one has to be eanum as the mail is in a few minutes. Please dont over eat until we can again together or I'm there to say stop or you'll be quite ill I know. The pirate costume idea is good but not the idea of having to bore ourselves with others on New Years night. Oh! to be alone for ages and ages and then – ages and ages. God bless WE sweetheart but I'm sure he does – he must. Your

DAVID

Wallis and the Prince saw in the New Year together at Melton Mowbray, at a house party given by the Colin Buists. Ernest had gone to Canada on business.

In a New Year note to Wallis, the Prince seems to hint at the dream of their marrying in 1936.

Edward to Wallis
1st Jan [19]36

Good morning my sweetheart

Thank God last night is over and lets go quickly this afternoon. Your lovely New Year message helped a boy a lot in his lonely drowsy and he was feeling sad. Give Mary an eanum note for me to keep until WE can be alone together again. Oh! my Wallis I know we'll have Viel Glück to make us *one* this year. God bless WE. Your

DAVID

The babies have new ribunds and say hello to the 'Eanum Oos'.

Wallis to Aunt Bessie
Thursday, Jan 9th   Bryanston Court

Dearest Aunt Bessie

It was thrilling to hear your voice on Xmas eve. It did make me want to see you so badly. We had a very nice Xmas – luncheon here and dinner with Betty Lawson Johnston. Then Boxing Night with the Humphrey Butlers[1] and Friday we went to Sir Philip Sassoon's[2] for the

1. The Duke of Kent's equerry.
2. A rich aesthete, socialite and politician, then Under-Secretary of State for Air.

145

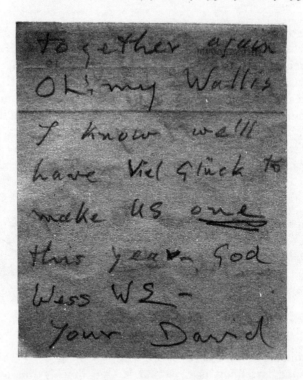

night and Saturday moved on to Sir Robert Vansittart's for another one night stand and then New Year's eve went to Melton to stay with Gladie [Buist] for the fancy dress party. The Prince returned from Sandringham for that party which really was very gay and a little like Warrenton. Horses have a peculiar effect on their owners as I've never seen the English so gay! It will be thrilling to see the Scanlons. I can't get over the jigsaw puzzle thing. What happened was that Walter Prendergast gave me 2 in south of France made in Chagrin Falls. They were the best I had ever seen. Then Aileen Winslow sent me 2 by Ian Russell, same make. The Prince loved them and they were a great help at week-ends so wired Aileen to send him a dozen and also I took one to Harrod's and asked them to order some as I'm sure they will be a hit over here. The two Aileen sent the Prince took to Sandringham and the King & Queen did them and have asked him for more. Ernest is away again for ten days. He says he may make some money. In that case I may be able to come to Washington. I have run into Thelma twice, all very agreeable and I'm sure could easily have her once more

146

sitting in the flat but think it far wiser to stay away from that gang now I'm clear. She has the most *awful* lot of people around her here and *Mala Brand* her best friend. I understand no one in NY accepts them at all. I shall always like Tamar and am sure she is the only decent member of the family. According to people here Gloria's giving up the money is only a gesture for the Supreme Court because if she wins she gets the lot with the child. I have learned to make that gooey stuff Mrs Bristol puts on the top of her ham. It's made of peaches. I will send the apple recipe on separate cover as I'm writing from the Fort where there has been a pompous week-end including the King's secretary and wife. I had a luncheon last week where Mr Phillips[1] from the State Department was a guest and heard some of the Washington news but so many strange names. You better begin to think of summer plans. Europe is much nicer than the US in summer you know. Take care of yourself. All love

WALLIS

From the Duke of Windsor's memoirs:
On Thursday afternoon, January 16, I was out shooting with friends in Windsor Great Park. An urgent note from my mother was brought to me in the field. 'I think you ought to know that papa is not very well', the note began, and in the calm way that I knew so well my mother went on to say that, while she herself did not consider the danger immediate, Lord Dawson (the King's physician), was 'not too pleased with Papa's state at the present moment'. She therefore suggested that I 'propose' myself for the coming week-end at Sandringham, but do so in such a casual manner that my father should not suspect that she had warned me of his condition.

From the Duchess of Windsor's memoirs:
I happened to be at the Fort that afternoon and was in the drawing room when he came in with the note in his hand. Without a word he gave it to me to read. He disappeared, and I heard him telephoning the pilot to have his aeroplane ready the next morning to fly him to Sandringham.

1. The future US Ambassador to Rome.

Edward to Wallis
Sat-y [18 January]   Sandringham, Norfolk

My own Sweetheart
   Just a line to say I love you more and more and need you so to be
with me at this difficult time. There is no hope whatsoever for the
King it's only a matter of how long and I won't be able to get up to
London tomorrow if he's worse. But I do long long [*sic*] to see you
even for a few minutes my Wallis it would help so much. Please take
care of yourself and dont get a cold. You are all and everything I have
in life and WE must hold each other so tight. It will all work out right
for us. God bless WE. Your

                                                                DAVID

*The following (Sunday) morning the Prince went to London to inform
the Prime Minister of the King's condition. He then returned to Sandringham.*

   From the Duchess of Windsor's memoirs:
   On Monday evening [20 January] I attended a movie given for
   charity with the Lawson Johnstons. During the showing, Lord
   Dawson's famous bulletin was read out: 'The King's life is moving
   peacefully to its close.'
   ... The Lawson Johnstons persuaded me to return to their
   place for a bite of supper. Shortly after midnight, as I was getting
   ready to leave, I was called to the telephone. It was David speak-
   ing from Sandringham.
   'It's all over,' he said.
   I could think of nothing better to say than, 'I am so very sorry.'
   Then he said, 'I can't tell you what my own plans are, every-
   thing here is so very upset. But I shall fly to London in the
   morning and will telephone you when I can.'
   It was only as I hung up that I realised that David was now
   King.

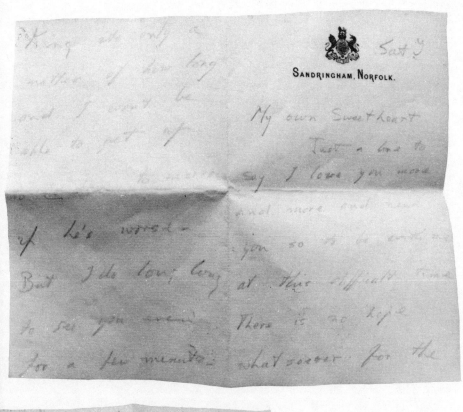

PART TWO

Wallis and the King

JANUARY–DECEMBER 1936

CHAPTER SIX

The New Reign
(JANUARY-FEBRUARY)

The Prince was now King and, for the first few days, Wallis saw little of him. His time was taken up by the ceremonies and formalities attendant on the change of sovereign; by the great and elaborate public spectacle that was his father's funeral; and by the task of having to receive the many distinguished foreign personages who came to London for the occasion. Only once were they alone together, when he briefly joined her as she was watching his formal proclamation from a window at St James's Palace. After that ceremony, she said to him: 'This has made me realize how different your life is going to be.' He replied that, however much this might be so, nothing could change his feelings for her.

Those feelings, indeed, were now intensified. The King acutely felt the strain of his lonely and exalted new position. To seek relief from his public burden he turned to his private emotional existence – and all of this was now invested in Wallis. She was the only person with whom he could relax or in whom he could confide. At first they could not be together as much as before: his royal duties were too pressing. But she was never far from his mind. He telephoned her whenever he could, and sent her amorous notes and flowers. He called upon her every evening at Bryanston Court. And they continued to spend their week-ends at the Fort, with a small number of guests drawn from their close circle of friends.

The accession of Edward VIII was greeted by his subjects with tremendous excitement and hope. His youthfulness, his charisma, his modernity, his interest in reform – all seemed to promise that the new reign would truly be a new age. His twenty-six years as Prince of Wales had given him an ideal training for his role, and had won him a unique place in the hearts of the people. Though deeply mourned, George V had been a figure of the Victorian past and intensely conservative in his ways. With Edward VIII, it was felt, a new spirit and style would enter public life. Wallis's letters to Aunt Bessie – and her one

*highly significant letter to the King around this time – show how
infected she was by the general euphoria, and how eager to help and
sustain him in his great task. But they reveal other things too.*

*It has been seen how, in 1935, Wallis had been tremendously fêted
by London Society on account of her friendship with the Prince. This,
however, was nothing compared to the social position in which she
found herself in January 1936. Now she was not just a princely
favourite, but the woman who had access to the ear and the heart of
the sovereign of the day. Thanks to the traditional silence of the British
press on the private life of royalty, her name remained unknown to
the public at large; but on the part of the official world and the
fashionable world, interest in her became obsessive. She was besieged
with invitations and flattering attentions – as well as with embarrassing
requests, for many people sought to use her as a sort of private communications service leading to the King, who being in mourning did
not appear in public and was inaccessible to all save his closest friends.*

*In considering the whole question of Wallis's role during the reign
of Edward VIII, it is important to bear in mind that – right from the
beginning – she was surrounded by flatterers (many of them possessing
distinguished social and public positions) who never stopped assuring
her of how much she was liked and what an excellent influence she
was considered to have on the monarch. Writing to Aunt Bessie on the
tenth day of the reign, she mentions that she has been inundated with
admiring letters; such of these as have been preserved in her archives
are indeed lavishly generous. Sibyl Colefax,[1] the hostess and decorator,
declared that she had 'grown every month more full of delighted
admiration for not only your immense wisdom & lovely common (so
miscalled!) sense, but also for your unfailing touch of being exactly
right in all judgments & in all kinds of moments in life at every angle'.
Margot Oxford thought she had 'every quality to be liked – you are
very natural, very kind, never pretend to know what you don't know
(a rare quality believe me) & a genuine desire to help the man you
love in his very difficult task'. Diana Cooper found her 'good and kind
and lovable – what more can one be?' No wonder Wallis writes to her
aunt that everyone has been 'too divine' to her, that she has been*

---

1. One of the great hostesses of her day and a notorious 'lion hunter', who brought an
extraordinary variety of people together at her house in Chelsea. A warm friendship developed
between her and Wallis based on their common interest in food, clothes and decorating. She
was the wife of Sir Arthur Colefax QC.

'*implored on all sides*' not to leave the King, that she is regarded as '*a good influence ... and right in the things I try to influence him to do*'.

These three women Wallis regarded as her friends, and they were in fact much attached to her; there were other so-called friends who wrote in similar vein, such as Emerald Cunard and Philip Sassoon, who a year later would claim barely to have known her. Yet Wallis does appear to have been genuinely popular in Society. Perspicacious political diarists of the period write of her in kindly vein. Meeting her with the Prince at the theatre a few days before the death of George V, Harold Nicolson[1] found her '*bejewelled, eyebrow-plucked, virtuous and wise*' and '*clearly out to help him*'.[2] '*Chips*' Channon[3] thought her '*a woman of charm, sense, balance and great wit, with dignity and taste*'.[4] Victor Cazalet[5] considered her '*the one real friend he has ever had. She does have a wonderful influence over him....*'[6] Of course, none of these people were aware, in the winter of 1936, of the King's desire to marry her. She appeared to be safely married to someone else. The general attitude towards her was rather like that of a family who are delighted that their head, with all his position and responsibilities, can rely on the support of an excellent and trusted secretary or housekeeper, but are not prepared for the news that he wishes to make her his wife.

We have seen that, writing to Wallis on New Year's Day 1936, the Prince had expressed his fervent hope that 'WE' might become 'one' that year. No doubt Wallis was greatly touched by such passionate declarations; but how seriously did she take them? Her intimate correspondence during the first weeks of the new reign contains some evidence that she regarded the King's marriage plans as a fantasy, and that she did not encourage them. Writing to him, she hopes he will '*cease to want what is hardest to have and will be content with the*

1. National Labour MP for Leicester, a former career diplomat and an author and journalist famous for his polished style. He was married to the novelist Vita Sackville-West.
2. Nigel Nicolson (ed.), *Harold Nicolson, Diaries and Letters, 1930–39* (Collins, London, 1966), p. 238.
3. Conservative MP for Southend, known in London Society for his waspish wit and lavish hospitality. He was an American from Chicago, married to a Guinness heiress.
4. Robert Rhodes James (ed.), *Chips, the Diaries of Sir Henry Channon* (Weidenfeld & Nicolson, London, 1967), p. 51.
5. Conservative MP for Chippenham, then thirty-nine, noted for his strong moral beliefs and his support of Zionism.
6. Robert Rhodes James, *Victor Cazalet* (Hamish Hamilton, London, 1976), p. 186.

simple way'. And writing to Aunt Bessie, she regards it as 'a tragedy that he can't bring himself to marry without loving' – that is, that he will not contemplate a suitable match with a woman other than herself.

Meanwhile, Ernest finds himself in a curious position. In the preceding twelve months, the emotional basis of his marriage had collapsed and he had transferred part of his affections elsewhere. But the man responsible for the disruption of his life with Wallis was now King; and Ernest, being solid, old-fashioned and half-American, worshipped him as such. On 21 January Ernest addressed a humble letter to his new sovereign, offering him, as a 'devoted, loyal subject', the 'warmest sentiments that friendship can engender ... in the ordeal through which you have passed ... to which I add my fervent prayer, God Bless Your Majesty'.

'Ernest has of course been marvellous about it all,' Wallis writes to Aunt Bessie. Domestic life at Bryanston Court went on as before – perhaps with fewer interruptions. But with the King's emotional claims on her now greater than ever, and his determination to remove all obstacles in the way of marriage, how long could it continue?

Wallis to Edward
[early February]   Bryanston Court

I am sad because I miss you and being near and yet so far seems most unfair. Some day of course I must learn to be always alone for I will be in my heart also I must develop strength to look at papers containing your photographs and accounts of your activities – and perhaps you will miss the eanum in your scheme. One can be awfully alone in crowds – but also perhaps both of us will cease to want what is hardest to have and be content with the simple way. And now I hear your machine which generally was a *joyous* sound because soon you would be holding me and I would be looking 'up' into your eyes.

God bless you and above all make you strong where you have been weak.

———————

'I send flowers to him.'

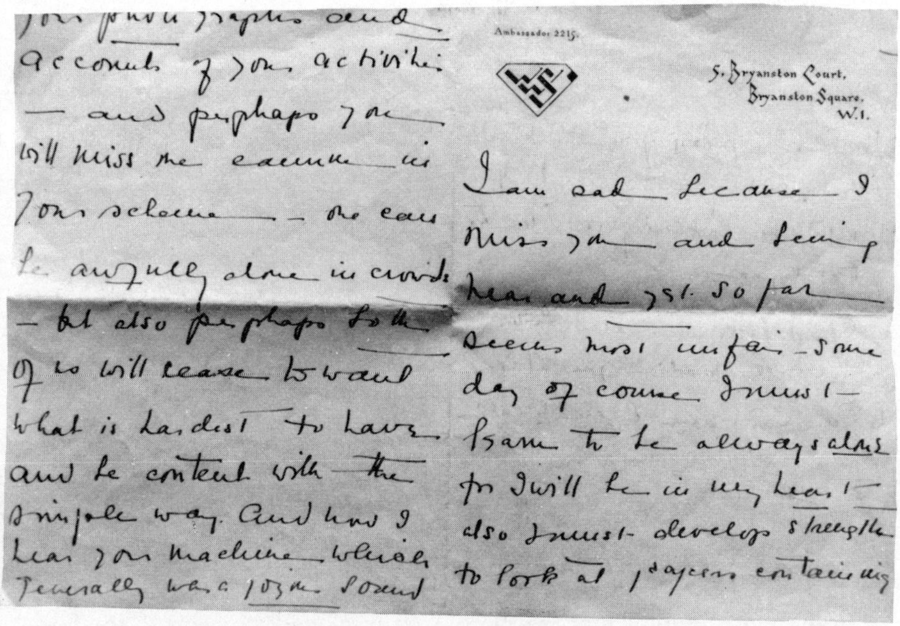

Ambassador 2215.

5, Bryanston Court,
Bryanston Square,
W.1.

I am sad because I miss you and being here and yet so far seems most unfair – some day of course I must learn to be always alone for I will be in my heart – also I must develop strength to look at papers containing

your photographs and accounts of your activities – and perhaps you will miss me easier in your scheme – one can be awfully alone in crowds – but also perhaps both of us will cease to want what is hardest to have and be content with the simple way. And now I hear your machine which generally was a joyous sound

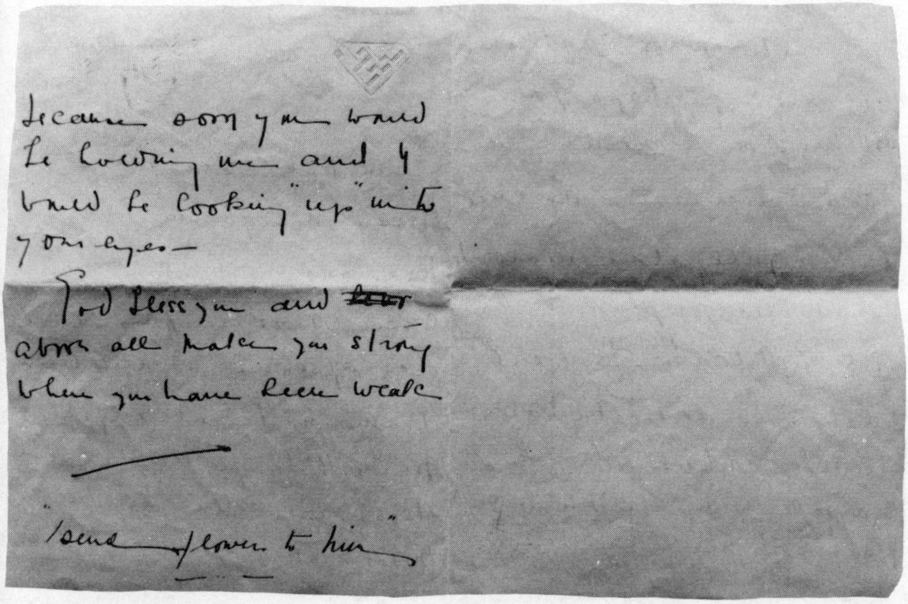

because soon you would be looking [at] me and I would be looking "up" into your eyes –

God bless you and ~~[illegible]~~ above all make you strong when you have been weak

"send flowers to him"

Wallis to Aunt Bessie
January 30th

Dearest Aunt Bessie

I can't remember when I last wrote but I know it was ages ago – but the last week has turned everything so upside down and everyone has been so keyed up etc. I have sent you the English papers so they will tell you the story of the King's death. It really was sudden though he had been more or less an invalid since his illness in 1928 – and the Prince thought him very feeble at Xmas. He was taken ill on a Thursday and died the following Monday at 12 midnight. I have had to be at the new King's beck and call, being the only person he has to really talk things over with normally, and it has all been a great strain. The ceremonies have been marvellous and impressive as only this country can produce and the proclamation of Edward XVIII [*sic*] the most picturesque thing – such costumes from the Middle Ages, the heralds looking like a pack of cards. The King has lost six pounds and the strain has been tremendous but things will adjust themselves now that the funeral is over and he will move to the Palace in about six months. In the meantime his office is there. Last week-end we went to the Fort and go again tomorrow where he will get the needed rest. Everyone including some of the cabinet ministers have been too divine to me and surely(?) I have really made some nice English friends. I am implored on all sides not to leave him as he is so dependent on me and I am considered to be a *good* influence believe it or not and right in the things I try to influence him to do. Of course I am very fond of him and proud and want him to do his job well and he is so lonely and needs companionship and affection, otherwise he goes wrong. Ernest has of course been marvellous about it all. He has the make-up of a saint and is much too good for 'the likes of me'. How things will work out now I can't say. Anyway don't worry your dear head about anything. I am enclosing a few samples of some of the letters I've had. Each is an example of 30 more I received. The one from Sibyl Colefax is especially nice. She is in her 50's.[1] Her handwriting is the top and the joke of London, so it will take you several days to read what she says. Please return the letters but keep all the snap shots as I have duplicates. I hear from Walter [Prendergast] that the Scanlons arrive on Tuesday. Unfortunately they will just miss [Bernardo] Rolland who

1. She was sixty-one.

has been here for a few days. I found a card here tonight from the Frazers. I shall do something about it as soon as I can but at the moment I am up to my neck in people all wanting more than ever to be friends and the days or the nights haven't been left open for days. Though the King is in mourning, everyone is over anxious to see that I am asked to all small dinners in the official world, all sending messages *via* me. Isn't it all funny and strange too? I'm just the same however and enjoying it all as a huge game – laughing a lot inside and controlling my tongue and sense of humour on the outside. I hope you are having a good time and that we will meet soon. All love,

WALLIS

Saturday, Feb. 1st   The Fort

Dearest Aunt B

I forgot to say in my letter that I would like one of those family tree things of the Warfield family and one of the Montagues. I know they are rather expensive to have done but I feel I should like to have them so will you find out who to go to to have them made up for one? I hope the histories of the two will stand up against these 1066 families here. Here one goes to the College of Heralds for these histories but I don't know at home. I think Cousin Lelia once 'vetted' the Montagues – which by the way when spelt with an e here means the Jewish family – the swell spell it without an e!! In haste and with much love

WALLIS

Monday, 9th Feb.   The Fort

Dearest Aunt B

As you see the week-ends continue only less people.[1] What effect being King will have on him seeing his friends as before remains to be seen when the Court goes out of mourning and the functions begin. Actually he has more free time in the evenings as the time of his going to public dinners etc is over but his days are much busier and far more interesting naturally being the boss. I think he will make a great King of a new era – and I believe the country thinks the same. Actually the old regime was a little behind the times but very dearly loved. The late King was not sociable nor the Queen and I'm sure this one will entertain more at the palace. It's a very lonely job – and it is a tragedy that

1. See Appendix 2.

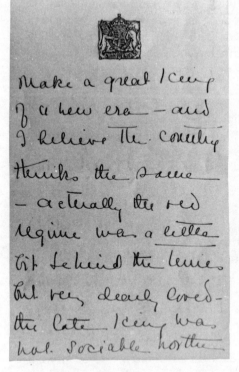

he can't bring himself to marry without loving. The English would prefer that he marry a Duke's daughter to one of the mangy foreign princesses left. However only the years and himself can arrange that for him. London is dull naturally. We all look like black birds. As I always wear so much black for economy I got into mourning with no expense. I shall wear it until the end of March – that is what we are all doing. I am much too busy as there are endless small dinners. The King dined at the flat last Wed and Thurs, and at the latter I had the Scanlons who had arrived the day before and we were just six – HM will not come if over – and afterwards went to York House where we all saw the film of the funeral procession. The Scanlons were thrilled and Gladys more out of breath than ever – and I thought making very little sense. She has not got around to bringing me my dress yet – which will be divine to pop out of black into. The King will move into Buckingham Palace end of Sept when Queen Mary goes to Marl-borough House. Foxy Gwynne has had someone's flat lent her in Paris and I may go over and stay for a week in March and get some clothes at Mainbocher at my good prices. I will send you some things for Sally but as you know I have been selling the old ones. Naturally I only get £20 or £30 for quite a lot – about the price of 2 new ones. Please take care of yourself in this cold weather I read of. Berta is back with numerous Grant relations this time. Poor May Osborne is dying of cancer. Berta and myself are going down Friday to see her. Miss Frazer has called but I actually haven't got round to having her in yet. I can't begin to tell you what the telephone is these days and Cain muddling everything up and still no housemaid! All my love　　　WALLIS

PS Marge Key had much to say about Anne.

[14 February]　　　　　　　　　　　　　　　　　Bryanston Court

Darling

So upset by the crack over the recipes that Mrs Ralph is now writing them out and Ernest will put in envelope and post as I am dashing off to Antoine's.[1] Yes, I do mean to have the families done by the people who do that sort of thing. It is only in case some old Court official wanted to know this and that – and *all English families* have that sort of thing – *and* we think it a good thing to have in reserve. I know in America there are people who make that research as I had a postcard from some man in Washington asking if I would like him to do it but unfortunately I threw it away. I really can't see why you get upset over the newspapers when men like Norman Davis, Phillips[2] etc. say no one believes the Hearst Press or all these sensational things that America produces. G. Trotter automatically retired from the then Prince of Wales' service this Oct on account of age.[3] There is an age limit for all the staffs of the Royal Family, otherwise they would be attended by people on crutches. And G came back and helped at the time of the late King's death. There has been no row of any sort. One gets tired of all these things and the only thing that saves most public characters is that they feel themselves above gossip. Look how Mr Baldwin has

1. The hairdresser.
2. US diplomats.
3. The rumour was that Trotter has been sacked owing to his coolness towards Wallis and continued friendship with Thelma Furness.

been attacked lately.[1] I suppose it has got him down. What then for the country? The clippings amuse me and Ernest and myself are keeping a collection, but as far as upsetting me they don't do that. I must dash now but will write again over week-end. All love,   WALLIS

Monday, Feb. 17th   The Fort

Dearest Aunt B

   Have just got over a rather political week-end here – Duff Coopers, Philip Sassoon, Ewan Wallace[2] – all cabinet – and Emerald Cunard who thinks she is the Prime Minister. My life is not so free these days – that is in speech as I can't express any views as they then all think the King must have said [sic] – so I just giggle and say nothing. He is having a lovely time transferring pictures here and lovely silver also. It will be a month before he does know all the treasures he owns. Gladys [Scanlon] finally got around to bringing me the lovely dress. I shall use it as a tea gown for Sunday nights in the country. It is a little too large but I can easily have it fixed. I haven't seen anything like it on this side and love it. The magazine came and I think the tone shows some improvement. Now that he is a step up I wonder what they will do to him? Berta [Grant] and myself went to see May Osborne. It is really so sad but she is so cheerful and brave. On the way back we stopped here and picked up the King. I thought Berta would faint from nerves. Gladys and Mike are having difficulty finding a house for their price, which has to accommodate 2 birds, 3 dogs and be in Mayfair and run on 3 servants. I have another new housemaid coming today. Can you beat it? I am afraid some of the difficulty is Cain who evidently is very hard to get on with especially since her illness – so I may have to let her go eventually. I am afraid this is a very dull letter but there is nothing to report. Ernest is well and may come to Paris with me if he can arrange his business to fit in at that time. I went to the first night of the Chaplin film and thought it too funny for words.[3] The King is having it at York House Wednesday night and 8 for dinner beforehand – more Cabinet. Why does Lelia have a shop – necessity

1. The Conservative-dominated National Government coalition led by Stanley Baldwin had won the general election in November 1935, but since then had been undermined by the Hoare–Laval affair, in which the Foreign Secretary had tried to do a deal with Mussolini over Abyssinia and had been repudiated by the British Cabinet.
2. Secretary for Overseas Trade and not in fact in the Cabinet.
3. *Modern Times*, which had just had its première.

or amusement? I hope you are well and happy. I wish you had a little car. I always worry over taxis and trains, especially to catch cold in. All love,   WALLIS

24 February   The Fort

Darling Aunt Bessie

Mike and Gladys [Scanlon] have just left. I am remaining on for lunch. Ernest has left for Newcastle for the night. I shall return to London in time for another of those endless small dinners. Gladys and Mike were a huge success and I had time to hear all the Washington news and gossip. How far away and foreign it all seems to me now. The difference in thought between the 2 countries is colossal. I feel unfortunately that I am out of tune and step with my own countrymen. I simply don't react the way they do to things, nor do I in the pure English way either. I seem torn between the 2 nationalities. I prefer the English mode of life, and dignity and wide outlook - but I prefer the US pep and sense of humour and detest their bourgeois morals. Gladys tells me the drinking is a caution - 8-9 cocktails before dinner - nothing with dinner - wines hardly ever used - and then more cocktails after. No wonder Anne went to the S.P.[1] One can't possibly have conversation of any intelligence on that diet. Gladys says they don't. We are still very busy with the X puzzles and Aileen has sent one of 1589 pieces - we finished a beauty with the Duff Coopers last week-end of 1200 pieces. I do think John's wife clever the way she has them cut and the subjects she selects. Next Sunday Foxy and myself go to Paris. I have 'little Ormund' a bit of money from the stocks I sold and E has produced a bit of money to aid my trip - and the King has got us wonderful rates at the Meurice[2] - *50 francs each* - 2 bedrooms and a sitting room. I can hardly wait to go. I am *so tired* of it all here and really terribly worn out - a continual round of questions. I also look forward to being away from the flat which has run so badly and with great effort this winter - and to my having dinner in bed - no people at last etc. - in other words a much needed rest with the days interesting. Do take care of yourself in the snow and ice - it is so dangerous. I only wish we could find some way for you to have a car. And what do you mean by a cut in your income? Has M[ary] A[dams]

1. The Shepherd Pratt nursing home, see letter to Aunt Bessie of 18 November 1935.
2. The discreet and fashionable hotel in the rue de Rivoli.

reduced it again? Ernest was so upset over poor Puzzle-Nuts' death and it was sweet of you to write him. He adores his Aunt Bessie. I shall try to get a picture for you – it's one of the more difficult subjects to approach. However this place is always a good setting for those things. All love,

WALLIS

Edward to Wallis
Thursday, two-thirty   St James's Palace, SW [mourning paper]

Hello my sweetheart. How are you? Missing a boy I hope. Here is the card for Kitty Brownlow's flowers. Hurry here please as a boy is longing to see a girl and will be all set and waiting at five thirty. Eanum?
    David says more and more.

[undated]   St James's Palace, SW [mourning paper]
My sweetheart
    Don't be long at the Savoy please and why not call for a boy here? He'll be waiting and longing to see you. You never sent Mr Loo but maybe you forgot. Anyhow if you don't call for me here telephone me and I'll be with you in a few minutes. Hello. Your

DAVID

Sunday   The Fort [mourning paper]

Good morning dear kind Wallis. Please say you are sorry for that impulsive gesture of throwing us so far into David's shoes. We both feel very hurt and sore. Please put us back on our chairs where we belong and David says for you to come down quickly.
Your loving babies

Wallis to Edward
[undated]   The Fort [mourning paper]

I can't believe anything so lovely could be given to a girl. I can't ever make you know how spoiled I feel. I only hope I can make you feel that I am always loving you working for you and with you and wanting everyone to realize the really fair person David is. I am your

WALLIS

[written on envelope:] Bring my yellow dawg to me please Sir

CHAPTER SEVEN

A Tangled Web
(MARCH–MAY)

The months of March to May 1936 represent the turning-point in the story of Wallis and Edward, and hitherto they have been shrouded in mystery. In February of that year Wallis seemed securely married to Ernest Simpson, and there was no sign that their marriage would not continue; by June, she had made up her mind to divorce him. In February, the King's idea of marriage to her seemed no more than a distant dream; by June, it had become a practical intention, and he had put in motion a definite plan whereby it might be realized. Neither of their memoirs, however, sheds any light on this dramatic transition. The Duke of Windsor says nothing about it. The Duchess merely remarks that it had now become clear to her that Ernest had found 'a new emotional centre to his life' – another woman – and she felt he ought to be 'free to pursue his new happiness, relieved of the weight of a dead marriage'. This, as will be seen from the correspondence which follows, was expressing in simple terms an extremely complex situation.

At the outset of the reign, Wallis seems to have hoped and imagined that things would carry on roughly as before – that she would preserve both her close friendship with the King and her marriage (such as it now was) to Ernest. However, neither the King nor Ernest were willing to tolerate the continuance of this situation. The King wanted nothing less than marriage to her, which would necessitate the removal of Ernest from the scene. As for Ernest, he had had enough. In 1934, he appears to have been content with an arrangement which put him into constant association with the heir to the throne; in 1935, he uneasily tolerated the sharing of Wallis with another; in January 1936, his reverence for the monarchy momentarily overcame his anguish over the fact that the new King was in love with his wife. But he could no longer put up with a state of affairs where the King laid constant claim to her presence and her affections.

According to an important eye-witness account, it was at a private meeting between Ernest and the King that matters were brought to a head, and apparently on the initiative of the former. This is the account of Bernard Rickatson-Hatt, Ernest's old friend from the time of his brief service in the Coldstream Guards, who was then editor-in-chief of Reuters.

It is worth recording Rickatson-Hatt's views on the affair as a whole, for he knew both of the Simpsons intimately. He thought Wallis's intention was 'to have her cake and eat it. She was flattered by the advances of the Prince of Wales and King and enjoyed his generous gifts to her to the full. She thought she could have them and at the same time keep her home with Simpson.' When Ernest tackled her on the matter, she always assured him 'that he could trust her to look after herself' and that 'she enjoyed the attention she received and there was no harm in it'; and Rickatson-Hatt believed that, 'but for the King's obstinacy and jealousy, the affair would have run its course without breaking up the Simpson marriage'.[1]

It is Rickatson-Hatt's specific evidence, however, which is important. It relates to an incident which took place a few weeks after the start of the new reign. One evening, Ernest went to York House to see the King. Wallis was not present – indeed, there is nothing to show that she even knew of the meeting – but Ernest got Rickatson-Hatt to come with him. At some point during the evening Rickatson-Hatt started to leave, but Ernest asked him to stay, and in his presence suddenly declared to the King 'that Wallis would have to choose between them, and what did the King mean to do about it? Did he intend to marry her?' The King then rose from his chair and said: 'Do you really think that I would be crowned without Wallis at my side?' That evening – according to Rickatson-Hatt's testimony as it has been recorded – a private arrangement was reached between the King and Ernest, whereby Ernest agreed to put an end to his marriage with Wallis provided that the King promised to remain faithful to her and look after her.

The date of this episode is obviously of crucial importance. Rickatson-Hatt's record is vague: he merely places it some time during the month of February. But it is reasonable to hazard a guess that it

1. Rickatson-Hatt passed this information to Walter Monckton in August 1940 (Lord Birkenhead, *Walter Monckton* [Weidenfeld & Nicolson, London, 1969], pp. 128 and 157), and, ten years later, to the editor of the Duke of Windsor's memoirs, Charles Murphy (*The Windsor Story* [Granada, London, 1979], pp. 137-8).

in fact took place during the first week of March. For on 1 March Wallis – as she had announced in her letters to her aunt – went off to spend a fortnight in Paris with her friend 'Foxy' Gwynne, on what was partly a shopping expedition and partly a rest cure after six hectic and exhausting weeks as the prop upon whom the new sovereign depended. Ernest remained behind in London – though he was due to join her in Paris for the latter part of her visit.

Did Ernest and the King take advantage of her absence to have things out? And if so, did she know anything of their confrontation? All that can be said is that, on 8 March, after a week in the French capital, she wrote Aunt Bessie a curious letter. Its tone is angry and depressed, and – for the first time – she writes of the King with a note of real exasperation.

Sunday [8 March]   Hotel Meurice, Paris

Darling Aunt B

Just a line to say that I've been here a week today and seem to have done nothing – in spite of the fact that Foxy and myself have attended strictly to business and have only been out 2 nights, one being last night. However I need not tell you the state of exhaustion, rage and despair that I have gone through and at the moment rather hope that the Germans will slap all the French couturiers, modistes etc.[1] Ernest arrives tonight and I suppose we will both return Friday unless he has to go to Hamburg on business. We go to Beatrice Cartwright's for dinner tonight – she is here in her flat. I am crazy to hear if you heard the King's broadcast and what you thought of it.[2] I shall write you in full next Saturday. Am simply too tired to do anything but lie down. I have stood for hours trying to get things done in a short time. There are lots of people here – unexpected old friends etc. I know how you

1. At dawn on Saturday 7 March Hitler had ordered his armies into the Rhineland in contravention of the Versailles Treaty. This caused consternation in London and Paris; but the general trend of opinion in both capitals (strongly reflected in the King's own views) was opposed to the use of force to reverse Hitler's coup.
2. The King's St David's Day broadcast on 1 March. In this address, the King departed from the text which had been proposed to him by the Government, to say: 'I am better known to you as Prince of Wales – as a man who, during the war and since, has had the opportunity of getting to know the people of nearly every country of the world, under all conditions and circumstances. And, although I now speak to you as King, I am still that same man who has had that experience and whose constant effort it will be to continue to promote the well-being of his fellow men.'

feel about this place so will say no more. Foxy goes off with Lord Dudley to Monte on Monday. He invited me but that little King insists I return and I might as well with the telephone about 4 times daily – not much rest. All love,

WALLIS

One may wonder whether her visits to the dressmakers, and the international situation, were the sole causes of her 'exhaustion, rage and despair'.

Having spent several days with Ernest in Paris, Wallis returned to England without him on Saturday 14 March. She and Ernest had doubtless discussed the future together; and the letter Wallis writes Aunt Bessie from the Fort after her return ends in a strange vein of fatalism. 'People must make their own lives ... and never having known security until I married Ernest perhaps I don't get along well with it knowing and understanding the thrill of its opposite much better....'

Meanwhile, Wallis's old friend Mary Raffray – whom Ernest had seen much of in America the previous autumn – suddenly and inconveniently proposes herself for a visit at short notice. Wallis writes with annoyance of this new complication – though she adds jocularly that Ernest seems keen on Mary, who might be suitable as his 'future bride'.

Monday, March 16th   The Fort

Dearest Aunt B

I got home on Saturday night and came here from the train. Ernest went on to Germany where I hope he won't be interned. Isn't it too tragic to think that nations are even contemplating war? Naturally the English as usual are calm and seem to think that nothing will happen for a few years anyway if then. However one feels uncomfortable. America is lucky to enjoy the exclusiveness the Atlantic gives her. I had a wire from Mary Raffray while in Paris asking if I could have her for a *short visit*. I had to say yes and promptly in return got a cable saying she was sailing last Sat on the Samaria. My life is so involved at the moment that I don't know what to do with her as I can't fit her night club mind into it and who is to take her on the town as I dine in old fogies' houses nearly every night and hear nothing but politics and personalities none of which would interest Mary and also that charming trait of the English never asking one's guests. Ernest returns next Saturday and is keen about the visit as he has always loved her. I suggest her to him as a future bride. I saw a lot of people in Paris but I was so tired all the time and couldn't make sense. The King sent his plane for all my things which was a help. I also filled it with langoustines for him – you remember his love of them at Biarritz. I am so worried about your blood pressure and please be sure to do exactly what the doctor tells you. What are your plans? Are you coming over to see us and if so when? My plans are indefinite. The King will I think take a house somewhere – naturally this is not for publication. His leanings are for Cannes again or at least that coast. Naturally the situation will influence all plans. Also some yachting is in the mind but as you know nothing is decided until 24 hours before. Anyway he would only leave late July to late August and then possibly open Balmoral. Gladys and Mike have a very nice house and are christening it tomorrow. I haven't seen anyone yet naturally and have told Cain to say I wasn't returning until tomorrow. The Hunters and Bates were here for the week-end and I sealed their lips. I can't bear the racket starting again. I had some rather good pictures taken for Harpers Bazaar while in Paris – I don't know which issue they will appear in. I suppose the recipes crossed on the way with your note – I hope they turn out successfully. I shall be without a cook middle of April and haven't yet found a housemaid. I shall send you a cheque for some flowers for mother at Easter. Cousin Lelia sent me a very nice note started in Wash and finished in Palm Beach. I hear your eyes are out on your cheeks. Do put them back and don't worry. As you know people must make their own lives and I should by now nearly 40 have a little experience in that line – as I wasn't in a position to have it arranged for me by money or position and though I have had many hard times, disappointments etc. I've managed not to go under as yet – and never having known security until I married Ernest perhaps I don't get along well with it knowing and understanding the thrill of its opposite much better – the old bromide nothing ventured, nothing gained. I might still be following ships. When will you come to see us? Love,

WALLIS

Mary arrived in England on Tuesday 24 March. The following week-end she accompanied Ernest and Wallis to the Fort.[1]

Monday, March 30th   The Fort

Dearest Aunt B

Mary is here and seems to be in a constant state of thrill. The Cunard Party was really a lovely one. Mary's clothes are rather naked for here – more night club types. We were here for the week-end with the Buists and Walter Prendergast. She and Ernest have now left for a tour of London. I am having 2 dinners this week – one of the Cannes party last summer and then one consisting of Lady Oxford, Lady Colefax, Emerald [Cunard], Alexander Woollcott,[2] Harold Nicolson and the Coxes[3] – it may be amusing and is at least literary. This week-end Ernest and self are going to Lord Dudley's. I am trying to hint at getting Mary asked. We haven't made plans for Easter but are asked here but E's mother is a problem as there is no one in London to be with her. I still haven't found out how long Mary will stay. We are absolutely jammed for clothes room as she has an extensive line of undress. I am so sleepy at the moment I can't keep my eyes open so please forgive this dumb scrawl. I just wanted you to know I was thinking of you. All my love.

WALLIS

From Harold Nicolson's diary, 2 April 1936:
I dined with Mrs Simpson to meet the King. Black tie; black waistcoat. A taxi to Bryanston Court; an apartment building; a lift; butler and maid at door; drawing room; many orchids and white arums.... Mr Ernest Simpson enters bringing in the King. We all bow and curtsey. The King looks very well and gay. It is evident that Lady Cunard is incensed by the presence of Lady Colefax, and that Lady Colefax is furious that Lady Cunard should also have been asked. Lady Oxford appears astonished to find either of them at what was to have been a quite intimate party. The King passes brightly from group to group.... I must say, he is very alert and delightful.... Mrs Simpson is a perfectly harmless type of American, but the whole setting is slightly second rate....[4]

1. See page of guest book reproduced in Appendix 2.
2. The distinguished American radio commentator and journalist.
3. Formerly joint First Secretary at the US Embassy in London with Benjamin Thaw, Raymond Cox had now become Counsellor at Buenos Aires.
4. Nigel Nicolson (ed.) *Harold Nicolson, Diaries and Letters, 1930–39* (Collins, London, 1966), p. 255.

The house party at Lord Dudley's during the first week-end in April was attended not only by Wallis, Ernest and Mary, but also by the King.

Edward to Wallis

[undated]   Himley Hall, Dudley, Worcs.

Good morning my sweetheart. How is your pain? How did you sleep and did you miss eanum? A boy has overdone the drowsel but is hurrying down to a girl. How [twice underlined] tired one is of people – they are exhausting. What shall [twice underlined] WE do today? More and more and more

DAVID

Edward to Wallis

[undated]   Himley Hall

THEY [twice underlined] say that THEY liked this bracelet and that THEY want you to wear it always [twice underlined] in the evening. THEY have told Mr Van Cleef[1] but are very sad THEY can't make christen or write tonight. A boy loves a girl more and more and more.

The next letter to Aunt Bessie gives no hint of trouble.

Thursday, April 14th   Bryanston Court

Dearest Aunt Bessie

I have neglected you the past 2 week-ends. I am in a state of collapse due to amusing Mary. The week-end at Lord Dudley's was very interesting and quite an experience for Mary – it has taken one seven years to work up to that sort of thing. There were 18 stopping in the house and all as the Corrigan[2] would say the creme. In fact she has met quite a lot of well known characters. At lunch at Emerald Cunard's she met

1. Of the famous firm of Paris jewellers, Van Cleef & Arpels.
2. The hostess Laura Corrigan from Colorado, who was the butt of numerous jokes in London.

Von Ribbentrop,[1] Ramsay MacDonald,[2] and poor Hoesch the German Ambassador who died a few days later. And speaking of sad things May Osborne died last night only 42 of cancer. We had a very quiet Easter party at the Fort with people from around the neighbourhood for dinner and Saturday HM had a film at Windsor Castle. That is his form of amusement these days, having films either there or in York House – a slight contact with the outside world costing a bit, but he is very rich now. Mary expects to go to visit Freddie Lewisohn at his villa at Cannes the end of the week and whether she returns to London is a matter of expense. *I am afraid.* Mrs Ralph's husband returns the end of May – a trying time as no good cooks are on the loose then having been taken for the so-called Season. I am awfully tired at the moment – so many people all the time and the job of amusing kings in mourning isn't easy. I don't think the Montagues are worth $250 so let it drop but thank you for the trouble you have taken. Perhaps if it means anything to the English they can pay for the information. Berta goes to South Africa with Lester tomorrow and Ernest is off to France again for a few days with 2 boys from New York. Betty's wedding is the 22nd.[3] I hope I won't have to face it alone. It snowed here the entire Easter holiday – can you beat it? All my love,

WALLIS

Such is the picture given to Aunt Bessie in mid-April: Ernest abroad once more on business; Wallis preoccupied by social events, by the entertaining of Mary, by her vocation of looking after the King. The only suggestion that all may not be well is contained in her reaction to the possibility that Mary may return to London later that spring – no more than three words, but ominously underlined.

However, when Wallis next writes to her aunt, on 4 May, the tone and content of her letter are startlingly different. What she delivers is nothing short of a confession, running to no less than twenty extraordinarily lucid pages in a calm, flowing, decisive hand. She explains to her dearest relative that her old life is over, and that she and Ernest

1. Hitler's adviser on foreign affairs, subsequently German Ambassador to London and Foreign Minister.
2. Prime Minister in the Labour Governments of 1924 and 1929–31, and of the National Government, 1931–5. By this time an old and broken man, though still in the Cabinet as Lord President of the Council.
3. The wedding of Ernest's niece Betty Kerr-Smiley to the art historian Christopher Hussey.

must go their separate ways; and that she must have the courage to discover where her affair with the King will lead her – though she seems to feel that the 'idea' which obsesses him will never be realized, and that she will be left in the end only with thrilling memories. In this letter she also reveals that the King has settled a substantial sum of money on her – enough to spare her financial worries for the rest of her life. Then, one week later, she writes another, shorter letter, revealing a dramatic fact which she has been holding back from her aunt: that Ernest and Mary have been conducting an open love affair in England – the resumption, indeed, of a liaison begun in America the autumn before. In the first of these letters Wallis says that divorce is something she is 'not contemplating at the moment'; in the second, she hints (though she does not directly say) that she has indeed begun to contemplate it.

For obvious reasons, Wallis does not tell her aunt everything – she does not wish to alarm and worry her, nor to provoke her righteous anger – and one may ask oneself whether she is being wholly frank. Is her parting from Ernest quite as amicable as she suggests? Is she quite as lacking in calculation as she represents herself to be, allowing herself to be carried along on a tide of fate? Is she as surprised and hurt as she claims by the behaviour of Mary and Ernest? The reader must draw his own conclusions. But, though much is evidently missing from the letter of 4 May, there is something convincingly spontaneous about her sweeping assessment of what has been, of where she now stands, and of what the future may hold.

Monday, May 4th   Bryanston Court

Dearest Aunt Bessie

I only wish I could say what I want and not have to write you for not only am I a bad writer but an impatient one. Please keep in mind that I want to see you more than anything in the world, only I don't think conditions here are such that would make you have a good time and in the autumn I hope all will be well and the weather is still good. It is hard I know for you to understand all that I am going to tell you, living so far away under an entirely different system but please do try to. I have of course been under a most awful strain with Ernest and H.M. for the past year and a half. It is not easy to please, amuse, placate two men and to fit into two such separate lives, which is what

I have been trying to do. The result is I am tired, nervous and irritable to say nothing of the old nervous indigestion returning from time to time. Ernest and HM have often talked the situation out so everything has been on a most friendly and arranged basis, Ernest having his own reasons for allowing the world to call him the 'complacent husband' but understanding the situation just a bit better than the world. The point is that I cannot continue along the same lines either, it is mentally and physically impossible, nor does the K or Ernest enjoy things as they are, though the latter *might* go on his way forever. And now to come to the point. I have had so much in the last 2 years in so many different and interesting ways which I won't go into – except to say that I am looked upon here by the majority of people in exactly the opposite way that the US press presents me. I can't have much respect for a nation that downs its own nationals and thus to belittle them in the eyes of the world. One's countrymen should be loyal. I haven't found them so and therefore like the Lindberghs[1] prefer to live else-where, so you mustn't see the situation through their eyes. In other words and really not in any conceit I say that here they consider me important and my position at the moment is a good and dignified one. Anyone in the public eye must be discussed, must have some enemies, and there is always jealousy. I try to create as little of the last two as is humanly possible. It would be extremely difficult to go back to life in Bryanston Court as it was before. In other words I've outgrown it and Ernest. So that, should I say I will give up HM tomorrow, I still could not make Ernest happy, as I would be discontented and always regretting having given him up and wondering what would have hap-pened if I hadn't. Also the affection which I had for Ernest has been interfered with and could not be recaptured under the circumstances. I am so very sorry for him and have tried to make things as easy as possible, and of course being a strong and noble character and a wonderful friend to me he will find his feet again and I feel that he should have the chance to find happiness again – especially when I know I can only make him unhappy by remaining 2 miserable people. We never fight and never have or will I trust. I propose to take a furnished house in the autumn and live alone for a while. Divorce I am not planning at the moment. Plenty of people live separately here

1. The aviator Charles Lindbergh and his wife Anne had lived outside the United States since the abduction and murder of their child in 1932 and their subsequent persecution by the American press.

Ambassador 2215.

5, Bryanston Court,
Bryanston Square,
W.1.

result is I am tired, nervous and
irritable to say nothing of the
old nervous indigestion returning
from time to time. Ernest and
H. M. have often talked the
situation out so everything has
been on a most friendly and
amicable basis – Ernest having
his own reason for allowing the
world to call him the "complacent
husband" but understanding the
situation just a bit better than
the world. The point is I cannot

and it does not create a stir. Now the other side of this is equally plain to me. Should HM fall in love with someone else I would cease to be as powerful or have all I have today. Perhaps I have made a few new friends and kept some old ones that would always be nice to me – but I expect nothing. I should be comfortably off and have had a most interesting experience, one that does not fall to everyone's lot and the times are exciting now and countries and politics madly thrilling. I have always had the courage for the new things that life sometimes offers. The K on the other hand has another thing only in his mind. Whether I would allow such a drastic action depends on many things and events and I should never allow him if possible to prevent a rather stubborn character to do anything that would hurt the country and help the socialists. In any case there is a new life before me whereas I can't go back to the old – nor can I continue as I am. My nerves are fast going, the demands on me are heavy from every quarter, and when one's personal life *also* requires so much management and tact – I can't do all therefore I must be on my own. I have discussed all this with Ernest. Naturally he is sad but sees my point, he knows HM's devotion to me is deep and of the right sort. His only fear is that he will go through with His Idea. I feel however these things solve themselves. May and June means that Ernest and myself will be working all this out besides carrying on with the world and I feel we will have to do it alone. I will go away to visit HM on July 23rd and then in September go to Balmoral for about 10 days – and instead of returning to Bryanston Court I will go to a house that I hope to be able to find before I go away. The financial side has been attended to for my lifetime so that need not worry you. These you see are my reasons for suggesting October to you. I am sure for the next few months my nerves will be in an awful state and in the autumn I should be in a better frame of mind. I am sorry to have to tell you all this for I know you worry so much – but you see I am 40 and I feel I must follow my own instincts as regard my life and am quite prepared to pay for a mistake. I know I can only control the financial side of the future and that I can't insure against heartache, loneliness etc. but if the worst happens I shall have to be like the Arabs and fold my tent and steal silently away – to travel and I generally find a few friends. Life is very full at the moment and should grow more and more so and I can only hope that HM will remain fond of me for some time – but I don't plan my future relying on that in any way. I am going away to Betty's [Lawson Johnston] for 5 days rest and diet – she has lent me her flat at Hove. I can't face the luncheons and dinners without a breathing space, with so many problems revolving in my mind. I am too tired to like anything by the time I've planned HM's dinners, listened to official things, continual thinking of the right people and right acts for him. I find I'm a flop when I have to deal with my flat. Somebody named Emily Yellot Blandford has written saying she has a daughter arriving in London. I can only remember Cousin Laurie Yellot. Do put me wise. And speaking of family matters, I shall of course pay the $150 for the Montagues! Cousin Lelia sent me Mrs Keyes. I found her so amusing and arranged for her to see the Queen Mary, which HM says he can arrange for you to travel in in October.

Darling, I hope this hasn't thrown your summer out and that you understand. It is better to have it all over before you come. So please write and say you will do the latter. I shall need you then to see me on my way.
All love,

WALLIS

11 May

Dearest Aunt B

I am very unhappy to think I have upset your plans but can't help but feel that when you have my letter and also the added complication which this one contains you will agree with me and also try to come in October. I realise that it is most annoying to have one's plans put off and you know I want to see you very badly but I feel I would at the moment be no pleasure to anyone. I didn't want to bore you with the trouble I have had with Mary and Ernest. It seems they had quite a fling last year in New York and arranged this appearance here – but I was kept in the dark. Anyway, to cut a long story short they behaved badly here and I soon saw that it wasn't me she had come to see. I did everything in my power to give her a good time. However, she and Ernest stayed up most nights alone until 5 or 6 a.m. and finally went off quite calmly for 3 days in a hired motor. I then had them followed and of course got the expected report etc. He now says he is in love with her and she has a service flat here. Isn't it all ridiculous? Anyway, we will work it all out *beautifully* I hope. I decided not to have Mary at the flat. She arrived while I was away for my rest from which I returned today. Ernest wishes me to have her here for all meals, parties, etc. – rather hard to take – but if it makes him happy I suppose it's only fair for me to do it. Whatever the result of it all is you may rest assured – everything will be conducted with dignity. This is written rather hastily as I came home. to find the desk high after ten days of no letters being forwarded. HM can always arrange for a cabin on the Queen Mary and I can make up any difference in the ticket from what you would have paid.

In haste but with all love,

WALLIS

Such are the main lines of the affair as they appear from the letters to Aunt Bessie. Fascinating and revealing as those letters are, they leave many questions unanswered. In particular, the whole matter of Mary's visit remains mysterious. Is her appearance on the scene purely fortuitous? Is it (as the letter of 11 May seems to hint) planned by Ernest as a means whereby he may put an end to his marriage (in accordance, perhaps, with his arrangement with the King witnessed by Rickatson-Hatt)? Is Wallis genuinely shocked to discover her husband and her oldest friend conducting an affair under her own roof, and is it this which resigns her to a separation she did not seek and finally to a divorce which she was otherwise reluctant to contemplate? Or can it be (as her remarks of 15 March on Ernest's feelings for Mary might be taken to suggest) that she is already aware of (or able to guess at) the liaison, and welcomes Mary's arrival as a means of keeping Ernest happy, or even of cutting her own ties with him? Is it reasonable to assume that both Wallis and Ernest wish to go their separate ways – but that each wishes first of all to be assured that, following separation, the other will not be alone but will fall into an enduring and satisfactory relationship: Wallis with the King unencumbered by Ernest, Ernest with Mary?

The motives of Wallis and of Ernest are not entirely clear: one must draw one's own conclusions. What is very clear indeed, however, are the motives of the King. Of his intentions there can be no doubt whatever. He is desperate to be married to the woman he so passionately loves and needs. Nothing matters to him except their eventual union: he is willing to contemplate all means to achieve that longed-for and sacred ambition. He is therefore determined to break up the marriage of Wallis and Ernest. To that end he is forever pressing, pleading, conspiring, cajoling – in his separate dealings with him and with her. Let us recall the words of Rickatson-Hatt, who knew them both well, that 'but for the King's obstinacy and jealousy' – or, putting it more charitably, but for the intensity of his love and his unshakable resolve to be united with the woman who meant all to him – Wallis and Ernest would have remained man and wife.

In her memoirs, the Duchess of Windsor writes that her decision to part from Ernest was taken entirely of her own accord, without any pressure or prompting from the King. It was merely a question of her 'freeing' Ernest from a situation which had become intolerable to him, of thus enabling him to pursue his own life. When she informed the King that she had decided to seek a divorce, she says, he 'replied gravely that, of course, it would be wrong for him to attempt to influence me either way, that only I could make the decision'. One is driven to the conclusion that such recollections in fact amount to chivalrous untruths, concocted in order to spare the Duke of Windsor's reputation and avoid the impression that the Simpson divorce was in any way collusive; and that, in reality, the King pushed her into divorce – at least to some extent against her own wishes and better judgement – and then took charge of the whole proceedings from beginning to end. The events and correspondence of the autumn of 1936 will be seen to lend much credence to this view.

There is a letter written by the King in the late spring of 1936 which gives striking evidence of his attitude. During the first ten days of June Wallis was in Paris again, accompanied this time by her friend Gladys Scanlon, the purpose of her visit being to buy clothes for the coming Season and rest after what had evidently been an emotionally turbulent time. On 5 June the King – who was spending the week-end alone at the Fort – wrote to her at the Hotel Meurice.

Edward to Wallis
Friday night [5 June]   The Fort. ERI.

Oh! my sweetheart it is so sad to return here without you. Hurry back quickly please and I know you will as you must feel how much you are wanted and missed back here. You have been away far too long and you mustn't ever go away again. WE have just had a lovely long talk but that is a poor substitute for holding tight and making drowsy. No and not making own drowsies either as we have had to do far too often lately. Oh! make your return come quickly as I know you want it to.

My talk with Ernest was difficult this evening but I must get after him now or he won't move. It's so unsatisfactory until its all settled and WE really are one and I can't bear your having to hear unpleasant things said as I'm just as sensitive as you are you know that. I know you will approve of A[llen]'s[1] plan but of course won't do a thing until WE can discuss it. Its the only way. I must make own drowsy now which I expect you are doing too and I only hope a girl is missing a boy as much as he is missing her. I'll finish in the morning. God bless WE.

Sat-y [6 June]

Good morning my sweetheart but again I've just been talking to you and you have accused me of extreme drowsiness. Make ooh! Its not a very nice day so I hope next Saturday will be. Ladbrook[2] is just taking this to London for air mail and I hope he'll be able to bring your Buick back for me to inspect and report on. Slippy is very aloof but that did not interfere with his botty house trick in the early morning. What a day you have and WE'll be so glad and happy when its all over and you are back to me again. I'll telephone around six o'clock. I'll be planting today I think but I've just got two of those d----d red boxes full of mostly bunk to read too. Take care of yourself my dear Wallis for your

DAVID

who loves you more and more

1. George Allen of the firm of Allen & Overy was the solicitor who dealt with the King's private affairs in London, who had been consulted about the best and quickest means whereby Wallis might obtain a divorce.
2. The King's driver.

Wallis and 'Mr Loo'

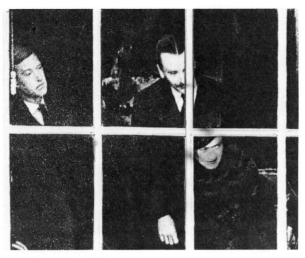

Edward VIII joins the woman he loves by a window of St James's Palace to watch his own proclamation as King, 1936. Behind Wallis stands Alan Lascelles, the King's Assistant Private Secretary

Ernest Simpson with Mary Raffray

With the Duke of York, following the coffin of King George V, 23 January 1936

On the *Nahlin* cruise, August 1936

Balmoral, September 1936: two studies of Wallis by Edward

Wallis and Aunt Bessie being photographed by the King
at the Fort at the end of November 1936

Every inch a King. Edward VIII dressed as an admiral for the State Opening of
Parliament, 3 November 1936

At the Villa Lou Viei at Cannes, 10 December 1936.
Left to right: Lord Brownlow, Katherine Rogers, Wallis, Herman Rogers

Edward, now Duke of Windsor, arrives in Vienna
to begin his exile, 13 December 1936

The Château de Candé

Wedding party at Candé, 3 June 1937.
Left to right: Fern Bedaux, Katherine Rogers, Lady Alexandra Metcalfe,
Aunt Bessie, Dudley Forwood, the Duke, 'Fruity' Metcalfe, Herman Rogers

WE are one

CHAPTER EIGHT

Indian Summer
(MAY–SEPTEMBER)

*There was no immediate separation. As Wallis had written to her
aunt, the months of May and June would be spent 'working things
out'. Ernest, while seeing Mary, stayed on at Bryanston Court and
continued to appear in public with his wife. On 28 May the names of
Wallis and Ernest both appeared, for the first time, in the Court Circular – along with those of the Prime Minister and Mrs Stanley Baldwin, the Duff Coopers, the Mountbattens and the Lindberghs – as
having attended a dinner given by the King at York House the previous
evening.*

*In her memoirs, Wallis tells us a number of things about this party,
which first brought her name formally before the British public. She
says that, 'as usual', she was responsible for the menu and the table
decorations. She remembers that the King declared to her that his
object in giving the dinner was to introduce the Prime Minister to 'my
future wife', to which she replied: 'You mustn't talk this way. The
idea is impossible. They'd never let you.' (The memoirs give the
impression that this was the first time the matter had been raised in so
direct a manner, but one may question whether this was so.) She
recalls that, on the night, she found the Baldwins 'pleasant but distant',
and that, as so often in the company of the great and famous in those
days, she was 'conscious of the assaying glance, the unspoken, probing
question beneath the polite surface of the conversation'. Finally, she
tells us: 'As best as I can recall, this was the last time that Ernest and
I were publicly together in David's company. Not long afterwards I
told Ernest that I was starting divorce proceedings.' However, the
correspondence shows that Wallis's memory was at fault on this last
point. The divorce petition was still two months away, and during
that time the Simpsons were to be together with the King on a number
of occasions.*

*The months of June and July were a busy time for the King, who
with the end of official mourning for his father had to face a mass of*

*ceremonial and the task of setting up his own Court. It was also a
troubled time in European affairs, with the coming to power of a
radical government in France and the outbreak of the Spanish Civil
War. For Wallis, it appears to have been a time of mental turmoil, as
well as uncertain health. (A serious recurrence of her stomach trouble
lasted from the middle of April to the end of June.) She seems to have
made her plans in a state of dream-like uncertainty, hoping that the
future would take care of itself.*

*But as she writes in her memoirs, she had 'little time for regret', for
her 'every hour was taken up by expanding social activities in London
and the week-ends at the Fort'. The first (and as it turned out, last)
Season of the new reign was upon her.*

Edward to Wallis[1]
12.vi.1936

Your eanum dawg and your David thank for the Buick ride and say
we are missing you terribly and holding you very tight indeed. We will
phone when we land and will be awaiting your call after the opera.
More and more always sweetheart.

Wallis to Edward

[undated, on mourning paper]   The Fort

David – you were sweet and dear to an ill girl last night. I am off to
the doctor at 2.30. Have arranged for this eve with a scene – but shall
expect you at 8.15 so as to make early drowsel. My love for you

WALLIS

Wallis to Aunt Bessie
Monday the 22nd [June]   The Fort

Darling – I haven't written for so long. There is so much happening
and I am being swamped with silly notes – but have a woman coming
in the mornings starting tomorrow to help me. I was just about to
write and say what a wonder woman you are to have written me your
first letter – when along comes the second one containing the explo-
sions. I couldn't understand better and I am sorry to be a source of
worry to you and not of pleasure – but please don't worry, because if

1. Following her return from Paris.

I feel I am making you unhappy it gives one more thing on my mind, which is very full of most involved things. I am much better – have found a doctor here who is doing me good – I have not got an ulcer but the type of stomach that needs care and I have a diet which evidently agrees as I haven't had a pain for a month in spite of busy times here. I must take a house. I could not have remained in the flat under any conditions. It is too difficult for the King to come to flats and I have been advised by Duff Cooper etc that house is necessary. I know the situation here better than you do so I must act from this angle. Mary I understand is staying here for the summer. I haven't seen her. I am really glad Ernest has someone to amuse him. Old Mr S[impson] had his gall bladder and 8 stones removed a week ago Friday and is doing very well – amazing at 82. I have been here ten days for Ascot – which was not brilliant, having rained at some time every day and the same people. We had a nice party here.[1] I have asked Mrs Howard to go to the King's birthday parade with me tomorrow – I sent a note but won't know until I get home tonight – I think the best and most English show of them all. Have the papers let up on me in the US or are you simply tired of sending them? I like to see what they lie about. Plan to come over some time in Oct. Naturally one can't find exactly what one wants in furnished houses, but I get the most comfortable going. All love,

WALLIS

PS Do the Drs at home believe in Hay's theory that you can't eat starch and proteins at the same meal?

At the end of June the King attended a large house party given by his friend the Duke of Marlborough at Blenheim. Both Wallis and Ernest were present too.

Sunday the 28th [June]   Blenheim Palace

Darling

This really is the most thrilling place to stay I have been in yet. Do you remember driving past? Mrs Howard went to the Parade with me and I think she enjoyed it. Everything is the same here. Mary remains on and Ernest seems to love her. Ernest however doesn't miss the chance of coming to places like this. Tomorrow I go to the Mount-

1. See Appendix 2.

battens and stay until Wed night. The South of France is still uncertain due to the conditions there[1] – so I really have no summer plans as yet though the house of Maxine Elliot[2] has been spoken of for it is next door to last year's villa. We return tonight after dinner. Jack Warner is in London and has brought the *Terrapin*[3] which was really delicious from the Vendome. Mrs Keyes writes Cousin Lelia may come over to visit her. The [Buckingham Palace] garden receptions are in July. We [*sic*] shall go to the first on the 21st. Tomorrow I go to the Mountbattens and the King inspects the Navy quite near Portsmouth. All my love,

WALLIS

PS We are having freezing weather.

There are four short love letters from the King to Wallis, written on successive days as they were staying with the Marlboroughs at Blenheim and the Mountbatens at Adsdean, to be read by her on retiring or waking.

Edward to Wallis
Saturday [27 June]   Blenheim Palace

My sweetheart
    This is to say good night and God bless WE Wallis. He will be missing Her as much as WE will be each other. Goodness me what a big house and what a lot of people. Tell Mary[4] to send a message when you are ready in the morning as I'll be scared to go down without you. Hold out arms and make long drowsel. No long talk as you must have some rest. A boy is holding you so very very tight always. More and More my beloved. Your

DAVID

1. The coming to power of Leon Blum's Popular Front government was attended by widespread political and industrial unrest.
2. Stage name of Jessie Dermot (1868-1940), an actress who had become an Allied heroine on account of her relief work in the First World War.
3. A species of diamond-backed turtle, regarded as a great gastronomic delicacy in the Southern States. Wallis's mother had been an expert in its preparation.
4. Mary Burke, Wallis's maid.

Sunday [28 June]   Blenheim Palace

Good morning we all say. How did you make drowsel and when will you be ready my sweetheart? Whiteman's band[1] has only just stopped and breakfast is now being served. The babies say hello too. Your

DAVID

Tuesday [30 June]   Adsdean, Chichester

Good morning my sweetheart. Miss me when you wake up. I am just off to inspect the sailors. The babies say they cant go in uniform and will Mary please give us 'face-hair' and some ribbands even if new. Kilts aren't ready. I'll hurry back to my Wallis. God bless WE. Your

DAVID

We say hello to Mr Loo too.

Wed-y [1 July]   Adsdean

Good morning my beloved. I do hope you slept well. I'm just going to play those six holes of golf with Dickie [Mountbatten]. I have no answer from the 'Queen Mary' re parcel for Mr A. J. Warner yet but will soon. What would a girl like to eat for dinner so as I can tell Mrs Mason?[1] I have to leave at 12 noon for Portsmouth. More and more your

DAVID

On 9 July the King gave another dinner at York House, where he was still living while his mother moved out of Buckingham Palace. This time the name of Mrs Simpson appeared in the Court Circular without that of her husband. The other guests included the Duke and Duchess of York; the Winston Churchills; Diana Cooper, Margot Oxford and Sibyl Colefax; the King's new Private Secretary Major Alexander Hardinge; and Sir Samuel Hoare, a veteran Cabinet Minister, who had recently been appointed First Lord of the Admiralty. The absence of Ernest indicated that he and Wallis had reached the point of separation. Wallis had now retained a well-known London divorce solicitor,

1. Paul Whiteman, the American bandleader.
2. The housekeeper at the Fort.

Theodore Goddard; in the preceding weeks, at the King's insistence, she had also consulted his own legal advisers, George Allen and Walter Monckton.

On 21 July, following well-established custom, Ernest Simpson and a female companion booked into the Hotel de Paris at Bray on the Thames. Ernest signed the register as 'Ernest A. Simmons'. The lady gave her name as 'Buttercup Kennedy'. (She was probably Mary Raffray, who had acquired the nickname 'Buttercup' in London on account of an item of floral headgear which she sported.) The couple took breakfast in their room and so were seen in bed together by the hotel waiters. On 23 July Wallis wrote Ernest a standard letter, to say she was aware 'that instead of being on business as you led me to believe you have been staying at Bray with a lady. I am sure you realize this is conduct which I cannot possibly overlook and must insist you do not continue to live here with me. This only confirms the suspicions I have had for a long time. I am therefore instructing my solicitors to take proceedings for divorce.' Ernest thereupon left Bryanston Court and went to live at the Guards' Club.[1]

The evidence was complete; and Theodore Goddard looked around for a suitable divorce list in which to set the case down for trial. Understandably, Wallis was intensely secretive about the whole affair. She mentioned the divorce to none of her friends; and in her next letter to Aunt Bessie, there is not so much as a hint that she and Ernest have even separated. She merely refers to 'a lot of tiresome business things' she has had to do, and her need of 'a holiday away from cares'.

Saturday, August 1st   The Fort

Darling

I haven't written for weeks but I really have been nearly crazy with visiting people. Some I hardly know but everyone telephones now. I had myself X-rayed from head to toes. They found a *healed* ulcer scar. I have an awfully good doctor and haven't had any trouble for 6 weeks. Have a diet - not too bad a one - the doctor is a German. I have gained some weight also, and feel better than I have for ages.

---

1. This account is based on the information subsequently revealed in court on 27 October 1936.

The shot [*sic*] at HM[1] and the upset summer plans have all been very disturbing. Also Ernest has been away so much [*sic*] that it has been difficult to make any plans – and there are some Americans who have been thinking of our flat. In that case I shall take a furnished house until after the Coronation. We are now going to the Dalmatian coast in a yacht chartered by the King and will be escorted by 2 destroyers – the same party intended for Cannes – possibly going to the Greek Islands and a visit to the King there – also perhaps to [the Regent] Prince Paul in Yugoslavia – all depending entirely on the political situation in Europe which changes from day to day – no place seems very safe for kings. I shall go to Balmoral in Sept stopping on the way first with the Duchess of Buccleuch and then the Sutherlands,[2] returning to London September 27th. Ernest has gone off to Scotland for a week with Mary and will be off to Italy in August on business. Everyone is tired after a really gay season. Miss Blandford telephoned[3] and I asked her in one day – but she had an engagement and I never could find time again. Please tell Lelia it is impossible to do anything about Robin[4] – I have tried in every way, but one evidently must put down at the time of conception. I shall write her soon. I feel sorry for Anne – on thinking over her life she seems to have made much headache for herself. I am expecting you any time in November or I may *run* over and collect you first part of that month. If I have taken a house it will not be before Oct 15th or later as the people don't want the flat until then. I have had a lot of tiresome business things to do and really feel the need of a holiday away from cares and people wanting things very badly. My job is too trying on the nerves for much relaxation – the tiny brain works overtime. I would very much like a few weeks in Washington entirely away from all of this so might possibly come over 1st of November for 2 weeks and we could return together. However I really can say nothing definite at the moment. I believe I leave here Sat for some port on the Dalmatian coast. The name of the yacht is Nahlin but letters had best go to the flat to be forwarded. The plan is

1. On 16 July, as the King was riding in procession on Constitution Hill after presenting new colours to the Guards, a loaded revolver was brandished at him by one Macmahon, an Irish journalist who wished to draw attention to some obscure grievance he nurtured against the Home Office. When a policeman tried to wrench the weapon from Macmahon's grasp, Macmahon threw it under the King's horse. There was no shot.
2. The beautiful Molly, Duchess of Buccleuch, and the Duke and Duchess of Sutherland.
3. See letter to Aunt Bessie of 4 May above.
4. Lelia had presumably hoped that Wallis could find a place for her son at Eton.

now to go as far as Constantinople and train from there, home by way
of Vienna for the ear doctor for HM. Be a little patient with me a
while longer – and also don't worry about me as I really am feeling
better than I have for ages – and once I get a little rest I shall be on
my toes. All my love,

WALLIS

*On 10 August the King and Wallis – with a party consisting of the
Humphrey Butlers, Helen Fitzgerald, Godfrey Thomas[1] and Jack Aird,
subsequently joined by the Duff Coopers, Alan Lascelles,[2] Lord Sefton
and the Herman Rogers – boarded the Steam Yacht* Nahlin *at Sibernik
in Yugoslavia for a four-week cruise along the Yugoslav, Greek and
Turkish coasts. During this otherwise pleasant and relaxing holiday
(in the course of which they met the rulers of the countries they visited)
they were recognized and mobbed everywhere, and photographs of the
King and Wallis together, often very informally dressed, caused a
sensation in the American and continental press.*

Thursday, August 13th

s.y. Nahlin, r.t.y.c.

Darling Aunt B

This won't reach you in time for your coming of age on the 16th –
nor I am afraid will a small silver gilt box with Jubilee Arms on it
that HM and myself have sent you. Anyway you know I shall be
thinking of my aunt and drinking her health. At last this poor tired
King got off. We left London on Saturday. Prince Paul met us at the
border of Yugoslavia with a very grand royal train. We stopped at his
house for a little while – then back on to the train and arrived Monday
morning at a small port where the yacht and 2 destroyers were waiting.
It is a lovely comfortable boat. We came north to see the inland sea at
Novigrad and are now on our way south stopping at Split to pick up
the corpses. Then we will be going on to the same places that we did
with Walter. We went ashore in a small quaint town – but even in
that remote spot HM was recognized and the local militia had to be
called out to deal with the crowd. Naturally it ruins exploring and
closely resembles the Pied Piper. I think the plans are to be in Scotland
on the 20th for ten days. I am still slightly indefinite due to indecision

1 and 2. Assistant Private Secretaries to the King.

of my winter. However any time you want to come there will be a room somewhere. Still feeling fine. All love,

WALLIS

Monday, Aug 24th   s.y. Nahlin, R.T.Y.C.

Darling

I haven't written because of the heat which is like the tropics and it is so sticky to write. We have been in such remote parts that there is very little to tell. We have bathed and slept and seen lovely mountainous coastlines [and] quaint little towns. At Corfu we dined with the King of Greece who has a house there for a month. We have seen Eric Dudley's party in two ports – otherwise just our party. At Athens the Duff Coopers and Butlers leave, Lord Sefton arrives, and the Rogers are coming as the Brownlows have to remain in London as his mother is ill. HM wired the Rogers two days ago and they are now on their way. Helen Fitzgerald is remaining the entire trip. I hope you have had a nice summer and will soon be over here with me. All love,

WALLIS

[Post card of Acropolis postmarked Istanbul, 5 September]

Too hot to write and nothing much to say. A lovely lazy holiday and interesting things to be seen. Love – W

After visiting the battlefields at Gallipoli, and stopping at Istanbul where they were entertained by the Turkish dictator Ataturk, the party left the Nahlin *and proceeded by train through the Balkans to Vienna, where they spent five happy days, the King meeting the Austrian Government.*

Edward to Wallis
[September]   Hotel Bristol, Wien

Good morning Wallis we all say. As you haven't phoned I guess you are still making drowsel. Just off Kinging with the babies. Miss me till I get back around one o'clock. Your

DAVID

On 14 September the King flew back to England from Zurich, while Wallis and the rest of the party went on by train to spend a few days in Paris.

CHAPTER NINE
The Divorce
(SEPTEMBER–OCTOBER)

Accompanied by the remains of the Nahlin *party – Lord Sefton, Helen Fitzgerald and the Rogers – Wallis arrived in Paris on the evening of 14 September, putting up, as on her two visits there earlier that year, at the Hotel Meurice. Almost immediately she began to suffer from a heavy cold and took to her bed. While she was languishing, her mail arrived, forwarded from London. It included letters from anxious friends – and from Aunt Bessie – enclosing sensational American press cuttings relating to the* Nahlin *cruise and to her forthcoming divorce proceedings. Reading these, Wallis (as she wrote in her memoirs) was 'amazed and shocked'. Her friendship with the King, and his intentions towards her, had become 'a topic of dinner-table conversation for every newspaper reader in the United States, Europe and the Dominions'. Speaking daily to the King on the telephone, she expressed what she later described as her 'deepening misgivings'. In her memoirs, however, she does not elaborate on these misgivings, merely remarking that the King assured her that there would be no public comment in England, and that the furore would soon die down.*

The truth was more dramatic. At this late hour – when her marriage to Ernest had broken down and he was living with Mary Raffray, when she had commenced divorce proceedings and a date had been set down for trial, when the King had shown himself determined to marry her when she was free and had settled a considerable fortune on her – Wallis was seized with a fit of clairvoyance and panic. Suddenly she woke up from the dream which had lasted two and a half years, and began to wonder fearfully where it was all going to lead. She contrasted the dull security she had known with Simpson with the unknown dangers (for him and for her) which lay ahead with the King. Though it is a theme which she tends to underplay in her memoirs – understandably, since it would hardly have been flattering to the Duke of Windsor to whom she was then married – the correspondence shows that, for the whole of that autumn, the idea of escape from her royal entanglement was constantly in her mind.

Why then did she not escape? The reasons were three: the King would not hear of letting her go; she was too fond of him simply to run away; and her determination was weakened by uncertain health and confusion of mind. 'The easy view is that she should have made him give her up', writes Walter Monckton. 'But I never knew any man whom it would have been harder to get rid of.'

There is a striking document – unknown up to now – which is proof of Wallis's state of mind at this time. On the night of 16 September – two days after her arrival in Paris – she wrote frankly to the King breaking off their affair, telling him that they could 'only create disaster together', and that she wished to return to Ernest Simpson. One may wonder to what extent she really believed such a return still to be possible.

It is interesting to compare this letter with that which Wallis had written Aunt Bessie on 4 May. There she wrote of the collapse of her life with Ernest and of chancing her fate with the King. Now she writes in exactly the opposite terms.

Wallis to Edward
Wednesday night [16 September]   Hotel Meurice, Rue de Rivoli, Paris

Dear David,

It is too stupid to have a cold at just this moment. However I am tucked up in bed feeling very very rotten. But I did have a trout and 2 ears of delicious corn. This is a difficult letter to write – but I feel it is easier than talking and less painful. I must really return to Ernest for a great many reasons which please be patient and read. The first being because we are so awfully congenial and understand getting on together very well – which really is an art in marriage. We have no small irritations one for the other. I have confidence in his being able to take care of me and of himself. In other words I feel secure with him and am only left with my side of the show to run. We each do our little jobs separately – with occasional help one for the other and it all runs smoothly no nerve strain. True we are poor and unable to do the attractive amusing things in life which I must confess I do love and enjoy – also the possession of beautiful things is thrilling to me and much appreciated but weighed against a calm congenial life I

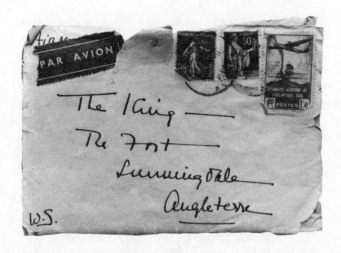

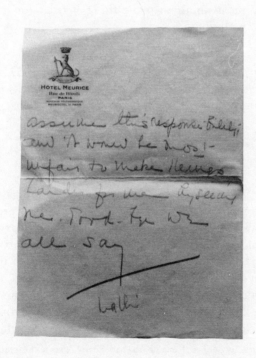

choose the latter for I know that though I shall suffer greatly now I shall be a happier calmer old lady. I have been here alone tonight but seen my friends (?) etc. I should rather have my husband than mere friends. No one can fill that place and no one can care (unless one has a family) so much. I know Ernest and have the deepest affection and respect for him. I feel I am better with him than with you – and so you must understand. I am sure dear David that in a few months your life will run again as it did before and without my nagging. Also you have been independent of affection all your life. We have had lovely beautiful times together and I thank God for them and know that you will go on with your job doing it better and in a more dignified manner each year. That would please me so. I am sure you and I would only create disaster together. I shall always read all about you – believing only half! – and you will know I want you to be happy. I feel sure I can't make you so and I honestly don't think you can me. I shall have Allen[1] arrange the return of everything. I am sure that after this letter you will realize that no human being could assume this responsibility and it would be most unfair to make things harder for me by seeing me. Good-bye WE all say

WALLIS

That same night, the King wrote to Wallis from the Fort. Though he had not yet received her letter, she had voiced the same doubts to him over the telephone. However, he took no account of them.

Edward to Wallis
Twelve-thirty a.m. [16 September]   The Fort

Good night my Wallis. Why do you say such hard things to David on the telephone sometimes? Hard things like you would prefer to have someone else with you tonight when you are sick that I would be bored that I dont understand you and lots of others which hurt me so and show that lack of faith and confidence in me which makes me so terribly unhappy.

I'm so sad tonight sweetheart for this and other reasons. First of all that you feel so ill and that I'm not there to look after you. Then that I wont see you before I go to Balmoral and not knowing when you

1. The King's solicitor George Allen. No doubt she particularly refers to the return of the money the King had settled on her.

Mrs Simpson

Hotel Maurice

Paris

France

THE FORT,
SUNNINGDALE, ASCOT.

Twelve thirty A M

Good night my Wallis

Why do you say such

hard things to David

on the telephone

sometimes. Hard

things like you would

prefer to have someone

else with you to night

will join me there. Oh! please make it quickly my darling because every moment we are separated is a sad and lonely one.

I'm not going to worry you or ask you to make plans when you dont feel in the health or the mood and the great thing is for you to get well again as quickly as possible. Our lovely holiday did do you good and now thats all undone. It makes me sick too. You see I do love you so entirely and in every way Wallis. Madly tenderly adoringly and with admiration and such confidence.

I feel like bursting tonight with love and such a longing to hold you tighter than I ever have before. Mr Loo and I are up here in our blue room and missing you like the dickens. Its hell but its lovely in a way too. Please try and trust me like you love me and dont have any doubts. I promise you there is not the slightest reason to. If only you could read into my lightening brain you would'nt. SHE does'nt doubt HIM.(hand is hiding face) so dont you doubt me.

I'm exhausted now and will try to make drowsel which I hope you will be able to do and I'll finish in the morning to send by air mail so as you can read all I have to say as quickly as possible. God bless WE

Thursday [17 September]

Good morning again my sweetheart as I've just talked to you. Your cold still sounds awful. Pooky demus! Please don't go out today though I know what a bore it is to be sick in a hotel. But its the only way to get through with it. I told you what a satisfactory talk I had with Allen last evening. Thank goodness WE have him to look after our interests. Its sad about Walter Prendergast being transferred. I've asked him to come and see me this evening at 6.30. I'm going to a building exhibition at Olympia on my way up to see people. Its pretty here now and there is a bit of color in the borders. How I wish you were here to see it with me. And the improvements to the house (which I don't pay for) are definitely good although not finished yet.

I don't know any more now except that I love you love you my Wallis but that you do know too. I'll be telephoning you again quite often. Your

DAVID

PS The Babies send you eanum flowers.

It is not difficult to imagine how the King would have reacted upon receiving Wallis's letter. Wallis evidently yielded to his blandishments, for when she writes to Aunt Bessie four days later she is about to leave for London on her way to Balmoral, and there is no hint of her attempted rupture with the King.

Wallis to Aunt Bessie
Monday [21 September]   Hotel Meurice, Paris

Darling

I have been here a week with the Rogers, Helen Fitzgerald and Hugh Sefton. The King flew from Zurich as it wasn't wise for him to touch France at the moment. The trip was absolutely the most interesting one yet – meeting dictators and kings along the line. And such lovely weather. I have wasted my time here for I picked up a cold bug in Vienna so stayed in bed until yesterday. Today we leave for England and tomorrow Scotland for the week. The Rogers are coming along. I see an amazing picture in Time of a block of *ten* houses saying it is *my* house. You will recognise the whole of the Regent's Park Crescent. They are fantastic. I have taken Mrs Stewart's house – which is what the English papers call 'not a large one'. It is the size of Upper Berkeley Street[1] anyway. You will come and see it. I have it until May 26th and move in Oct 7th. We have rented the flat very well. I had a letter from *Both Wise Mary* – can you beat it – saying her daughter would be in London end of Sept. I have written her that unfortunately I will be in Scotland. I am in a great hurry so please forgive as I am trying to do everything this morning. All love

WALLIS

Before proceeding to Balmoral with the Rogers, Wallis stopped for a day in London to see her solicitor, Theodore Goddard, and discuss the arrangements for her divorce. Since a London divorce would involve some delay, her petition had been set down for hearing at Ipswich Assizes on 27 October, where she would be represented by one of the most celebrated King's Counsel of the day, Norman Birkett. To qualify for the jurisdiction of the Ipswich tribunal, she would have to take up residence in the County of Suffolk during mid-October; Goddard had arranged for her to take a furnished house at the coastal resort of Felixstowe. If she received her Decree Nisi at Ipswich on 27 October, she would be eligible to apply for her divorce to be made absolute six

1. The town house which Wallis and Ernest had rented at the start of their marriage.

*months later, at the end of April 1937; and it would therefore tech-
nically be possible for her to remarry before the Coronation, due to
take place on 12 May. In his memoirs, the Duke of Windsor strongly
implies that this was no mere coincidence, and that he himself had so
arranged matters as to make it possible for him to marry her before
he was crowned.*

*On 23 September Wallis and the Rogers arrived at Balmoral, where
they stayed for a week. The other guests were relations and aristocratic
friends of the King, including the Mountbattens and the Kents. Wallis
wrote in her memoirs that she enjoyed her stay; and, indeed, this was
to be the last really happy interlude that she was to know for some
time. No doubt some eyebrows were raised at the mention of her
presence there in the Court Circular, and at the fact that the King
fetched her from Ballatar station on a day upon which he had declined
to open a hospital in Aberdeen. But it is not true, as scandal has
suggested, that she behaved as the mistress of the house, except in one
particular: as had now become usual for her, she took charge of the
planning of the meals and the evening entertainments.*

*An amusing exchange of notes survives from this time. The King
sent Wallis a list of neighbouring worthies who would be attending a
film show that evening, with the message: 'Darling – here are the
people who are going to bore us for eanum time tonight.' She replied
on a scrap of Balmoral writing paper: 'DDD – have you thought of
changing the film as all the nuts have seen it – WE can see in London.'*

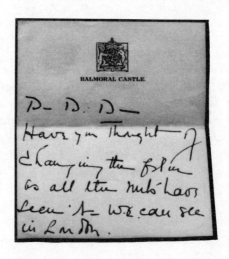

On 1 October Wallis returned to London, staying at Claridge's while her furnished house in Regent's Park was being got ready for her. The week-end of 9–12 October she and the King were at the Fort with a party of friends. Following this week-end, Wallis took up her residence at Felixstowe, occupying a banal villa on the shore. George and Kitty Hunter, her best and oldest English friends, came with her to keep her company.

It was an unpleasant time for her. She was not feeling well. She was depressed by the house, by the atmosphere of an out-of-season bathing resort, and by the stormy weather. She was under strain because of the atmosphere of secretiveness which surrounded the whole business, and the prying attentions of the journalists who had quickly discovered her whereabouts. She was deeply worried by the mounting hostile gossip concerning herself and the King, of which she was told by the Hunters. Once again, she was plagued by fears and doubts, and wondered whether she ought to continue with the case and with the King. 'Do you feel you still want me to go ahead?' she wrote to him. '... Isn't it best for me to steal quietly away? ... I can't help but feel you will have trouble in the House of Commons and may be forced to go. I can't put you in that position. ...'

Wallis to Aunt Bessie
[On Bryanston Court writing paper, but from Felixstowe. Undated.]

Darling
Please forgive everything but I have been and am having a bit of trouble at the moment and I feel it is better not to worry other people so haven't written. I want you to come over and I'll tell you about things so pop on a boat after Nov 1st and come to see me. I can never put foot in the US on account of all the publicity. I am sorry you are in the dark but it is best for you to be that way. I love you and everything will eventually be all right – just now I'm having a bad time. I am at Felixstowe on the North Sea for ten days. The Hunters are with me. I will make up any difference in fare on the Queen Mary than you would pay on a smaller boat. Love,

WALLIS

Wallis to Edward

[On Claridge's writing paper, but from Felixstowe]
Thursday [14 October]

My dear

This is really more than you or I bargained for – this being haunted by the press. Do you feel you still want me to go ahead as I feel it will hurt your popularity in the country. Last night I heard so much from the Hunters that made me shiver – and I am very upset and ill to-day from talking until 4. It nearly ended in a row as naturally it wasn't pleasant things I heard of the way the man in the street regards me. I hear you have been hissed in the cinema, that a man in a white tie refused to get up in the theater when they played God save the King and that in one place they added and Mrs Simpson. Really David darling if I hurt you to this extent isn't it best for me to steal quietly away. Today Ernest called up to say he was deluged with cables from the US press and also that it had been broadcast in America last night. Mala Brand had also called. We can never stop America but I hope we can get small announcements after it is over from Beaverbrook which will be your Friday's job should we decide to go ahead. I can't help but feel you will have trouble in the House of Commons etc and may be forced to go. I can't put you in that position. Also I'm terrified that this judge here will lose his nerve – and then what? I am sorry to bother you my darling – but I feel like an animal in a trap and these two buzzards working me up over the way you are losing your popularity – through me. Do please say what you think best for all concerned when you call me after reading this. Together I suppose we are strong enough to face this mean world – but separated I feel eanum and scared for you, your safety etc. Also the Hunters say I might easily have a brick thrown at my car. Hold me tight please David.

But the King would not hear of the divorce being abandoned. He himself was preoccupied with efforts to ensure that it received no significant press publicity in England. So far the British newspapers, true to their traditional reticence about the private lives of royalty, had (in contrast to their American and Continental counterparts) made no reference to Wallis's friendship with the King; but could this silence be continued in view of the mass of overseas comment on the Ipswich proceedings? On Friday 16 October – as anticipated in Wallis's letter

– the King received Lord Beaverbrook, the influential proprietor of the Daily Express, *at Buckingham Palace. Beaverbrook later recalled the interview:*[1]

The King asked me to help in suppressing all advance news of the Simpson divorce, and in limiting publicity after the event. He stated his case calmly and with great cogency and force.

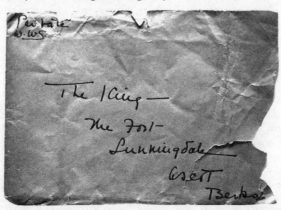

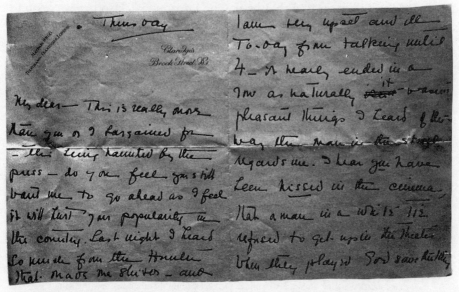

1. Lord Beaverbrook, *The Abdication of Edward VIII*, ed. A. J. P. Taylor (Hamish Hamilton, London, 1966), pp. 30–31.

The reasons he gave for his wish were that Mrs Simpson was ill, unhappy and distressed by the thought of notoriety. Notoriety would attach to her only because she had been his guest on the *Nahlin* and at Balmoral. As the publicity would be due to association with himself, he felt it his duty to protect her.

These reasons appeared satisfactory to me, and so I took part in a negotiation [with other newspaper owners] to confine publication of the news to a report of Mrs Simpson's divorce, making no mention of her friendship with the King.

On Friday evening, following this satisfactory meeting, the King went to Sandringham to prepare for a shooting party which was to take place there the following week. A note he wrote from there on Saturday, however, suggests that Wallis had returned to London for the week-end, and that the King intended to go and see her there on Sunday evening.

Saturday [17 October]   Sandringham, Norfolk

This eanum note to welcome a girl back and to say that a boy loves her more and more and that he will be hurrying back to her very soon now. Oh my sweetheart what a nightmare these days that are thank God ending now have been. I will telephone tomorrow afternoon to say when I arrive God bless WE my Wallis Your

DAVID

As soon as the King returned to Sandringham from his brief reunion with Wallis, he received an urgent request for an interview from the Prime Minister, Stanley Baldwin.[1] He thereupon left his shooting party, which had now gathered, and (so as not to arouse the curiosity of his guests) saw the Prime Minister at the Fort on the morning of Tuesday 20 October.

Affable but nervous, Baldwin – after much circumlocution – asked the King if he could prevail upon Mrs Simpson to withdraw her divorce petition, which had given rise to so much gossip and anxiety and foreign press speculation. The King disingenuously replied (as he re-

1. The correspondence would appear to clear up a minor mystery here. Baldwin had been trying to contact the King all Sunday evening, and on learning that no one knew the King's whereabouts, concluded that he had probably gone to see Mrs Simpson at Felixstowe. He was right, except that his tryst with Wallis was in London and not at Felixstowe.

called in his memoirs): 'I have no right to interfere with the affairs of an individual. It would be wrong were I to attempt to influence Mrs Simpson just because she happens to be a friend of the King.' Baldwin did not press the point or enquire further, and the meeting broke up having achieved nothing.

At the time, the King does not appear to have told Wallis about this ominous episode. He continued to send her amorous and encouraging notes.

Saturday [24 October]   The Fort

These three gardenias are eanum but they say enormous ooh and that a boy loves a girl more and more and is holding her so tight these trying days of waiting. Far the hardest is not being able to be together and one is so lonely and cut off. But it will be all over soon now my sweetheart and it will be so lovely and exciting when it is.

I know it sounds easy to say dont worry but dont too much please Wallis. I'm doing half the worrying and looking after things this end. Oh! how I long for you here and everybody and everything at The Fort misses you too dreadfully. Its a lovely day only THEY did'nt make the sun come out alas. God bless WE my beloved sweetheart. Your

DAVID

Tuesday 27 October was the day of Wallis's divorce hearing at Ipswich. According to her memoirs, she had spent a sleepless night full of self-questionings. 'I paced the small floor for hours, wondering whether I was doing the right thing, whether my recklessness of consequences had betrayed me, whether I was right in my confidence that what I was about to do would bring no harm to the King.' When she arrived with her solicitor at the courthouse the following morning, they were greeted by a crowd of several dozen reporters.

The brief but nerve-racking proceedings which followed have been admirably described by H. Montgomery Hyde in his biography of Norman Birkett:[1]

1. H. Montgomery Hyde, *Norman Birkett* (Hamish Hamilton, London, 1964), pp. 456–8. Birkett – who was a curious choice in that his public fame was liable to increase the likelihood of sensational publicity – had discussed the case privately with the King on a number of occasions, most recently at the Fort on 24 October.

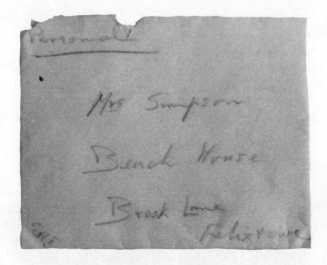

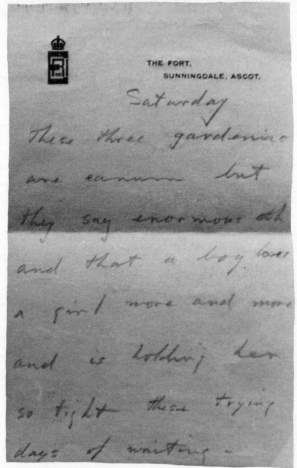

Special precautions had been taken by the local police to control the admission of spectators, and none was allowed into the gallery facing Mrs Simpson,[1] only a handful being accommodated in the seats behind her. This arrangement, added to the general air of tense expectation and excitement in the courtroom, somewhat puzzled the judge, Mr Justice Hawke, who observed irritably, as Birkett got up to address the court, 'How did the case come here?' After some whispers from the Clerk of Assize, the judge was heard to reply, 'Yes, yes, I see,' but he did not attempt to conceal his hostility when Mrs Simpson went into the witness box. There she answered the few questions her counsel was obliged to put to her, with an understandable nervousness.

She said that she and her husband were married at Chelsea Registry Office in 1928 and afterwards lived at addresses in Berkeley Street and Bryanston Court in London W.1. There were no children of the marriage. Her case was that she lived happily with her husband until the autumn of 1935, when there was a change in his manner towards her. According to Mrs Simpson, he became indifferent to her and stayed away at week-ends. She eventually consulted her solicitors ... and she subsequently received information upon which the petition was based. Evidence was also given by two waiters and a hall porter at the Hotel de Paris at Bray. The name of the woman concerned was not read out in open court.[2]

'Well,' said Mr Justice Hawke, when he had heard this recitation, 'I suppose I must conclude that there was adultery in this case.'

'I assume that is what your Lordship has in mind', said Birkett.

Suddenly the judge's bored expression changed to one of palpable annoyance. 'How do you know what is in my mind?' he asked. 'What is it I have in mind, Mr Birkett?'

'I think, with great deference,' replied Birkett quietly, 'that your Lordship may have in mind what is known as "ordinary hotel evidence", where the name of the lady is not disclosed. I thought that might have been in your Lordship's mind.'

1. There were in fact two women sitting in the otherwise empty gallery above the judge's dais, who turned out to be his wife and a friend of hers. The judge himself - to add to the uncomfortable atmosphere of the courtroom - was suffering from an audible cold.
2. The name given in the petition was Buttercup Kennedy. This does not appear to have been the name of a professional corespondent, but rather the pseudonym under which Mary Raffray had booked into the Hotel de Paris with Ernest Simpson.

Again the judge's demeanour changed, as he became amenable to counsel's suggestion.

'That is what it must have been, Mr Birkett. I am glad of your help.'

'The lady's name was mentioned in the petition, my Lord,' continued Birkett, 'so now I ask for a decree nisi with costs against the respondent.'

'Yes, costs against the respondent, I am afraid,' the judge agreed with some reluctance and after some hesitation. 'I suppose I must in these unusual circumstances. So you may have it, with costs.'[1]

'Decree nisi with costs?' Birkett repeated, to make sure.

'Yes, I suppose so,' said Mr Justice Hawke.

Following this ordeal, Wallis made her way through the crowd of journalists outside and returned immediately to London.

---

1. Wallis later reimbursed these costs to Ernest, in accordance with an agreement between them.

CHAPTER TEN

The Crisis
(OCTOBER–DECEMBER)

It is unfortunate that, as the historically exciting and controversial period of the Abdication crisis unfolds and the story of Wallis and Edward reaches its climax, the letters to Aunt Bessie temporarily cease; for, responding to her niece's call, she arrives in England aboard the Queen Mary on 9 November. Nor is there much opportunity for written exchanges between the King and Wallis, who are preoccupied with great problems which they discuss together constantly. Nevertheless, their surviving unpublished personal communications of this period – while they are not extensive, and do not by any means tell the whole story of the Abdication – are of considerable interest and importance, shedding as they do new light on their relations and reactions at this dramatic time. In particular, there is a long and imploring letter written by Wallis to the King four days before he gave up the throne, to which neither of them refer in their memoirs.

It is beyond the scope of this book to give the political history of the Abdication in any detail. What follows is no more than a summary of the main events from the viewpoint of the two persons principally concerned, incorporating the new material.

Having returned to London on Tuesday 27 October following the affair at Ipswich, Wallis installed herself at the handsome regency house in Cumberland Terrace which had been prepared for her in her absence. That evening the King dined with her there, and told her of Baldwin's visit to the Fort a week earlier to express concern over the divorce – news which greatly alarmed her.

Superficially, life seemed to proceed normally during the first half of November. The King discharged his duties as sovereign. He opened Parliament on the 3rd, took part in the Armistice Day ceremonies on the 11th, and made a highly successful visit to the Home Fleet at Portland on the 12th and 13th. Wallis's London social life continued, as did the week-ends at the Fort. But beneath the calm surface a storm was brewing, for the proceedings at Ipswich had released a torrent of speculation concerning the King's intentions towards her. So far this was more or less confined in England to smart society and official circles, for the newspapers remained silent and Wallis's existence was unknown to the general public. But this press silence could not continue indefinitely, for gossip was spreading quickly and the royal affair had already aroused massive public interest in the United States.

There was in fact one British publication which did mention 'the King's matter' – the weekly news magazine Cavalcade. *Wallis referred to this with some anguish in a scribbled and undated note which she sent the King around this time.*

Wallis to Edward
They are selling Cavalcade *in the streets of the city.* Think of the harm among *that* class. Goddard says it is a libel. Something must be done at once. I hope your pain is better and that soon we will be able to be happy although now one's eyes are sad & worried. I long to be gay and open with everybody. Hiding is an awful life. I send Mr Loo.

Wallis's archives show that, during these days, she received numerous letters from friends and fashionable acquaintances – Sibyl Colefax, Margot Oxford, Lady Londonderry, the Duff Coopers, Philip Sassoon, 'Chips' Channon and others – sympathizing with her in the difficult situation in which she found herself. They begged her not to let gossip and publicity distress her; they assured her how much she was liked and how good she was thought to be for the King. It is also clear that some of these letter-writers had frankly asked her whether the King intended to marry her – and that she had replied that, as far as she knew, he had no such intention. She would later be reproached for her lack of candour on this subject; but it is hard to see what else she could have said, given her loyalty to the King and the need to scotch rumour. Besides, it is far from certain how far she herself believed, even at this stage, that it would come to marriage.

One of the most welcome letters she received was from Herman Rogers, to whom she had written in a depressed state from Felixstowe. 'I can't tell you how sorry we are that you should have to go through this dismal time', he wrote from Cannes on 28 October.

I wish you had asked us to stay around – or to come back, if we could have been of any help to you. You know we'd have been only too glad to. That goes for the future as well – and please remember it if you ever need us. You are still my one living example of a perfectly wise and complete person. We are with you always.... Come to us if and when you can – or call us if you want us.

It would not be long before she would have need of this generous offer.

Another person from whom Wallis heard was Newbold Noyes, the editor of the Washington Evening Star, *who had finally married her second cousin Lelia in 1935. Noyes wrote[1] that the publicity she had been receiving was 'unfair, unpleasant, shabby' but that he might be able 'to get the wheel started in the other direction' and so 'make every American intensely proud of her'. He offered 'to fly over for a few days to talk over the whole problem', which would become 'very serious ... unless proper steps are promptly taken'. Wallis accepted this offer, and – on the strict understanding that he should reveal nothing about his privileged contacts, and that he himself should write nothing more than a character sketch of Wallis based on his previous knowledge of her – Noyes was invited to the Fort that November, where he discussed the situation both with her and the King. When the Abdication came, however, it was too much for Noyes to respect these confidences and miss the chance of the unique scoop which lay in his grasp. He then wrote a series of sensational and widely syndicated articles based on the private conversations he had had at the Fort, which (though favourable in tone) gave the impression of being Wallis's and Edward's authorized account of their affair. Edward was furious, and Wallis (who felt obliged to issue a disclaimer) never forgave Noyes.*

On the evening of Friday 13 November the King, having completed his successful visit to the Home Fleet, joined Wallis and Aunt Bessie at the Fort. There he found awaiting him an outspoken letter from his Private Secretary, Major Alexander Hardinge, warning him that the press would shortly break silence 'on the subject of Your Majesty's

1. In a letter to Aunt Bessie dated 20 October, for Aunt Bessie to take to London to show Wallis.

friendship with Mrs Simpson', and that the Government were meeting 'to discuss what action should be taken to deal with the serious situation which is developing'. Hardinge advised that, in order to avoid a political crisis, Mrs Simpson should go abroad 'without further delay'. In his memoirs, the Duke of Windsor wrote of his reactions to this letter:

> I was shocked and angry – shocked by the suddenness of the blow, angry because of the way it was launched, with the startling suggestion that I should send from my land, my realm, the woman I intended to marry.

He did not immediately show the letter to Wallis; but he discussed it with his old friend and adviser Walter Monckton, through whom he was henceforth to conduct his relations with the Government.

On the evening of Monday 16 November the King saw Baldwin again, this time at the King's instigation. The Prime Minister came to the point and said that whomever he married would have to be Queen, and that the British people would never accept the twice-divorced Mrs Simpson as Queen. The King then announced that he intended to marry Mrs Simpson as soon as she was free: this had become an 'indispensable condition' to his 'continued existence'. If he could marry her as King, he would be 'happy and in consequence perhaps a better King', but if the Government opposed the marriage, then he was 'prepared to go'.

Over the next twenty-four hours, in separate interviews, the King communicated this drastic decision to his mother and his three brothers, all of whom were deeply shocked. He asked Queen Mary if she would receive Mrs Simpson, which she refused to do. He also (with Baldwin's permission) consulted two members of the Government with whom he was friendly – the War Secretary, Duff Cooper, and the First Lord of the Admiralty, Sir Samuel Hoare. Hoare assured him that the Cabinet would be solidly behind Baldwin in opposing the marriage. Cooper suggested that the King shelve the marriage issue until after the Coronation, when the position could be reconsidered; but the King could not agree to such a course, which he considered tantamount to 'being crowned with a lie upon my lips'. Following these various meetings, the King departed, on the night of 17 November, on a two-day tour of the depressed areas of Wales, in the course of which he uttered his celebrated remark that 'something must be done' about unemployment.

What meanwhile of Wallis? When the King showed her Hardinge's letter – which he did on the 15th – she was (as she later wrote) 'stunned'. She wanted to follow Hardinge's advice and go abroad, but the King would not hear of such a thing. As she wrote in her memoirs:

> Now it was my turn to beg him to let me go. Summoning all my powers of persuasion, I tried to convince him of the hopelessness of our position. For him to go on hoping, to go on fighting the inevitable, could only mean tragedy for him and catastrophe for me. He would not listen. Taking my hand, he said, with the calm of a man whose mind is made up: 'I'm going to send for Mr Baldwin to see me at the Palace tomorrow. I'm going to tell him that if the country won't approve our marrying, I'm ready to go.'
>
> I burst into tears. . . .

Wallis goes on to say that, tempted though she was simply to flee abroad and vanish from the King's life, she did not do so, partly because she loved him and felt she could not abandon him, and partly because, not fully appreciating the King's constitutional position, she could not understand how the Government could make so popular a monarch give up his throne over such an issue. Besides, any intention she may have had to take flight was now deflected by a new and unexpected proposal.

While the King was absent in Wales – that is, on 18 or 19 November – Wallis was invited to lunch at Claridge's by Esmond Harmsworth, heir to Lord Rothermere's Daily Mail *press empire and chairman of the Newspaper Proprietors' Association. Harmsworth knew of the King's desire to marry her and of the problems involved, and wanted to suggest the solution of a morganatic marriage – that is, marriage of a kind once common in German royal states whereby she would become the King's wife but not share his royal rank, perhaps taking one of his subsidiary titles as, for example, Duchess of Lancaster. While such a proceeding would not be very flattering to her, it might be a means whereby the King could realize his marriage project yet be kept on the throne.*

Wallis seems to have been at first bewildered by this idea, then fascinated by it. The following week-end at the Fort (Saturday the 21st to Monday the 23rd, a week-end they shared with Aunt Bessie and the Hunters), she urged it upon the King. The King was at first uneasy about the project, but eventually – either because of her persuasions or because he was desperate – took it up with great enthusiasm. As morganatic marriage was unknown to the Common Law, legislation would be needed, both in Great Britain and the self-governing British Dominions; and he was warned by some of his advisers, notably Beaverbrook, that by asking for such legislation he would be 'putting his head on the block' by giving his home and overseas governments the chance to tender binding and critical advice on his marriage plans. Having made up his mind, however, the King was determined to see the matter through. On 25 November he saw Baldwin again, and authorized him to put the proposal to the British Cabinet and the Dominion prime ministers.

The Cabinet met in special session on the 27th; despite a plea on the King's behalf from Duff Cooper, the proposal was unfavourably regarded. Telegrams were sent to the Dominion prime ministers asking for their views; in the opinion of some historians, these telegrams were so framed as to make unfavourable replies (which Baldwin in any case appears to have solicited through private channels) inevitable. On Wednesday 2 December Baldwin saw the King to tell him what he had already gathered, that none of his governments would be willing to agree to a morganatic marriage, and that only three choices now confronted him: renunciation of Mrs Simpson; marriage contrary to the advice of his ministers (who would thereupon resign); or abdication.

Some days prior to this, Wallis had left London for good. As her notoriety grew, the atmosphere at Cumberland Terrace had become oppressive, with threatening letters and telephone calls, and an ever-increasing crowd of gapers and reporters outside the door. She was now feeling seriously ill with the strain: she seems in fact to have suffered something of a nervous breakdown. On Friday 27 November – the day the Cabinet met to discuss the morganatic marriage proposal – she and Aunt Bessie departed, at the King's suggestion, to make a prolonged stay at the Fort.

In her memoirs, Wallis charts the progress of the crisis, but says little about her own feelings in the days which followed. In fact, those days seem to have marked a psychological turning-point for her. Removed from the crowd of flatterers by whom she was surrounded in London, able to brood in solitude upon her predicament, she apparently decided that she must do what she felt she ought to have done two weeks earlier, and remove herself abroad and from the King's life as soon as she felt well enough to travel. She expressed this decision in letters written three days after her arrival at the Fort to two of her best friends, 'Foxy' Gwynne and Sibyl Colefax – letters which bear eloquent witness to her state of health and mind at that moment.

To Sibyl Colefax
Monday [30 November]

Darling Sibyl,

I have been put to bed for a week's true isolation policy. I am very tired with and of it all – and my heart resents the strain – so I am to lie quiet. I heard from the Bonners[1] that you had Miss Flanner[2] to tea. ... I am planning quite by myself to go away for a while. I think everyone here would like that – except one person perhaps – but I am planning a clever means of escape. After a while my name will be forgotten by the people and only two people will suffer instead of a mass of people who aren't interested anyway in individual feelings but only the workings of a system. I have decided to risk the result of leaving because it is an uncomfortable feeling to remain stopping in a house where the hostess has tired of you as a guest. I shall see you before I fold my tent. Much love,

WALLIS

To 'Foxy' Gwynne
Monday [30 November]

Darling Foxy,

Everything is wrong and going more wrong – and I am so tired of it all. Even the heart has been acting up and I have been put to bed for a week's complete rest – no calls, no callers. The US press has

1. An American couple who lived in Paris and who had recently spent a week-end along with Sibyl at the Fort.
2. The American journalist Janet Flanner who wished to interview Wallis.

practically ruined two people's lives however – they go on pounding away – it does get one's morale down. I think I shall remove myself when I am well enough for a small trip and give it all time to die down – perhaps returning when that d - - - - d crown has been firmly placed. I want to see you so much and hear your news which must be cheery and happy. So when I can I'll ring you. Much love,

WALLIS

So at last, it seemed, Wallis had made up her mind to leave. Writing to her aunt in May, she had said that she would know when to 'fold her tent', and now (for she uses the same expression writing to Sibyl Colefax) she recognized that the moment had come. That recognition, indeed, had dawned some weeks earlier. In September she had written to the King that they could 'only create disaster' together; in October, she had thought of giving up her divorce and 'stealing quietly away'; in mid-November, her instinct had been to follow Hardinge's advice to go abroad. Now, belatedly, she had formed a definite intention (if the letters of 30 November are to be believed) to remove herself from the scene. All she needed was a few days to recover her strength.

But it was too late. Events were moving too quickly for her. On the night of Wednesday 2 December – which was cold and foggy – the King took her for a stroll on the terrace of the Fort after dinner. He told her of his interview with Baldwin that day, which seemed to leave no choice between abdication and renunciation of her, the second of which courses was unthinkable to him. He told her too that, following a public remark by the Bishop of Bradford concerning the King's need of divine guidance, the press were about to break silence – and the crisis was about to become public.

The following morning the storm broke. All the newspapers were full of the royal marriage issue, and the general tone was one of disapproval. The King agreed that, now that her existence and his problem had become universally known, she ought to leave the country. She telephoned Herman and Kitty Rogers to invoke the hospitality and protection which they had generously offered her earlier that autumn. Hurried arrangements were made for her to proceed secretly to the Rogers' villa at Cannes in the company of the King's old friend and Lord-in-Waiting, Lord ('Perry') Brownlow, and Inspector Evans of Scotland Yard. With these protectors, Wallis left the Fort that afternoon for the cross-channel ferry at Newhaven. Aunt Bessie remained behind, as did Slipper (who would be an emotional link in the months of separation that followed). The King's last words to Wallis (as she recalled) were: 'I don't know how it's all going to end. It will be some time before we can be together again. You must wait for me no matter how long it takes. I shall never give you up.'

Before leaving the Fort, Wallis had discussed with the King one final plan by means of which he hoped to save his crown. This was that he should broadcast an appeal to his people and put his problem frankly to them. He was going to propose such a course of action to Baldwin that evening, and hoped to make the broadcast the following day. His idea was then to withdraw from the country for a period to allow public opinion to form on the subject of his marriage, delegating his authority to a Council of State. But it seems that Wallis wanted him simply to state in the broadcast that he was giving her up.

This appears to be the meaning of a curious short note written by Wallis to the King as she was about to depart from England, on Fort writing paper. Presumably it was written in Lord Brownlow's car during the trip from the Fort to the coast, and (since it is in an envelope without stamp or address) given to a servant who would be able to deliver it to the King. It reads:

Wallis to Edward
Be calm with B[aldwin] but tell the country to-morrow I am lost to you but Perry and myself can discreetly manage. We will let Bateman[1] know.
   A big-big oo'oh

The events surrounding the King over the next few days are complex in fact but simple in essence. On the night of 3 December, a few hours after Wallis's departure, he informed Baldwin of his wish to broadcast – to be told that he could not constitutionally do so without the consent of his ministers, which would not be forthcoming. After that, there was never any real doubt that he would abdicate. Churchill and Beaverbrook (both political enemies of Baldwin) tried to get him to fight the Government, and this caused him to hesitate for a moment; but he had no wish to make a stand which would have split the

1. William Bateman was the King's private telephone operator at Buckingham Palace, who had been instructed to give priority to all calls and messages from her.

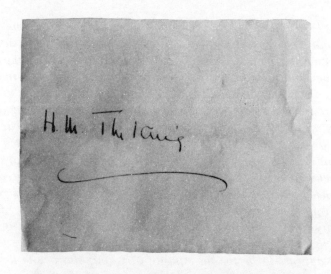

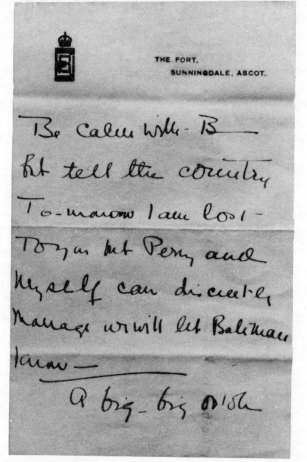

216

country. By the time Wallis arrived at Cannes in the early hours of Sunday 6 December, his mind appears to have been made up. All he now hoped was that he might be able to secure certain conditions for himself and for Wallis before taking the final step: the right to a pension, and to the future occupancy of the Fort when he returned to England; the right of his future wife to share his royal title; and, above all, an Act of Parliament making Wallis's divorce absolute immediately, so that he could join her and marry her as soon as he abdicated. In the event, he had secured none of these conditions by the time he signed the Instrument of Abdication on the morning of Thursday 10 December – though at one moment it had seemed possible that the Government would agree to the last of them.

Wallis's journey to Cannes was nightmarish. Even before she left England she was thrown into confusion by the urgent advice of Brownlow that instead of going abroad she should retire to his house in Lincolnshire, from where she would more easily be able to influence the King against abdication. This (to her subsequent regret) she declined to do, on the grounds that it would be resented by the King as an underhand manœuvre. No sooner had they disembarked in France than Wallis – in spite of the measures which had been taken to keep her journey secret – began to be recognized; and before long an army of newshounds were on her trail. As the party tried to shake them off, a fantastic flight ensued, with sudden changes of route, frantic near-encounters with their pursuers, and hurried, clandestine departures from hotels and restaurants. Throughout the two days they spent on the road under these agitated circumstances, Wallis (who allowed herself to be guided by Brownlow) was in a state of mounting anxiety over the fate of the King. Several times she tried to ring him to plead against abdication and suggest some other course of action; but owing to the faintness of the lines and the fact that such telephoning had to be done from public places, this was hopeless. Finally, at two o'clock on the morning of Sunday 6 December, their Buick – with the King's chauffeur Ladbrook at the wheel – drove past the crowd of reporters who had discovered their destination and through the gates of Lou Viei, the Rogers' villa, Wallis crouching on the floor of the car with a rug over her head.

From the Duchess of Windsor's memoirs:
Herman and Katherine were at the door.... Katherine put her arms around me and led me inside where a fire was blazing in the living room. I was back among friends. ...

For days several hundred reporters and photographers were deployed around the house like a besieging army. The Rogers were followed wherever they went; inquisitive telephone operators, in the pay of the reporters, listened-in on their telephone conversations; and attempts were made to bribe their servants. The eavesdropping on the telephone became so bad that Perry [Brownlow] had to protest to the Préfêt of the Alpes Maritimes, and in consequence the French Foreign Office in Paris sent down two of its own operators to the Cannes exchange to handle telephone traffic with the villa. Katherine and Herman bore the burden they incurred from my presence with unfailing kindness. I have reason to be grateful to them as perhaps to no one else on earth, with the exception of Aunt Bessie. ...

The villa was a twelfth-century monastery upon which Katherine and Herman had lavished loving care and imagination. It is situated on a stony ledge slightly below the crest of a hill. Photographers equipped with long-range lenses had stationed themselves on the higher ground, and some were even perched in the trees. If I wished to preserve my privacy, Katherine warned when she joined me in my room for Sunday breakfast, I had better be careful to stay away even from an open window. 'The French police want to be helpful, and Herman will do his best,' she added, 'but for a while, at least, you had better regard yourself as a prisoner.'

From the moment of her arrival at Lou Viei to the moment (on 9 December) when the King formally notified the Government of his irrevocable decision to abdicate, Wallis (by her own account) was engaged in a desperate and unremitting struggle to escape from him and so keep him on the throne. She pleaded with him on the telephone, speaking in a prearranged code. She issued a signed press statement saying that she 'wished to avoid any action or proposal which would hurt or damage His Majesty' and that she was prepared 'to withdraw from a situation that has been rendered both unhappy and untenable'. Esmond Harmsworth, who was staying nearby, suggested that she give up her divorce so that the King could not marry her; her solicitor Goddard – in an episode still surrounded by mystery – flew out from England with the same suggestion; and she was willing to agree to this if it affected the King's decision. She even planned, with Brownlow, to vanish to the Far East.

Many have tried to see an element of mere posturing in these efforts; though those who were in closest touch with her at the time, Brown-low, Goddard and the Rogers, never doubted her sincerity in wishing to save the King by disappearing from his life. What is unquestionable, however, is that all these endeavours were utterly futile, and that nothing could deflect the King from an action upon which he was now inflexibly determined. When she said she would go away, he replied that he would follow her wherever she went. When she read her press statement to him, when she threatened to give up her divorce, he assured her it would make no difference. In response to her pleas that he give her up at least for the time being, he read out a note prepared by his solicitor, George Allen: 'The only conditions on which I can stay here are if I renounce you for all time.'

Among the Duchess of Windsor's papers there exists a remarkable document. It is a letter written by her to the King, fifteen pages long, and dated 6 December – the day of her arrival at Lou Viei. Indeed, since she hopes he may receive it (by air mail) that same evening, it was probably written immediately upon her arrival. It is barely coherent, and proof of the mood of exhaustion and despair in which it was composed. Reading it, one must remember that its aim was not to explain her motives to posterity, but to try and affect the King in the obstinate and unreasoning state in which he was.

Wallis to Edward
Sunday [6 December]   Lou Viei, Cannes

Darling

I am sending this by air as I think it important you have it before. I am so anxious for you not to *abdicate* and I think the fact that you do is going to put me in the wrong light to the entire world because they will say that I could have prevented it. Chips [Channon] has telephoned that the cabinet have decided to force an answer by 5 today so I am sending this by air. If you will just give Baldwin my plan. If he turns it down then you have yours and the world could know a second compromise was turned down. My plan in detail is that you would say I [the King] shall stand back of everything I have said[1] (this saves you and me in the eyes of the world because naturally if you did not make this clear you would be a cad in the eyes of the world and I would be the woman well you know that was turned down – so that sentence printed in every newspaper saves that) to go on with the main theme – I will repeat again what to say to Mr B. I stand back of everything I have said but I do not wish to create a situation within the country so I therefore will not press this issue at the moment but reopen it in the autumn. Then if in the autumn they turn it down your plan[2] comes into action. I ask you to put that to Mr B so that no one can say we haven't tried in every way to do our duty in such a big cause. Personally I think he will turn it down and then we have the glorious other[3] but surely if it should go we will make the sacrifice of not seeing each other for that length of time. In fact we can arrange to secretly through our friends. I feel so terrified of what the world will say and I again repeat that they will say I could have stopped it. Also I don't see how anyone has the power to push the decree forward so be very careful that people would not insinuate the one legal reason – also the money – and the right sort of name with HRH. Don't be carried away with the idea alone that things can happen for us so quickly – all those 3 things must be bound up impossible to find a flaw.[4] My idea might go in Oct so it would appeal to the world. We would have made a gesture which is sporting fair. If B turns it down in Oct – there would be an uproar. No one but Baldwin and the dominions want you to go and as the Aga Khan telephoned they haven't given you a fighting. The people in the press are clamoring for a word from you. You owe it to them to tell them something and if you made that gesture by radio – by October Mr B couldn't afford to say no and I think the Dominions could be won over. Think my sweetheart isn't it better in the long run not to be hasty or selfish but back up your people and make an 8 month sacrifice for them. Then they will give you what you want and if they can't we will be vindicated in the eyes of the world and no one can say you shirked and ran

1. The offer to abdicate.
2 and 3. The alternative of abdication.
4. Wallis refers to the notion that abdication, if it takes place, should be coupled with measures to provide for her final divorce decree and his pension and royal title – an outcome for which the King and his advisers were working (in vain) at this time.

Sunday

1

LOU VIEI
CANNES

Darling. I am sending this
by air as I think it will get here
you have it before. I am

so anxious for you not to abdicate
and I think the fact that you
do is going to put me in the
wrong light to the entire world
because — they will say that I
could have prevented it. Chips

away when the people were rallying to your aid. Mr Baldwin has misrepresented your case already in Parliament – by keeping repeating into their heads I must be Queen.[1] You must speak and tell the plan of the Duchess[2] and my plan. Don't be silenced and leave under cloud I beseech you and in abdication no matter in what form unless you can let the public know that the Cabinet has virtually kicked you out by repressing 2 proposals. I can't support you unless you tell the country the 2 proposals. I must have any action of yours understood by the world but hidden by B we would have no happiness and I think the world would turn against me. When now we have their sympathy. I worry too about the legal side because that would be a tragedy if they refused me [a divorce]. This plea is to beg you to submit my idea to B. If he refuses – I have spoken to you so there is no more to say except I'm holding you tighter than ever.

W ALLIS

Wallis's plan, therefore, was that they should remain parted, and the King should cease to press his marriage plans, until the autumn of 1937; and that he should meanwhile keep his throne. But there is evidence that, in proposing this plan, she was playing for time not just for the King but for herself; and that she in fact hoped to extricate herself altogether from the King's fatal friendship. This, at all events, was what she wrote in effect to her confidante Sibyl Colefax a week after the Abdication:

18 Dec.   Lou Viei

Sibyl darling

I still can't write about it all because I am afraid of not conveying the true facts as brain is so very tired from the struggle of the past two weeks – the screaming of a thousand plans to London, the pleading to *lead* him not *force* him. I knew him so well, I wanted them to take my advice. But no, driving on they went headed for this Tragedy.

---

1. On 4 December, Baldwin had announced in Parliament: 'The King himself requires no consent from any other authority to make his marriage legal. But ... the lady whom he marries ... necessarily becomes Queen. She herself therefore enjoys all the status, rights and privileges which ... attach to that position, and with which we are familiar in the cases of Her late Majesty Queen Alexandra and Her Majesty Queen Mary; and her children will be in direct succession to the throne.'
2. The morganatic marriage proposal.

If only they had said, let's drop the idea now and in the autumn we'll discuss it again. And Sibyl darling in the autumn I would have been so very far away. I had already escaped. Some day if we ever meet I shall tell you all. The little faith I have tried to cling on to has been taken from me when I saw England turn on a man that couldn't defend himself and had never been anything but straight with his country. . . .

It was a stricken and defeated Wallis who awaited the ex-King's farewell broadcast on the night of Friday 11 December.

From the Duchess of Windsor's Memoirs:
As the moment approached, everyone in Lou Viei, including the domestic staff, gathered around the radio in the sitting room. David's voice came out of the loudspeaker calmly, movingly. I was lying on the sofa with my hands over my eyes, trying to hide my tears. After he finished, the others quietly went away and left me alone. I lay there a long time before I could control myself enough to walk through the house and go upstairs to my room.

PART THREE

Wallis and the Duke

DECEMBER 1936–JUNE 1937

CHAPTER ELEVEN
December

Having given up the throne in order to be able to marry the woman he loved, and taken an emotional leave of his family at Windsor Castle after his famous broadcast, the newly-styled Duke of Windsor left England, sailing from Portsmouth in the early hours of Saturday 12 December aboard a Royal Navy vessel. By a strange irony, however, it was impossible for him to join Mrs Simpson – the motive for his sacrifice – who remained at the Villa Lou Viei at Cannes with her friends the Rogers under a virtual state of siege. Now that he had made public his desire to marry her, it was essential (under the laws which then existed) that they should not meet until Wallis's provisional decree of divorce from Ernest Simpson had been made absolute, otherwise the whole proceedings might be jeopardized. And the six-month delay which would enable her to apply for her Decree Absolute would only be up on 27 April 1937. The Duke therefore made for Austria, where Baron Eugene de Rothschild and his American wife Kitty had offered him a refuge at their castle near Vienna, Schloss Enzesfeld. There he began the lonely vigil imposed upon him until the day when he could be reunited with his beloved. It was to last more than twenty weeks.

Throughout that period of enforced separation, Wallis and the Duke spoke almost every evening (and sometimes several times a day) on the telephone. It was not an ideal means of communication. Calls between Cannes and Enzesfeld took up to an hour to put through, and were frequently cut off without warning; the line was often so faint that one had to shout to be heard; there were constant interruptions from operators; and freedom of speech was curtailed by the risk of eavesdroppers. Fortunately, these unsatisfactory talks were supplemented by regular letters to each other, and some three dozen of these (along with letters they wrote at the time to Aunt Bessie and others) have been preserved in their archives. While these letters do not always by themselves tell a continuous story – 'hot news' was generally exchanged, albeit with difficulty, during the daily conversations – they must surely rank among the most extraordinary documents in the annals of romantic correspondence, enabling us as they do to observe the reactions of two persons who found themselves in a unique situation.

What is remarkable about the Duke's side of the correspondence is that it shows him to be a man in the grip of sheer euphoria. This was a factor which had startled the ministers, advisers and relations of the abdicating sovereign in the last days of the crisis: far from appearing to be depressed by his predicament and its tragic outcome, he had been in a positively jolly mood – 'as if he were looking forward to his honeymoon', as Baldwin remarked after their last meeting. Once the deed was done, this mood seems to have possessed him completely. Perry Brownlow, who saw much of him that autumn, found him 'exalté to the point of madness'. His euphoria stifled all regret. There can be no doubt that he was dazed by recent events ('a nightmare like a bad dream one hopes never to have again'); that he found the long trial of separation agonizing ('as hard and as trying as two people have had to endure'); and that the slow realization that he had become an outcast from his country and family (which he had not anticipated) came as a bitter blow to him. ('If I ever hear another word of that old bromide "The English are a nation of sportsmen" I'll yell the place down.') None the less, all these feelings were overborne by a pervasive sense of joy and liberation at the prospect of spending the rest of his life with the human being who was the centre of his universe. 'It's all so lovely Wallis and so dear and sweet and sacred', he writes in his first post-Abdication letter, 'and I'm really happy for the very first time in my life.' And again in his New Year's letter: '... although it is still a matter of weary months to wait it is lovely to have 1936 behind us and only this and many more happy years together to look forward to.' His fervour of anticipation has a note of religious ecstasy about it: God will bless them, he never ceases to assure her; he prays in Austrian churches for their future together.

Wallis's feelings were very different. The dramatic event which had for him been a liberating step on the path to happiness was to her a catastrophe of unimaginable proportions. She was shattered by her failure to dissuade him from his terrible action. 'I have fallen back exhausted from the struggle to prevent this great tragedy,' she writes to Kitty de Rothschild. 'One felt so small not to be able to make him

*stay where he belonged – and then the world to turn against me –
because I fought a losing battle.' She realized that – for all her efforts
to make him give her up – she would be blamed for what had happened: this fact was brought home to her relentlessly every day by the
mountain of hate mail (including assassination threats) which arrived
at Lou Viei; by the attitude of many she had thought her friends; by
the way she was shunned by English society on the Riviera; and by
endless hostile comment in all the world's press, which painted a
picture of her which she found unrecognizable. In her memoirs, the
Duchess of Windsor wrote of how forlorn and abandoned she felt at
this time – a time of heartache and terror:*

The enormity of the hatred I had aroused and the distorted image
of me that seemed to be forming in minds everywhere went far
beyond anything I had anticipated even in my most depressed
moments.... To be accused of things one has never done; to be
judged and condemned on many sides by people ignorant of the
controlling circumstances; to have one's supposed character day
after day laid bare, dissected and flayed by mischievous and mer-
ciless hands: such are the most corrosive of human experiences.

She wrote too of how she surmounted her trial:

I survived at Cannes by mastering my own emotions. What is
called for is a kind of private arrangement within oneself – an
understanding of the heart and mind – that one's life and purposes
are essentially good, and that nothing from outside must be
allowed to impair that understanding.... I learned that one can
live alone.

*Wallis's letters of the period reveal much of this anguish – as well
as of her efforts to overcome it. But they also reveal something else –
love for the Duke of Windsor. She had wanted to give him up, and he
had abdicated against her strongest wishes. She had listened to his
speech in tears and with horror. But in the letter she writes him the
following day, there is no hint of recrimination. She writes tenderly,
echoing his feelings for her. 'My heart is so full of love for you
and the agony of not being able to see you after all you have been
through is pathetic.... Your broadcast was very good my angel and*

it is all going to be so very lovely.... I hope you will never regret this sacrifice....' Her thoughts of him are protective and possessive. She is anxious for his safety on the Austrian roads and ski-slopes. She is jealous of the few women he sees, even including his hostess at Enzesfeld. Her own woes gradually dissolve in anger as she observes the chilly treatment meted out to her husband-to-be. While the Duke's mind is fixed on a coming eternity of bliss, she sees their love in terms of a heroic solidarity: all the world is against them, but they will 'find a new strong life built on our lonely love which has stood a test to prove its greatness'. She senses that she is following him into a life of nothingness, but she does not retreat for an instant.

If her letters sometimes sound a trifle admonishing in tone, one must remember, first, that he looked up to her and wanted to be led by her; and secondly, that he was in a state of hopeless unreality, which virtually forced her to take charge of him. The whole situation was strange in that, while the circumstances which existed had been willed by him and not by her, it was she who now found herself cast in the dominant role. There is something utterly childlike in his infatuation for her; and now more than ever their relationship is seen to be that of mother and son rather than of ordinary lovers.

Wallis to Edward
Saturday [12 December]

Darling

My heart is so full of love for you and the agony of not being able to see you after all you have been through is pathetic. At the moment we have the whole world against us and our love – so we can't afford to move about very much and must simply sit and face these dreary months ahead and I think I shall have to stay here. It may be safer than moving and a house is more protection than a hotel from the press and the fanatics. I am thinking where is the best place for you because you must have people with you always. The Hunters would come out also Perry & Kitty [Brownlow], the Buists etc. A man called Bedaux – Americans – have offered their place to you. It is near Tours. The Rogers say it is lovely. Perhaps it is too near here. Then I hear Ralph Grimthorpe has offered you his house at Sorrento Italy. I also hear that Lincoln Ellsworth[1] has a lovely house in Switzerland which you could probably get – and in my opinion Mimizan[2] is safe. I don't think you will be happy long at Enzesfeld and besides you couldn't stay forever. I think after Xmas the limit. Anyway we will find something for you my darling and I am feeling all your feelings of loneliness and despair which must face you on this new beginning. If we could have been together during the waiting it would have been so much easier. I long for you so. I hear that there is an organization of women who have sworn to kill me. Evans is investigating. We must not take any risks because to have an accident come now would be too much to bear – so please be a 'sissy' about protection. I am. There is nothing I can begin to say about Perry's friendship for us. It has been absolutely marvellous in every way. Do tell him.[3] I can't because I begin to cry, I have never seen anything like it. I don't know your name but rather hoped it would be The Prince [sic] of Windsor. I suppose we will have difficulty about a name for poor me as York [sic][4] I don't suppose will make me HRH. Above all we want to have a dignified position no matter where we are. That is also important to the throne. Your broadcast was very good my angel and it is all going to be so very lovely. Make ooh! It is cruel the laws are such that we can't see each other until April. However everything must be done to try and placate the legal side. I can't believe the Government would want more scandal and everything raked up again at the time of the Coronation. Some of the papers – Times, Telegraph, Morning Post – have been disloyal to you and foul to me. However it is all over now. I hope you will never regret this sacrifice and that your brother will prove to the world that we still have a position and that you will be given some jobs to do. I am sending Ladbrook home as he wants to go but he will come out to you anywhere and you must have a car. I am engaging a local chauffeur. I think the detectives hate the job but I must have them and if the Home Office withdraws them I shall have to have two out and pay them. Monckton or Allen could select them and I shall pay out of the

1. The American polar explorer, who had visited King Edward shortly before the Abdication with an offer to buy his ranch in Canada.
2. A shooting-box belonging to the Duke of Westminster on the French Atlantic coast north of Biarritz.
3. Brownlow was about to leave Cannes to join his master at Enzesfeld. He may have been the bearer of this letter.
4. Throughout the weeks that followed, Wallis continued to describe the Duke of Windsor by his old title, and the new King and Queen as the Duke and Duchess of York.

savings account. It is worth it God knows with all these threatening letters. I love you David and am holding so tight.

WALLIS

Hello everybody – and a pat to Slippy Poo.

The 'man called Bedaux' referred to by Wallis in her letter was an old friend of the Rogers, an ingenious Frenchman who had taken American nationality and made a fortune by developing industrial time-and-motion systems. His wife was American, from Michigan. For the time being the Duke had to refuse their offer of a sanctuary at Candé, their château in Touraine, but the offer remained open.

Wallis now had to confront a new misery. She received word from her solicitor, Theodore Goddard, that one Francis Stephenson, an elderly solicitor's clerk of Ilford, Essex, claimed to be able to show cause as to why her divorce should not be made absolute, and that on 10 December he had Entered an Appearance at the Divorce Registry in London to this effect. Stephenson (as Goddard surmised) was no more than a malicious mischief-maker: he subsequently confessed that the evidence on which his intervention was based was mere gossip, and he withdrew his Appearance only a few days after entering it. But it was dismaying for Wallis to realize that there were those who were intent on wrecking her divorce and so making her marriage to the Duke of Windsor impossible; and that, under English law, their allegations, however spurious, were liable to be officially investigated.

Wallis to Edward
Monday [14 December]   Lou Viei, Cannes

Darling

It is practically the last straw the intervention. I didn't think the world could put more on two people whose only sin is to love. I look a hundred and weigh 110 – you won't love me when you see the wreck England has made me. I now have the Sunday papers in which your mother makes a colossal denial of statements in foreign press saying she had seen me. It is a cruel denial. I made it 2 weeks ago to the US press but of course it got no headlines. The world is against me and me alone. Not a paper has said a kind thing for me. Can we survive the attack and will we have or you have enough loyalty left by your family to help us with the legal things because your mother has placed me in a worse position than ever and practically says she would not accept me. It is plain that York guided by her would not give us the extra chic of creating me HRH – the only thing to bring me back in the eyes of the world. It is despair for me to have been so badly treated. I enclose you a kind letter from Ava[1] and all my love my darling. It's just my feelings are so very hurt by these headlines. All love once again

WALLIS

Wallis to Edward
December 18th   Lou Viei

My darling
  I have decided to sit in the villa walking in the garden – an occasional drive. So much scandal has been whispered about me even that I am a spy that I am shunned by people so until I have the protection of your name I must remain hidden. Nothing but scandal talk and bitter looks follow me. So this is my 4 months of exile and I must face it. The Rogers are nearly exiles as nobody asks them on account of me. Never mind. If we keep our poor heads and our health everything will be ours. So my darling please be more than careful in everything and the less we are seen the better. We want to get our names off people's lips. That England could have turned on the Prince of Wales has been a cruel blow to my faith in mankind. However we will find a new strong life built on our lonely love which has stood a test to prove its greatness. The anguish and loneliness of these months will be terrifying but we must take it and use our last remaining strength to endure it. I love you my own dear David.

WALLIS

Wallis to the Baroness Eugene de Rothschild
December 18th   Lou Viei

Dear Kitty
  (I must call you that under these very tragic circumstances that have brought two strangers so close together.) First I wanted to say I think it noble of you to have the King [*sic*]. I know how I have ruined the

---

1. Basil, 4th Marquess of Dufferin and Ava (1909–45), a junior government minister.

December 18ᵗʰ

LOU VIEI
CANNES

My darling —
            I have decided
to sit in the villa walking
in the garden — an occasional
drive — so much scandal
has been whispered about me
even that I am a *spy* that
I am *shunned* by *people* —
so until I have the protection
of your name — I must remain

normal life of the Rogers – the newspaper notoriety is appalling and disgusting and nothing but lies as a general rule. This will of course in time cease but I feel for you at this moment. Only the knowledge that you are doing an act of great kindness can take the edge off your feelings of resentment at having your privacy invaded. I have talked to the King and am sure all the things you spoke to me about are completely under control. He is not really at all what people said of him in his younger days and I can assure you he will also be all right after you have gone. This letter is disconnected but after the strain of the past few weeks I have lost my continuity of thought and I have fallen back exhausted from the struggle to try and prevent this great tragedy and sadness for all concerned. One felt so small not to be able to make him stay where he belonged and then the world to turn against me – because I fought a losing battle. Dear Kitty – be kind to him. He is honest and good and really worthy of affection. They simply haven't understood.

Edward to Wallis
22nd Dec. 1936   Schloss Enzesfeld, A.D. Triesting

My own darling
   I just dont know how to begin to write to you when I have so much that can only be 'oohed' and said. Oh! my sweetheart the thought of the next four months separation is an agony and just not possible to think about. I am forcing myself to pretend that I'm only away from you because I'm on a job in this country and you cant come here for business reasons! Otherwise I would have gone mad already and I've only been here ten days – ten days that have passed very slowly and with the most monotonous precision. But who cares darling how they are spent and maybe they will pass quicker later on. And now we have Christmas the nearest we have ever been to spending it together although we are further away in distance. But a boy is holding a girl so so tight Wallis. 'Poor things' that we are just now but not 'so stupid' only 'so lonely'. Oh! 'pooky demus' WE say. The thing that worries me is that although you have the Rogers and Mary – oh! and I forgot Aunt Bessie – you are so cramped at Lou Viei and have'nt as much room to circulate and walk around as Mr Loo and I have. He sends you millions of dog kisses and thanks you for the pat you sent him. He is very well and has a lovely time on the golf every

afternoon and then eats an enormous dinner and has his Bob Martin[1] every two or three evenings. But he misses you terribly too. I must say the Rothschilds are very kind and hospitable and allow me to lead my own life here by never expecting me for lunch or to sit and make conversation after tea. It is luxuriously comfortable and as you know the food superb. But I am neither eating nor smoking too much and the 'pipe line' is very short!! Oh! my beloved I am only living for the 27th April (maybe sooner who knows) and only live now for our telephone talks in the evening. WE have to thank God for that instrument just now or it really would be just too unbearable. I seem only to have talked about me till now. I know what hurt feelings you have had and that has made me so unhappy. But that was the fault of the King not of David not that it stops the hurt feelings. I could not have believed how cruel and inhuman the American newspaper business is until one has been their 'meat' as WE have. Even the one man we thought our friend Noyes[2] has let us down too. I'm afraid that we must face the fact that WE will be news value until some time after that dear sweet day when we will 'officially' belong to each other. Oh! Wallis why must we wait so long? It's so cruel. But now I must not say that because we have been through so much for each other and for our perfect happiness that we can take this last through the longest and most trying lap of the course as bravely as we have faced the World the last two months. Its all so lovely Wallis and so dear and sweet and sacred and I'm really happy for the very first time in my life. I worry about you though so far away at Cannes without my protection and you will be careful won't you? Please – please! 'Everybody' – all of 'US' here – send all of 'YOU' oohs enormous oohs for Christmas and we are all of 'US' so sad we can't send each other any presents. HE (I hide face) Eanum and Pig (I hide face again) and all the toys miss YOU ALL at LOO VIEI more than they can say. It's pathetic but we'll just have to write this Christmas off and make up for it by so many lovely happy ones in the future. I will go to Church in Vienna on Friday for eleven o'clock service and pray so hard that God goes on blessing WE for the rest of our lives. He has been very good to WE and is watching over US I know. I have so much more to say my sweetheart but I want you to get this for Christmas so will

1. A brand of conditioning tablets for dogs.
2. See above, page 209.

enclose it in a cover address to Herman and mail it now. I love you love you Wallis more and more and more and am holding so tight. Your   DAVID

Edward to Aunt Bessie
22 December 1936   Schloss Enzesfeld

Dear Aunt Bessie,

Thank you so much for your very sweet letter written from London before you left.[1] And you must have been as glad to get away from London as I was. Those last two weeks were indeed a nightmare like a bad dream one hopes never to have again. I do hope you found Wallis better than you expected. What a ghastly time she has had poor darling. That thought as you know was the only one that really worried me. However it does seem to be quieter at Cannes now although I'm afraid the American newspapers will never lay off till next summer. Oh! for next summer and the next four months are going to be as hard and as trying as two people have had to endure. But we are brave and can go through with anything when we have each other and our perfect happiness to look forward to. So you will look after her all this time of separation I know. It would be fine if you could come here for a little visit later on. It is a very comfortable house and the Rothschilds very kind and hospitable. They go to Paris around tenth January I believe so any time after that date it would suit you to come here. Mr Slipper is very well and is a grand companion but I only wish Wallis could have him. But she can't on account of the Rogers' scotties so that's that. I'm afraid that Newbold Noyes turned out to be the worst friend we could have in trying to be a good one. It's too bad

---

1. Dated 17 December, Aunt Bessie's letter to the Duke read as follows:
Sir,
    Before I leave London tomorrow – and who knows when I may see it again – I want to send you a line to tell you how constantly I have held you in my thoughts since you left, and, Sir, with what affectionate regard you will always remain there. I go to Cannes tomorrow and I dare to hope that before 1937 is very old I may be privileged again to see you.
With all good wishes I am, Sir,
    Your obedient servant
                                                BESSIE L. MERRYMAN

Shortly afterwards Aunt Bessie arrived at the Carlton Hotel at Cannes to be near her niece, where she remained until her return to the United States early in February.

they dont seem to have the first ideas of dignity or humanity. I hope Ulick Alexander[1] and Mr Carter[2] were able to help you after I had gone. I hear the Hunters or at any rate Kitty has not be nice about us. But who cares!

And now I send you my very best wishes for Christmas – and may 1937 and the succeeding years be very happy ones for us all.
With love from

EDWARD

Wallis to Edward
[late December]

Darling

Give this to whoever is doing the job. It was a large jar of the nuts we like from Honolulu so you can have them say how much you like them. I am getting rather worked up about what support we are going to get from your family for our wedding. It is so important – everyone around me realizes the importance of it re announcement etc. After all we have done nothing wrong so why be treated that way. It is not the first marriage to a commoner in the family. Really David the pleased expression on the Duchess of York's [*sic*] face is funny to see. How she is loving it all. There will be no support there. All my love

WALLIS

PS I've had an Xmas card from Mae West!

At the end of December Wallis heard from Ernest Simpson:

I did not have the heart to write before. I have felt somewhat stunned and slightly sick over recent events. I am not, however, going into that, but I want you to believe – I do believe – that you did everything in your power to prevent the final catastrophe.

My thoughts have been with you throughout your ordeal, and you may rest assured that no one has felt more deeply for you than I have.

1. Keeper of the Privy Purse, the Court official who looked after the royal finances. He remained a loyal friend to his ex-master, who had appointed him to his post.
2. A clerk in the Privy Purse Office, who looked after the Duke's affairs in London.

For a few pence each day I can keep *au courant* with your doings....

...And would your life have ever been the same if you had broken it off? I mean could you possibly have settled down to the old life and forgotten the fairyland through which you had passed? My child, I do not think so.

CHAPTER TWELVE
January

1937 was the year that the Duke of Windsor hoped to become 'one'
with his beloved; but it opened with his having to face some harsh
realities. In his own country, his decision to give up the throne for love
had been greeted with intense and widespread dismay. There were
many who deeply sympathized with him, and believed that he had
been the innocent victim of a base intrigue. But there were many others
who, having had such high hopes of him, now felt let down and
betrayed. The fact that the man born to be King appeared to have
thrust the crown upon a shy and reluctant successor was the cause of
general resentment – not least within his own family. Then there were
those (particularly among the 'Establishment', a word then just coming
into use) who had always disliked the ex-King for being too original
and democratic, wayward and impulsive, who were happy to see him
go and did not want him back. The Duke did have his well-wishers
and partisans, more than is commonly supposed; but, as the shock of
the Abdication wore off, the general feeling towards him – particularly
in the corridors of power and at the Court of the new King and Queen
– was one of hostility.

The Duke had no regrets: he believed he had taken the only hon-
ourable course open to him under the circumstances, and looked not
to the troubled past but a happy future. As it gradually dawned on
him that he had become an outcast, his main reaction was one of hurt
bewilderment. So obsessed was he with love, such was his state of
exaltation, that he did not really understand what was happening to
him. One by one the blows fell – that he would no longer be able to call
upon the Court, even for secretarial assistance; that he would not be
given a pension in the new Civil List;[1] that his family would not be
attending his wedding; that his future wife would not be allowed to
share his royal rank; that he would be unable in effect to return to his

---

1. The parliamentary vote of Crown funds to members of the Royal Family, which then took
place at the outset of each reign.

own country – to be greeted by him with a kind of outraged bafflement.

In these circumstances, Wallis became his passionate defender. She knew to what extent the Abdication had come about through his own obstinacy, and she had warned him – in her letter of 6 December – what the consequences would be in terms of his popularity. But she now feels nothing but love for him. She is out to protect him. She writes of the Abdication as a noble gesture, for which he has been rewarded with nothing but shabby treatment. She calls down curses on his enemies, on 'Baldwin's rotten politics', on his family who seem to ignore him. She opens his eyes to the realities of the situation. She encourages him to stand up for himself. Her judgements may seem at times somewhat naïve or even hysterical, but there can be no doubt that she is out to do her best for her man and to secure a dignified future for their married life together.

Meanwhile their separation becomes increasingly painful, and their sense of longing for each other ever more intense. Edward remains at Enzesfeld, where he enjoys the unwanted society of his hostess and is joined in the middle of January by his old boon companion 'Fruity' Metcalfe. Wallis remains at Cannes, where the press siege lifts sufficiently for her to visit a few friends on the Riviera such as Somerset Maugham and Daisy Fellowes. They begin to think of where they will marry and where they will live afterwards. But there is still the divorce....

Mrs Simpson

Lou Viei

Cannes

SCHLOSS ENZESFELD
N. D. TRIESTING

1st January 1937

Hello! my sweetheart - Such a very happy New Year I wish for WE from the fastness of my 'exile' - my exile from you and not from England my darling and although it is still a matter of weary months to wait it

is lovely to have 1936 behind us and only this and many more happy years together to look forward to - Oh! WE will make it - this separation but by jolly it is hard and a terrible strain - If it wasn't for that unsatisfactory telephone then I really would go mad - Oh! poor everybody WE all say and HE is so

scared of loosing his hairpin that he does want HER to hurry and send him another to secure the old one - I'm giving this to Storrier to take to you to-morrow evening along with an earnum New Year present (the two feathers were for (Christmas) in which you will find three letters for you and some monograms to choose one from for note paper etc. Have a good talk to Storrier and then he'll return to report the situation and you could give him a letter for me if you have written one - I'll have to watch out for our interests in England like the dickens

as there's not much for her
to do and B is of course
a slight extra expense to
the Rogers — I'm worried
over Herman having to go
to the nursing home — for him
the unpleasantness and for
you the loss of protection
But you'll be able to
arrange something — I'm glad
its quieter for you too now

although we still have loyal
friends like Walter and Ulick
and of course E R Peacock
and Allen — Oh! how hopeless
writing is when WE have so
much to say and arrange
about the future — May be
it would be better for
Aunt Bessie to return now

from the newspaper end but it will
all boil up again in April damn it.
Mr Loo sends a lot dog kisses and
I send a four leaf clover. Its a
cultivated plant but there were
two on one root and I have kept
and pressed the other. Oh! "make
ools" to think you'll hold this
piece of paper — God! how I love
you love you my Wallis my
bloved sweetheart more and more
and more — I'm holding so tight
all the time until that dear,
lovely precious day — oh! God make
it come quickly and bless WE
this year and always — Your David

Edward to Wallis
1st January 1937 [year underlined 4 times]   Schloss Enzesfeld

Hello! my sweetheart. Such a very happy New Year I wish for WE
from the fastness of my 'exile' – my exile from you and not from
England my darling and although it is still a matter of weary *months*
to wait it is lovely to have 1936 behind us and only this and many
more happy years together to look forward to. Oh! WE will make it
– this separation but 'by golly' it is hard and a terrible strain. If it
was'nt for that unsatisfactory telephone then I really would go mad.
Oh! poor everybody WE all say and HE is so scared of loosing [*sic*]
his hairpin that he does want HER to hurry and send him another to
secure the old one. I'm giving this to Storrier[1] to take to you
tomorrow evening along with an eanum New Year present (the two
feathers were for *Christmas*) in which you will find three letters for
you and some monograms to choose one from for note paper etc.
Have a good talk to Storrier and then he'll return to report the situation and you could give him a letter for me if you have written one.
I'll have to watch out for our interests in England like the dickens
although we still have loyal friends like Walter [Monckton] and Ulick
[Alexander] and of course E R Peacock[2] and [George] Allen. Oh! how
hopeless writing is when WE have *so* much to say and arrange about
the future. Maybe it would be better for Aunt Bessie to return now as
there's not much for her to do and is of course a slight extra expense
to the Rogers. I'm worried over Herman having to go to the nursing
home – for him the unpleasantness and for you the loss of protection.
But you'll be able to arrange something. I'm glad its quieter for you
too now from the newspaper end but it will all boil up again in April
damn it. Mr Loo sends a lot dog kisses and I send a four leaf clover.
Its a cultivated plant but there were two on one root and I have kept
and pressed the other. Oh! 'make ooh' to think you'll hold this piece
of paper. God! how I love you love you my Wallis my beloved sweetheart more and more and more. I'm holding *so* tight all the time until
that dear lovely precious day – oh! God make it come quickly and
bless WE this year and always. Your

                                                          DAVID

1. Chief Inspector Storrier of Scotland Yard, the Duke's detective.
2. Sir Edward Peacock (1871–1962), the Canadian banker who was Receiver-General of the
Duchy of Cornwall and had for some time been the Duke's private financial adviser.

Wallis to Edward
Friday night [1 January 1937?]

Darling sweetheart

I couldn't bear hearing you cry – you who have been through so much and are so brave. My baby it is because I long to be with you so intensely everything becomes so magnified. Darling I love you. Come to me soon.

Wallis to Edward
Sunday [3 January]   Lou Viei

Darling Sweetheart

Sometimes I feel as though my heart would burst if I didn't see you. But we must be brave and keep sane for a few more months. I am so distressed over the way your brother has behaved from the first and is certainly giving the impression to the world at large that your family as well as Baldwin and his ministers do not approve of me. I do think now that the deed is done your family should not give out such an impression. Even in the speech[1] he took the opportunity to convey that idea. I realize it is put there by the politicians whose game it is to have you forgotten and to build up the puppet they have placed upon the throne. And they can succeed, because just as they had for months an organized campaign to remove you – and how cleverly they worked – so have they one to prove they were right in what they did and the first step is to eliminate you from the minds of the people. I was the convenient tool in their hands to use to get rid of you and how they used it! Naturally we have to build up a position but how hard it is going to be with no signs of support from your family. One realizes now the impossibility of getting the marriage announced in the Court Circular and of the HRH. It is all a great pity because I loathe being undignified and also of joining the countless titles that roam around Europe meaning nothing. To set off on our journey with a proper backing would mean so much – but whatever happens we will make something of our lives – but since you have been so trusting all along perhaps now you are beginning to realize that you can't go on being and then have praise after you are dead. You must employ their means to accomplish your ends – and after Feb I should write your brother

1. Baldwin's speech to the House of Commons at the time of the Abdication?

a straightforward letter setting forth the reasons for him not to treat you as an outcast and to do something for me so that we have a dignified and correct position as certainly befits an ex-King of England who really only left to get what the present one was lucky enough to have. Up to the present the only person in the drama that has made a big gesture is you. Frankly I am disgusted with them all. I am sending you the clippings. Do read them carefully. Some are to make you laugh, some to make you think and the nasty ones to have the papers apologize. Please keep them all – not on the floor. I haven't seen Mr Storrier as yet as he hasn't arrived so will leave this open to write more. I love you more and more.

Monday [4 January]

I have my lovely bag now. As much as I like it and the dear warm letter I would rather Storrier had brought me you and ooh. It made me sad to be on the yacht once again and to see the rocks where we spent such a happy afternoon from the Rosaura. I think so much of all the beautiful times we have had together only I can't bear to think of the Fort. I cry so hard especially when the vivid picture of you peeping out to see what sort of day it was [*sic*]. Darling it is so funny to be homeless and not have our lovely things all around us. We will though that is the only thought to have. I hear Thelma is writing your life and also what a bad influence I had upon it – ten thousand pounds from Hearst – Gloria has just finished hers for the same sum. Naturally they do not write them – they tell the facts to a journalist. I had very bad luck in finding a scent for you. The shops are really bad here. I send you the only one I could find. I should think by April 15 we could meet somewhere as I think anyone would intervene before then. However we must be guided by advice. I know you are going to be even more bored than I will. Your life has been led at such a great and busy pace that inactivity will be very trying for you my loved one. The buttons have not been fixed as you like them but Storrier could take them to England and have Cartier do them. I said last night I don't like any of the drawings – so have Lambe[1] write to Sindon[2] to

1. Commander (subsequently Admiral of the Fleet Sir) Charles Lambe (1900–60), the equerry who had joined the Duke in Austria, where his main task was to answer the hundreds of letters which arrived daily.
2. Presumably the London stationer who had made a die-stamp of the Duke's monogram.

send you some. 'She' sends the hairpin which 'she' says she found very comfortable and hopes 'he' will. I hide my face but send you all love.

WALLIS

Wallis to 'Foxy' Gwynne
Sunday [3 January]   Lou Viei

Darling Foxy,
    Thank you for your sweet letter and wire. Somehow I didn't think you'd play rat! I'm now in 1937 feeling stronger and braver about the future and I'm taking a few 'rat' names. Now two I've been given several times surprise me – that is the Buists – and I haven't heard from them. So just answer me yes or no.[1] It won't make trouble and it is only for future guidance. Please thank that sweet Dottie Sands – she has been so kind, and I don't know her address. And please tell me the name of that face woman in Paris. I shall be here until the spring – am making no plans, it seems a waste of time. Daisy is here and I do some boating with them and have been to Willie Maugham's. Outside of that the boredom is appalling but healthy after 2 years of 3 a.m. nights. Much love,

WALLIS

[undated]

Darling
    Here it is. It is really too unkind. Something must be done to put it out of the people's mind in England that your family are against us. I can't stand up against this system of trying to make me an outcast in the world. After this I doubt if anyone speaks to me.

Wallis to Edward
Tuesday Jan 13th [which was in fact Wednesday]

Darling
    I have just read in the paper that Lambe is to return to London on the 19th. Who is coming out in his place?[2] You cannot be alone with

---

1. In spite of their temporary silence, the Buists had in fact remained loyal and would resume their friendship with the Duke and Wallis.
2. Lambe was replaced as equerry by Major Douglas Greenacre of the Welsh Guards, who was in turn relieved in mid-February by 'Jack' Aird.

247

Fruity. In the first place he is not capable of handling the post and dealing with servants etc. In the second place it is necessary you have an equerry at all times. Why is London and your brother especially neglecting you so? They are behaving as if you were on the worst possible terms. Are they going to do nothing for you from their end? Up to now the dealings with London have been far from satisfactory and an attitude of complete indifference. It is impossible from Austria for you to find equerries. Surely you have some friends or your family to send someone to you. You must not be there alone with Fruity: I won't have it. I am enclosing some clippings which I want you to read. I am glad an Englishman agrees with me. It's the first time. I love you and think about you every minute. We are certainly being beaten on all sides and one has some pride about continually telephoning and grovelling. Can't Godfrey [Thomas] come or some of your old staff? I feel Perry [Brownlow] is more important later for us. Again my love

WALLIS

Wallis to Edward
Thursday the 21st [January]

Darling

I really am too nervous about those icy roads. You read of accidents on them nearly every day – and it does take the top in chauffeurs to negotiate them. That and the skiing combined is making me lie awake at night. However you must do it all I suppose or go mad with boredom. I get absolutely insane some days with waiting. Everything is so empty and as one can't move about in a normal fashion on account of so much staring by people and the attitude of scores of the English here and the wondering whether they should speak or not – all snobs, all afraid of getting in wrong with the new order. I have never been in such an ignominious position in my life. Mr King – Canada's Prime Minister – has seen it his duty to get up in whatever they have in Canada and announce that he told 'Mr Baldwin that the people of Canada would not approve King Edward VIII's marriage to Mrs Simpson whether she became Queen or not'. How can Prime Ministers speak for the people when they have never even asked them? I haven't had one nasty letter from there – and lots hoping you would become Governor General. I have a horoscope from Switzerland today

- most dreary - saying many more obstacles were to arise for me this year ... [page missing] ... is quite long and boring but we have so many arrangements that must be made and carefully made. A clergy-man in Alberta says you're very naughty that you broke up a home there. Now which one of the many was she? We all say 'good-bye' and send our love to all of you.

PS Aunt B has seen the kitchen here also. We are horrified. Anyway there is a different dog ill each day - and such dogs - they 'mell'! However I hope to remain well until March as think the hotel would be difficult besides expensive. I long for my own house.

Now came another unpleasant shock. On 21 January Theodore God-dard wrote to Wallis to say that Sir Boyd Merriman, the President of the Divorce Court, had ordered the King's Proctor, Thomas Barnes, to investigate the Intervention of Francis Stephenson in her divorce suit - notwithstanding the fact that Stephenson had purported to withdraw his Appearance. 'I do not think you need be worried by this', wrote Goddard. 'I propose to give the King's Proctor every facility in the matter, as after all we have nothing whatever to hide.' Wallis replied on the 23rd: 'I seem to be engaged on the greatest obstacle race of all time. I shall try not to worry. Nor am I afraid to fight any intervention.... I am surprised that one can investigate something which does not exist.' In a letter of 26 January, Goddard added: 'My own view of the matter is that the President, having had cognisance of the intervention, feels that he ought to have the matter investigated because he has had this notice, and to allay any public criticism.' All that would happen, he thought, was that Barnes would see Stephenson to hear his 'evidence'; and once it was established there was none, 'we shall hear no more about it'. In fact (as a memoir of the Attorney-General, Sir Donald Somervell, reveals)[1], Barnes was at that moment in the process of conducting a full investigation of the circumstances of the Edward–Wallis relationship - including the interviewing of servants and the crew of the Nahlin *- with a view to establishing whether Mrs Simpson had been guilty of adultery.*

In the midst of this depressing matter, Wallis had found what she thought might be a suitable place for their reunion and (should all be

---

1. Quoted in H. Montgomery Hyde, *Baldwin* (Hart Davis, MacGibbon, London, 1973), pp. 566–70.

well) their marriage – the Villa La Cröe at Antibes which its owner, the newspaper magnate Sir Pomeroy Burton, was prepared to let them have for a few months at a modest rent. She had also received a letter from her friend 'Chips' Channon suggesting that they buy Wasserleonburg, Count Munster's castle at Carinthia in Austria, as their future residence.

Edward to Wallis
26-1-37   Schloss Enzesfeld

(How do you like this note paper? I couldn't take the old stuff any more.)

My Sweetheart

This is just to say good meesel and that I love you more and more before I make another drowsel. I enclose an eanum frog for the thirty first to live in your bag with the fat Vienna frog. The silly man hasn't copied my writing as I told him to but anyway its what I want to add for 1937 opposite my oval picture. Oh! golly how the days do drag but the skiing does help pass the time and I really am being very careful. But it's terribly cold and that's another reason for longing for the Spring. Oh! there's so much to say and arrange and I must go South to you for a little after the Civil List[1] unless the boys advise us it will complicate and that would be too cruel and ridiculous for words.

The Baroness [de Rothschild] and Rex leave here in a week thank goodness. Of course she would have gone with Eugene if she had had any tact and was'nt such a stupid woman. Otherwise this place has the best possible under these trying circumstances [*sic*]. I hate to think of you living under the conditions you've just described to me. 'Pooky demus' WE say and I'll be glad when you move. My sister and Harewood[2] will be arriving in a fortnight and I'll be able to give them a lot to say and arrange for our wedding when they return. And then of course I'll write and explain myself too.

1. Before the Abdication, the Duke had been advised by the Government that any meeting between him and Mrs Simpson before her divorce became absolute would prejudice his chances of obtaining a pension in the new Civil List due to be voted in the spring of 1937. In the event, he received nothing in the List anyway.
2. The Duke's sister, Princess Mary, and her husband the Earl of Harewood, a Yorkshire landowner. They were to be the first members of his family to visit him in exile – but they would not bring him the good tidings for which he hoped.

Please show the new eanum frog to HER as HE has seen it!! How HE longs for house and make soon HE says too. God bless WE my beloved Wallis. Remember what the eanum frog says and that I love you more and more. Your

DAVID

Edward to Wallis
Half-time! 21-1-37   Schloss Enzesfeld

My own beloved sweetheart
After WE had shut down our telephone last night I designed the enclosed 'W' which I send along for your approval. You will see how it is taken off and fits over the 'E' (No 5) that you have chosen for me too and if you like it with either the eanum or the big crown above (I like the eanum best) will you please send it direct to Mr Sindon and I will have him telephone me to explain it all to him. I am becoming quite a detailist. I am longing for your letter darling but really am scared about the drains and 'mells and filth where you are. People are extraordinary but I don't expect many people's houses would stand close scrutiny or inspection. But I know how you and I feel about any sort of 'pooky demus' so have Mary[1] be as careful as she can and I really cant see why you dont talk straight to your hostess and you can always blame it on their servants and report badly on them. Thats good about the Burton house for that sum for two months and how lucky the name is 'La Cröe'? is that right? I am going to Vienna now for Dianabad[2] hair cut and a talk with Selby[3] over the European situation because not having access to FO telegrams just now and despatches or Cabinet papers I like to know what is going on and he does. I hope to have word from Hugh Thomas[4] from Paris tonight and I'll tell him to thank the French authorities for your police protection as well as make arrangements for sending out stores and any of our things by bag or anyway via the Paris Embassy. WE wont ever do anything rash but I cant see what could possibly prevent the Easter Bunny from fetching 'us all' down from the ice and snow to you all

1. Wallis's maid Mary Burke, who had accompanied her to Cannes.
2. The principal steam bath in Vienna, of which the Duke was an habitué. After the *Anschluss* he helped its Jewish chief engineer emigrate to England.
3. Sir Walford Selby, British Minister to Austria.
4. The Duke's old friend and sometime Assistant Private Secretary Hugh Lloyd Thomas, then Minister at the British Embassy in Paris. He died a year later in an accident, aged forty-nine.

and Mr Loo too. And that's such a long way off too and this separation seems so endless and drives one crazy with missing and longing and then the stupidity of it all. No two grown up people have ever had to endure such a thing and sometimes I feel its such an insult to our intelligence!! I shall be glad when Walter [Monckton] comes and my sister and Harewood too because I can find out and tell them so much. God bless WE my sweetheart and hold tight. I love you so dearly and want you so desperately. Your

DAVID

Wallis to Edward
Wednesday [27 January]   Lou Viei

Darling

Here is this morning's clipping from a French paper. I do think it the limit that it should come out that Baldwin won't let your brothers visit you – and I think the King ought to send one simply to show Baldwin and the world. It's really too much. Baldwin ruining your family affairs as well. Must he keep on humiliating you. Your brother should not allow it. You can see it is copied from the English papers. My love

WALLIS

Wallis to Edward
Thursday the 28th [January]

Darling

I have just returned from Daisy's [Fellowes] in the worst storm I have ever seen, lightning etc. You can imagine a girl on that Monte road! There is so much to say that is important. I hate writing – and the telephone really is difficult. First I am enclosing a letter from Chips which explains the Austrian Schloss situation very clearly and I think we can trust him for taste and comfort plus his experience in the country. I would not consider buying the Munsters but I would definitely consider renting it for 4 or 5 years as I am convinced if we did not want to go there every summer I am sure we could always let it. What they ask when renting you would have to find out and I should think Jackie [Aird] a good one to write to Paul Munster or Greenacre since it looks rather risky to wait – read Chips' letter carefully – the handwriting needs careful study. The next thing is about the matter I scribbled to you about in pencil. I met a number of Englishmen at Daisy's today – among them Sir Ian Malcolm (Suez Canal) a Lord somebody etc. Everyone is under the impression that you and the family are not on good terms and that they are not behind you and the reason is that they have all seen in the papers where Baldwin refused to allow either of your brothers to visit you and that had the King been back of you he would have sent Kent in spite of Baldwin. I remained silent. It all hurt so much. I only wish one of them would come for a few days to show the world. You can see yourself it is Baldwin playing politics because if your brother makes no public demonstration then the country thinks Baldwin more right than ever. Surely you deserve some consideration and it is this Government that is trying to squash you with your country. You must fight them and your brother be made to see the injustice. He can help you that way and there is no reason for the government to win there. It is wicked and nothing but Baldwin's rotten politics and there is no reason to bring them into family relationships. If it continues the answer is a book – which will let England see how they are being hoodwinked by Mr B. You cannot allow that man to finish you – and believe me that is the idea. It makes me boil because your brother is letting them get away with it. Can't you make him see it? All my love

WALLIS

Wallis to Edward
[no date, but in reply to the Duke's letters of 26 and 27 January]

My sweetheart

I love the new frog and so does 'she' – the diamond nearly put her eye out!! I am enclosing a letter from Peggy Munster with the address for Paul M as well. Maybe you can still rent it. Certainly we don't want to own anything until we know what is going to happen. I am sure they will rent it to you for say 3 years. Anyway do deal with it quickly as you see what the situation is. I long for you and love you but become eanum suspicious of 'all of you'. It is odd the hostess remaining on. Must be that fatal charm! Daisy is dying to see you. I advise against it not from jealous reasons but you know what the press and the gossip would say – as we know her reputation is not too steady. She wants us to send presents and messages by her. I shan't do either – but you could talk on the telephone without having to see her.

The fact is to be polite because she has been kind to me – and I really don't think you need ask her to the house – but certainly talk on the phone. If there was any way to get to Wasserleonburg by train it might be worth the trip to see what one was taking for a few years. Oh darling will we ever be together again? It is so hard on the nerves.

WALLIS

CHAPTER THIRTEEN
February

At the start of February Edward and Wallis came to a decision about their wedding. Instead of renting La Cröe on the Riviera,[1] they would be married at Candé, the luxurious castle in Touraine which had been offered to them fully staffed and free of charge by its owners Charles and Fern Bedaux, friends of the Rogers. In her memoirs, the Duchess of Windsor tells us that the Duke – still imagining at this time that his wedding would be attended by his family – in fact left the final choice to the King, who agreed that Candé would be the more dignified setting. The plan was that Wallis should leave Cannes and install herself at the château in the first half of March; and that Edward, in order to be nearer her, would go and live at Saint-Saens, the Duke of Westminster's estate in Normandy, until he could finally join her.

As they impatiently awaited their respectives moves, February turned out to be a particularly difficult month for both of them. With no news of the continuing investigations of the King's Proctor, Wallis became increasingly worried over whether she was going to succeed in obtaining her divorce. It was made clear to the Duke that he would not receive a pension in the Civil List; and – though he was visited at Enzesfeld by his sister Mary and his favourite brother, the Duke of Kent – his relations with his successor continued to deteriorate, the King no longer wishing (or as the Duke later surmised, no longer being allowed) to speak to him on the telephone.

Wallis to Edward
[early February]

Darling
   I love you and here is your lesson for Sir Pomeroy Burton (Chateau

---

1. They did in fact take the villa in the spring of 1938, and remained its tenants for some ten years.

la Cröe, Antibes (AM), France).[1] I am sure we have done the wise thing and I also believe from the point of view of the servant problem we will be better off as it would be difficult to train an entire new staff in a strange house and at Candé they have the butler that gets them. The food here is the end – the dirt grows worse – and I can't get my diet. Also I think I shall enjoy a change of scene and grounds to walk in. I think it would be a good idea for Storrier to meet me there and look over the staff and start the ex-police officer on his duties etc. From the feminine side it will be difficult about hair, face, nails etc and very expensive having people from Paris. However some of the savings that I've made must make their appearance. I enclose the proofs of Beaton's article that is going to appear in US Vogue. See about the crosses and the cairn in the article. I miss you and long for you.

WALLIS

You should order some paper with the new design. More dignified.

Wallis to Edward
Saturday, Feb 6th

Dearest Lightning Brain

   I don't know what English papers you take in but you never seem to know what's going on. I enclose some clippings. It will be the last blow if they take Knight of the Garter away from you. That is what they did to Beauchamp[2] and people of that sort. I think the Civil List looks stormy in view of the position Mr B has put you in with the country. All the papers report more or less like this one from the Telegraph. I must advise writing your brother instead of the telephone. I think with a slow brain such as his that he doesn't take in ideas as quickly as you speak and then the constant yelling which one has to do is apt to get on the nerves of a highly strung person. I know it's hard for you to write but feel that at this critical time in our lives you must make every effort and force yourself to do unpleasant tasks. I think we spend too much money on telephone calls which we may

---

1. Wallis enclosed the text of a polite letter she wanted the Duke to send Burton, regretting that they would not be taking his villa that spring but hoping to look over it at some future time.
2. The 7th Earl Beauchamp (1872–1938), a distinguished Liberal statesman, who had been obliged to resign his offices of state and flee abroad in 1931 owing to a homosexual scandal.

need badly some day. I think we ought to only speak once a day except for something important that arose. I think you should write your brother telling him what a good thing it would be if he saw Somervell and simply let him know that anything in the way of holding up my decree absolute would be most objectionable to him. I agree with letting the old man go on but we want Somervell warned so that he can suppress any suit should Merriman find a small technicality to bring it on. I think he will ... [words illegible] ... his mind to stop it. Also the hypocrisy of the church is amazing. The Rector of St Mark's Church is going to marry Dottie Sands twice divorced in his church. So what? Why you have been singled out to be crucified I can't see. If there was one decent bishop your brother should send him to marry us. If not why play with the Church of England? Let's have something else. If you read Bedaux's letter you will see that we will have to make arrangements with the Catholic church to use the chateau chapel so that by the end of March we must know about a clergyman coming out so as to start negotiations. I hope to get there by the 10th. Perhaps you could come by the 15th if we are assured nothing will happen. It isn't against the law to see each other properly chaperoned. It is all too much the desire to reduce us to a pulp. I have a letter from a woman in Paris saying 'Die Kitty' has arrived full of new rumours, additional gossip, etc. I can only pray to God that in your loneliness you haven't flirted with her (I suspect that) or told everything about yourself – finances, family matters or hurt feelings over your brothers treatment of you because Paris will be full of that and once on the telephone she hinted to me that London wasn't treating you well – and also once hinted about the pipe line. I know my sweet you have a way of telling too much to strangers and heaven knows the Rothschilds were that when you arrived. Darling – I want to leave here I want to see you touch you I want to run my own house I want to be married and to you.

WALLIS

Wallis to Edward
Sunday the 7th [February]

Darling

I am enclosing Goddard's letter[1] which explains clearly the position we are in. As you will see unless Walter [Monckton] & your brother take some steps we will not know the King's Proctor's intentions until about April 24th. Surely if it is unwise to touch Merriman can't Barnes the Proctor be approached in some way and let him know that the King does not wish any case against. Frankly I don't think he will find one – but it is absolutely necessary to know what is going to happen some time in March. As you see if I have to bring it up again on the defended list it can be a matter of a year or more before I would be free. I think the only thing for us to do is to go ahead with our plans and then if on April 24th the blow is struck we will have to deceive them. I can't believe that Walter, Somervell etc. can't find out the result of the King's Proctor into Mr Stephenson's intervention [*sic*]. Will you return Goddard's letter for my file on this subject. I enclose also some information from Bernard [Rickatson-Hatt]. I can't believe that either the King or Walter [Monckton] are doing anything to make it known to Barnes – or Walter doing any underground work to find out the result of the interrogation for it must be finished by now. The Telegraph takes up the Garter. I hope you won't have that taken away also. How they are humiliating us. Can't your brother see that if he is as fond as you say of you? Why allow all the knocks in the world. The Telegraph also adds you are not expected back in England for a considerable time. I blame it all on the wife – who hates us both. All my love and of course we will meet in March now.

WALLIS

Having spent six weeks at the Hôtel Carlton at Cannes to be by her niece, Aunt Bessie returned to the United States on 3 February. The letters to her now resume.

1. Wallis had asked her solicitor to explain what form the King's Proctor's investigations would take and when their result would be known. Goddard replied (4 February) that the King's Proctor made his enquiries 'entirely on his own account' and was not required to inform anyone of their result. If he discovered evidence of collusion or adultery, nothing would be known of this until three or four days before the divorce was due to be granted, when he would 'enter an Appearance' and 'propose to show cause why the decree should not be made absolute'. He would then 'file a plea' in support of his contention, the Petitioner would have to reply to this, and the whole case would then have to be heard again, with the usual delays.

Wallis to Aunt Bessie
Wednesday, Feb. 10th   Lou Viei

Well darling, we all miss you very much and hope you have faced the
newspapers with your usual success. Nothing new is happening here.
The fate of the decree is still hanging fire of course, which makes life
uneasy. The weather is perfect now and I have taken 3 walks but the
golf goes on. We had ten for dinner last night, quite a gala. We have
decided to go to Candé provided one goes anywhere and have told the
Burtons – which passed off pleasantly. I think I'm lucky not to have to
deal with the servant problem as the butler there does it. The Rogers
have been very good over their disappointment and the house is to be
added to anyway. We found the glove and a letter from Katherine. I
have sent them both off. The scrapbook cost $500 so we declined that
with thanks. Good luck with NJ. I'll let you hear the minute I know
anything myself. With much love

                                                    WALLIS

Wallis to Edward
Sunday the 14th [February]

Darling

Here is the letter I neglected to enclose in my last scribble. We still
have to have Miss Hussey twice a week and my desk looks the same
with the personal letters. I see I also had a letter from Lloyd Tabb. He
is the next to write about me – harmless and stupid. We or I at least
hope to leave here on the 8th getting to Candé the 10th. I can't help
but feel I am never going to live any place but Lou Viei. Lately more
people I know have pased this way returning from Africa and next
week-end I am going to spend at Mr Maugham's without the Rogers
(not asked) as Sibyl Colefax is to be there. Thus leaving if all goes well
only one more week-end here! I long to hear how the storm broke and
hope you have survived it well. All love

                                                    WALLIS

As yet no plans.

Wallis to Aunt Bessie
[15 February]   Lou Viei

Darling

Here are the Noyes' letters to you and which they wired me to open before sending on to you.[1] As you see Lelia's is too rude to consider ever seeing her again as far as I am concerned. Newbold's far more restrained and his the confused side. As you know all the rumours they speak of were denied from here. Naturally they have no idea what the situation was from Cannes and that we got all the rumours including the baby one.[2] We also denied rumour that I had had a row with H.R.H. The Noyes treat the rumours as true and that they didn't use them – it's all fantastic – but Newbold and myself you can clearly see simply did not understand each other. I did say I thought he could have done something to correct stories. I did say he could write about me – you know it all – but what came out was quite different. The King did say he hoped Newbold could help *me* with the U.S. press. There it all ends. Newbold's letter I do understand. Lelia's I think an impertinence. Love

WALLIS

Edward to Wallis
18th February 1937   Schloss Enzesfeld

My own beloved sweetheart I really dont know how many letters I owe you – and I've been very idle about writing. I'm sorry Wallis and please don't stop writing as I love your letters. I only wish my pen flowed like yours does. Its lucky I have such a good telephone voice though I have to admit that I'm licked when 'the bird' really gets going. Oh! darling, one really does wake up some mornings wondering whether one will keep one's sanity if this separation goes on much longer. This place has got on my nerves now despite the comfort and you have'nt even got that! I must get out of here before Easter what-

1. After Noyes' newspaper articles had been published in France in January in a particularly sensational manner, Wallis had issued a press statement disowning them. Noyes protested in the form of a bitter letter to Aunt Bessie destined for Wallis's eyes, as did Lelia, who implied that she was encouraging her husband to sue Wallis for libel.
2. When Theodore Goddard saw Wallis at Cannes on 9 December 1936, there had been a press rumour to the effect that he was, or was accompanied by, a gynaecologist who had come to deliver her of a child.

ever happens and if you approve (only only if you do) I might go up to some quiet Ski-Ort when the snow has gone from the Semmering on my way to France. I have heard of one or two unfashionable places where there are no trees or dangerous obstacles and I would get fit and full of health. However we'll discuss that later on and in the meantime I have a lot of business on hand as 'the boys'[1] arrive tomorrow and Paul Munster is here to discuss Wasserleonburg. Of course I won't decide a thing without consulting you my darling you know that and nobody is going to be able to slip anything over a boy. Two minds that work along the same lines as ours do are so much better than one and they shant take advantage of our separation to get me to agree to whatever they have to propose all by myself. I'll know by tomorrow night so will be able to tell you all about it before you go away for a more difficult week-end telephonically. Then 'der Kent' is by way of paying a visit some time next week[2] but I've not heard from him. Perry arrives 26th and I'm looking forward to seeing him and maybe you would like him to go to you wherever you'll be. I've just had a nice wire from Bend Or[3] who hopes to get my letter in Mimizan. I hope so too. How he does move! It would be fine if we could get the 'Cutty Sark'[4] for a while this summer but 'die Schwester Anna'[5] would be better than no yacht at all. But we'll see. What a lot WE have to do and how lovely its all going to be Wallis. My first job will be to fill in that 'trench' between your eyes a bit and I know I can ... [one page missing] ... good for Queen Elizabeth and the Duke of Norfolk downwards!! But who cares and WE will be back in our full glory in less time than WE think. It is a terribly difficult time for both of us my beloved one but dont let it get you down. I know it sounds easy to say that but I have all the responsibility and its never going to get me down and only makes me fight all the harder. And WE'll win despite them all. I know WE will so hold tight and go on trusting a boy and never take any notice of anything or rotten gossip that any foul woman or women may try to spread. I hate them all darling and despise them all so. So you do so too and never never believe a word of it because it never never would or will be true. That's all and now I must have tub and dress for this Anglo–American stag dinner at the Grand Hotel.

1. Walter Monckton and George Allen.
2. The Duke of Kent stayed at Enzesfeld from 24 to 28 February.
3. The Duke of Westminster.
4. The Duke of Westminster's yacht.
5. Daisy Fellowes' yacht.

The boredom but its a change from here – a rest for the chef and maybe useful and interesting for a boy. I'll write again quickly and till then know that I love you love you Wallis always more and more. I know that I can make you happy for all time my sweetheart and that is a terribly big thing to say. Still I say it. God bless WE. Your own

DAVID

HE says his voice has been very bad lately and to tell HER that its the fault of the 'telephone bird'.

Wallis to Edward
Friday the 19th [February]

My darling here are two more letters. One from England is quite mad. The other is from Paris but I send it to you as the French have funny detective habits! I want to get away from here so badly. It really has been uncomfortable to a degree – also boring and then there is Katherine – hard as nails. I will feel better having a house to run etc. I imagine it is quite safe to go to Paris for a few days – at the Meurice.

WALLIS

Wallis to Aunt Bessie
Sunday, Feb 21st   Villa Mauresque, Cap Ferrat, A.M.

Dearest Aunt Bessie

I have come here for the week-end with Somerset Maugham as Sibyl Colefax here also. It is a marvellous change and heaven to have a pretty bedroom. As far as I know we leave Lou Viei March 8th, arriving at the chateau the 9th, where the owner Mrs Bedaux is going to receive us. The butler there has got all the staff which has been a great help but which I imagine I'll change some when I get there. My other plans are completely unmade. In the first place I am not to be allowed to see the King [sic] before April 28th and as the telephones get more impossible every day it is hopeless to make plans or for him to have any decent talks with London. Then no one seems to know what is going to be the divorce verdict. So one can only be patient and try not to let it get one down. The King hopes to be able to get the Duke of Westminster's house near Dieppe from March 20th on but it is only an attempt to be in more direct communication with London and me. Actually it is 200 miles from Candé (Monts near Tours, France). I have asked Herman to ask the secretary many times for the address but nothing has happened so far. They are very busy with their plans. The estimates were too expensive so now comes the cutting down. The mad woman they still have at the bottom of the hill but Katherine won that round. We will probably go to Paris for four days. I have asked Gladys & Mike [Scanlon] to come for Easter and maybe Gladie, Colin [Buist] and Foxy. Gladie and Foxy are in Marrakech now and could stop on their way back. No one knows the place. I've just sent vague invitations that I am going to have a house of my own somewhere. I don't regret for a moment the decision to go to Candé. The Riviera has a cheap air about it no doubt and the reputation of being the world's playground. It will be more dignified to be in the country. I should book the reservation on the boat arriving April 30th or if you can get on a boat landing Cherbourg or Havre around that time so much the better as it's less journey this end. What is so awful you will have to be on the water before I know whether I get the decree absolute and if I don't get it naturally I don't know just where I'll hop off to to get one. With much love

WALLIS

Wallis to Edward
[undated]

Darling

Here is the thing about the divorce from the US papers. I cried myself to sleep last night. No talks to a boy – and today all the lines are down to Cannes – damn the French. I really can't continue to carry on with all of England taking cracks at me and no decent society speaking to me. What have I done to deserve this treatment? I have never had a word said in my defence or kind word in the press. Surely your brother can protect me a bit – not to be the butt of musical comedy jokes on the radio etc. If they knew your family approved our wedding when free, things would be so different for me. I do feel utterly down. It has been such a lone game against the world for me and a woman always pays the most – and you my sweet haven't been able to protect me. You can see how worried I am over the divorce. There must be a way to find out what the King's Proctor is going to do. David darling all my love

WALLIS

Surely he has finished his investigation by now?

Wallis to Edward
Sunday the 28th [February]   Lou Viei

Darling

Another day gone thank God! What a dreary life we lead and the waste of time is so pathetic. I am enclosing my English love letters. 2 of the same ilk I tore up as Herman didn't think they were traceable as the handwritings were so bad. It will be a relief to move away from the English gossip of this small place. It does hurt sensitive girls you know. The new address is Chateau de Candé, Monts (I&L) France, tel. Tours 18-40. The station is Tours but as there are several stations the one to alight at is St Pierre des Corps and the train that is the best is the Sud Express. I am so anxious to hear just what arrangements Westminster leaves for you at Saint Saens. I may be able to help you with extra servants if necessary. I am also suggesting that you have the chauffeur with the Ford wait and come to you there. This scrawl is being written on my lap in the dungeon known as the drawing room so forgive its looks. Only one more week here. I am afraid the Riviera is ruined for me. It has been so sad this trip and I'm sure you'll never want to see Enzesfeld again either. I want to see you so much my sweetheart some days I feel I can't go on alone.

CHAPTER FOURTEEN
March

The first days of March were taken up for Wallis with preparations for the move to Candé.

Wallis to Fern Bedaux
1st March 1937   Lou Viei

Dear Mrs Bedaux,

It is frightfully difficult for me to convey even one tenth of what I feel about your and Mr Bedaux's kindness and generosity to the Duke of Windsor and myself. When we meet perhaps I can make you realise a little of it. I am so looking forward to our arrival at Candé the ninth and I hope you will not have a shock at the size of the caravan. I am afraid I must warn you that if our move is detected before my arrival you may have an awful struggle with the press. We are so used to it here that it has ceased to be upsetting – but the first encounter is a shock. Anyway the answer is always the same – 'you don't know anything'. There is one more thing I wanted to tell you – that suddenly a night watchman for indoors may appear from London a day or two before the Rogers and myself arrive. I hope Hale[1] has not had too difficult a time with the staff. I am told they are difficult to find. I am looking forward to running house once again. It is the thing I adore most, so you can feel that Candé is in interested hands. Again my most grateful thanks and appreciation.

Yours sincerely,

WALLIS SIMPSON

Edward to Wallis
3-III-37   Schloss Enzesfeld

Hello! my sweetheart.

I have no news except what you already know that I love you love

---

1. The butler at Candé.

you more and more. I'm so terribly scared by these filthy letters you are receiving but we mustn't let them get on our nerves. Only for God's sake be careful and not take a chance and we'll see later on whether it is wise for a girl to go to Paris without a boy. It will be such a huge relief when we have both moved nearer to each other even if the d-d law still says we cant meet before 27th April. It will all be so much easier and cheaper too and Bend Or now says he will leave some staff behind and his friend Charles (not George!) Hunter says we can get any more we want. And then Herman can anyway come to see me and it will be nearer for Allen and Walter etc. I do hope you will have a good drive across France darling and that you will be able to elude some of the news hounds. I am afraid that to even hope you could get away with it entirely would be futile.

As I write your letter and enclosures arrive. God's curses be on the heads of those English bitches who dare to insult you. Oh! it makes me so sick and scared and I'm so far away and cant protect you. But Herman has written such a nice letter and that helps eanum. Please thank him. I love yours sweetheart and how right you are about my feelings for this place. Maybe WE can make the Riviera all right again together but not for a long time. I enclose an eanum mascot for your cosy motor for the trip next week. Your chauffeur can nail it on some place and I have one exactly like it for mine. Storrier will be returning to me soon and then I'll send him down to see how you are and of course you can't possibly go to Paris without him. I'm just going to Vienna with the boys for a Dianabad a blow from old Neumann[1] and then a boring dinner with the old gents of the 'Jockeiklub'. I'll telephone from the Bristol at 7 o'clock. God bless WE Wallis and may HE protect us both now and always. But please please take care as I do love you so. Your

DAVID

Wallis to Edward
Saturday, March 6th   Lou Viei

My darling

I have your note and the ladybird setting on the 3 which has already been put in the Buick. It is something to be moving – especially away from an atmosphere where Michael Arlen[2] refused to dine at the same

1. An eminent Viennese ear specialist whom the Duke consulted.
2. The fashionable London novelist of Armenian descent.

party where I am – but it is a trying time especially with the horror of a hitch in the divorce. England would do anything to me in their smug fashion. They won't blame themselves for letting you go by not granting the one thing you ever asked of them but place it all on me. It is a cad's attitude and they are a nation of cads where women are concerned. I've always said that – and of course the jealousy, which is the dangerous side. My sweetheart I enclose you a letter which explains itself. I wonder if Scotland Yard can't have this anti-Simpson organisation traced. You know I heard of it in the very start from a man named De Courcy[1] who I believe is a lobbyist – I didn't actually as I was here and he came to see Aunt B and terrified her. I think they ought to do something about it as it crops up from time to time. Perhaps he could be interviewed in some way. The Hunters unfortunately don't know his address – but maybe it could be found through the House of Commons – though he is not a Member. I don't know myself what is meant by a lobbyist. Evans is supposed to have sent on Miss Campbell-Smith's letter to the Yard about the organisation. She wrote to him personally what she had heard. I don't suppose however Scotland Yard would bother much about me. I love you my darling one.

WALLIS

This sounds very much like the De Courcy idea – as he also said powerful and with money you know what the latter means. Paying well for killing.

Wallis to Aunt Bessie
Saturday, March 6th   Lou Viei

Dearest Aunt Bessie

You can imagine our excitement here with the big move scheduled for Monday, all the secret arrangements etc re the van for the luggage etc. We hope to be safe from the press until Tuesday at least. We are spending Monday night at an old chateau off the beaten track not touching Lyons on the way. The staff engaged at Candé sounds nothing short of Buckingham Palace and as it is only for we 3 & perhaps a few week-enders it seems a waste for they have told the King [*sic*] he cannot see me until after the 27th & also there is no way to know

---

1. Kenneth de Courcy (born 1909), a right-wing political journalist who became a friend of the Duke and Duchess of Windsor.

what the King's Proctor is going to do until we put in the papers for the decree absolute and that is only a few days before the 27th so everything as far as wedding plans is just as when you left. The King is going to leave Austria around the 20th and going to the Duke of Westminster's house near Dieppe about 200 miles from Tours. We hope there to have a clearer telephone. Also he is closer to London etc, etc. I should think you will just have to make up your mind whether to gamble on the wedding the same as I have to. So I suggest the boat arriving the 30th Villefranche because if nothing happens I should naturally leave Candé and could meet you somewhere and also the wedding would not be before the first week in May at any event and maybe not until after the Coronation. I haven't read N[ewbold] N[oyes]'s article[1] yet but was glad to know your age at last! I can't remember whether I gave the address - Chateau de Candé, Monts (Indre et Loire), France. Mrs Bedaux is meeting us there. Naturally life is one series of difficult complications. Everyone in London is busy with the Coronation & it is hard to get any answers to anything & a very trying time on the nerves for everyone concerned. This paper has given out and mine is packed. All my love

WALLIS

Wallis to Edward
Sunday, March 7th

My darling

I have come to what I think a very wise decision from everybody's point of view. Especially I think it best for WE and that is what we so often say on the wretched telephone - that we are working for that only. I have decided that we must not be married until after the Coronation. My reasons are as follows. It is going to be very difficult to get things properly arranged from London. Every one is working full blast - highly keyed up. We are unimportant compared to the show they are trying to bring off. Once successfully accomplished they will turn their attention to you and the whole atmosphere will be cleared. Also from the press point of view we would not be properly handled. Their attention would also be on the other. Afterwards we will have a better chance. It also proves there was no great hurry for the marriage, Mr B. wrong, and it is more dignified to the whole world

1. A magazine article which Noyes had written to supplement his newspaper series.

and we have time to watch the other event and make ours perfect. We shall lose trying to do it beforehand and it puts the cards across the channel. If I were with you I could make you see all these things. You must believe in this – it is all intuitive – but I know right. Now from our point of view we do not have to be separated and you will come to Candé the 28th and we will make every arrangement together and it is an excellent quiet place to be on May 12th etc etc. We do not have to have more separation under this plan. My idea would be that you would inform your brother that it was your plan and ask him to announce the engagement on May 5 and also the date of the wedding which I suggest for May 19th – both included in the one announcement. Also whoever is coming can then arrange their engagements accordingly. I mean Kent etc. Perhaps we may get a few presents in the week between!! – but I'm quite sure you'll agree that this is the dignified and better method – no rush ever and dignity – and I am keen to let them have their show. All moods everything will be better and no world criticism and the earliest we could arrange things anyway would be the 4th of May and this only makes two weeks later and we are together all the time and will have gained much sympathy and dignity. It is a clever move my beloved and I'm sure you will agree with a girl who lives for the day when you will call her your wife. Say yes and then write your brother a few days after you are settled at St Saens – giving dates so that there is no excuse of short notice etc. All my love

WALLIS

From the Duchess of Windsor's memoirs:
Early in March [on Tuesday the 9th], Katherine, Herman and I left for Candé, at six o'clock in the morning. In another car following behind us were two French detectives of the Surêté, whom the French Government had thoughtfully assigned to protect me (Inspector Evans having long before returned to Britain), as well as Katherine's personal maid and mine. It was pouring rain as we left, and we travelled in a downpour all the way north. We stopped overnight at Roanne, finally arriving at the chateau in the grey dusk of the next afternoon. To avoid reporters who, we had been warned, were already posted at the main gate, we entered the grounds by a back entrance, and my first glimpse of Candé was pleasing – grey walls and slim turrets in the slanting rain.

Mrs Bedaux was at the door to meet us. She struck me as an unusually handsome woman, graceful and poised. 'I was afraid', she said, 'that this rain would delay you. You must be tired and chilled. Tea is ready, if you want it.' ... Seldom in my life have I known a person to show more kindness to a stranger....

Fern Bedaux led us through a small entrance hall into what she called the library – a large panelled room, with a handsome fireplace in which several large logs were blazing. We were famished: the tea refreshed us. Among her other admirable qualities Fern exhibited tact of a high order. She asked nothing about my wedding plans, only remarking that she would be leaving the next day and she hoped I would stay at Candé as long as I desired. 'Now let me show you around,' she said. 'The chateau is not quite so large as you may think. There will be time for you to rest before dinner.'

The drawing room, spacious and high-ceilinged, with oak panelling, was more formal and, I thought, less attractive than the library. At one end was an organ. Off this room was a smaller salon, very French, with pale panelled walls and Louis Seize furniture. I instantly decided that this was the room in which I would be married. The dining room was downstairs – a kind of taproom, with immense hand-hewn beams, very old, and with an equally ancient oak table flanked on either side by long, low benches. Adjoining the main part of the house, and reached by a narrow passage and a flight of stone steps, was a small guest apartment. Fern Bedaux suggested that the Duke might like to have this apartment when he came from Austria.

Then she showed me her own bedroom, a rather spacious room, with a cream-coloured *boiserie* and having an excellent view of the grounds. Since she would not be there, she asked me to use it as my own. Adjoining the bedroom was a small sitting room with a daybed that Mr Bedaux used. Herman decided to take this for himself. He had slept in a room adjoining mine with a gun under his pillow ever since I had arrived from England, more than three months before. Upstairs were several other bedrooms, of which Katherine took one.

Having shown us around, Fern Bedaux left us to change for dinner. The long ride in the rain had tired me, and I lay down on the big bed, hoping to snatch a nap before my bath. But my mind persisted in running haphazardly over the innumerable questions in my life and David's that were still unresolved. Where would we start our life together? What to do about our things in Great Britain? Would there ever be a reconciliation between David and his family? How to deal with the renewed onslaught of the press that the marriage was certain to bring?

There was another question that troubled me still more. Who would marry us?...

In the midst of these melancholy reflections the telephone rang. It was the butler to say that *'Son Altesse Royale'* was calling from Austria. 'Darling,' came a clear voice across the width of Europe, 'I am so glad to find you safely at Candé. Was it a difficult trip?' I ceased to be afraid.

However, the day after her arrival at Candé, Wallis received further upsetting news. It came in the form of a handwritten letter from the loyal and vigilant George Allen.

8th March 1937   3, Finch Lane, London E.C.3

Dear Mrs Simpson,

Do you mind if I mention something which is troubling me a great deal?

When I was at Enzesfeld, H.R.H. told me of his projected move to the Duke of Westminster's chateau somewhere in France. I do not know exactly where it is, but I imagine it is within about 300 miles of Tours. I advised H.R.H. very strongly against any move which would take him into the same country as you were in, prior to the D[ecree] A[bsolute]. So long as he was in another country – say Switzerland or even Belgium – even though he was just over the frontier, all would be well, but if he should come to stay in France itself, then all the old suspicions & allegations will be revealed with heaven knows what consequences.

You realise that my only desire & objective is to secure your D.A. & subsequent marriage & I am quite confident that these will be seriously threatened if you allow to arise a situation which will compel the authorities here to think that H.R.H. and you are meeting & they will refuse to believe otherwise, & so will the public at large, if you are within range of each other in the same country.

I realise, of course, all the exasperations and chronic inconvenience of your present locations where telephoning is difficult, & there is no reason why you should not be much nearer to each other, but in different countries for the time being.

I hope you will be happy and comfortable at Tours.

Yours very sincerely,

A. G. ALLEN

Wallis to Edward
Wednesday the 10th [March]   Chateau de Candé, Monts (I&L)

My darling one

I can hardly bear to send you the enclosed letter from Allen because I know how sad it will make you. But it speaks for itself and I don't think we can afford to take a chance in any way – so what can a boy do is now the problem. If your hostess does not return until April 10th that would only give you 17 days there with her – if it would not be awkward to ask to remain on. I don't know whether she has asked you to do that. The other solution would be Belgium as it is the nearest to me. I don't know whether you could write the King of Belgium and ask him if he knew of a place you could have or whether he has one he could lend you for a month – otherwise I think it best if it is all right with Kitty to remain where you are and we will simply have to go on screaming over the telephone. Anyway we can make the more definite arrangements from here and you can write the first ones to your brother about dates, announcement etc. It is too distressing but Allen is not an alarmist and we simply can't afford to do a thing. Oh darling this is a hard time. I am better off now away from all the smallness of Cannes and will just sit here in the greatest comfort and such expense. I am sorry we have got the extra chauffeur and night watchman though the latter is perhaps necessary – if the chauffeur turns out well and is not too young I will let the French one go back to Cannes and then I will just have the two. This place is bristling with servants and much too much food – but when Mrs Bedaux leaves I shall deal with the chef. It is awful about St Saens and I don't know what excuse you will give except to say that you have been advised that it is better for you not to go to France at the moment – don't say why as it might get repeated and make some hurtful gossip. I shall remain here I think unless it became a great expense to have them come to me. I don't think there is danger in Paris only it starts the press again and the photographs. I shall be anxious to hear what you decide to do my darling and if it is to stay on – perhaps you ought to telephone Kitty. Of course I don't know what was said about your length of stay when she left. Make come quickly please – and I do love you so much and long for the day we can meet.

WALLIS

I enclose another of those letters.

Wallis to Aunt Bessie
Thursday the 11th [March] Candé

Dearest Aunt Bessie

We had a very successful and peaceful trip here stopping the first night at a charming chateau which is an hotel with heavenly food. Mrs Bedaux met us and she is awfully sweet and attractive and she left today. This is quite a business, the top in luxury – and expense, I am afraid. The servants seem excellent but I imagine do you in the eye. Katherine far prefers Lou Viei I can see. I've never tasted such lovely food. One eats too much, that is the trouble. There is golf, fishing and riding but nothing can be indulged in as the weather is foul – floods and wind. I don't care. I was so glad to leave Cannes. I have decided one thing and that is that I shan't be married until after the Coronation. I think it more dignified and it won't mean any longer separation as the King [*sic*] can come here and stay after the 27 of April & we will have a decent time to plan things correctly and also London will be able to give more time to us once the big bubble has burst on the 12th. I should not be married before May 18 which would give you time before leaving to know whether I get the decree. You could book now on the Italian lines and try to arrive around the 8th of May. The King is very restless and planning to move somewhere. Unfortunately, having made all arrangements to go to the Duke of Westminster's house near Dieppe, Allen yesterday sends word he can't come to France as no one would believe we weren't going to meet. It is all too unkind – so now new arrangements have to be made. He is very disappointed. It is certainly a difficult and trying time in every way for us. I have decided not to touch Paris. It is easy for the things to come to me here. Write me soon and excuse me if anything seems strange I say or do but there is something new to deal with each day. All my love

WALLIS

Wallis to Fern Bedaux
15th March 1937   Candé

Dear Mrs Bedaux,

I can't help but write you a few lines to tell you how happy I am here. It is the first time I have been able to use that word since December. The peace of Candé and the protection of its lovely grounds have made me live again. I have fallen in love with every inch of it. We are expecting you any time this week.[1] I shall have a friend here who has come from Rome to see me. Again I want to thank you and Mr Bedaux for what I now know has amounted to saving my life – and certainly any sense of proportion in regard to the people of this strange world.

WALLIS SIMPSON

As Wallis busied herself at Candé with preparations for the still uncertain wedding, the Duke made plans to move from Enzesfeld at the end of March to a hotel at St Wolfgang near Salzburg. Meanwhile he had been visited at Enzesfeld (11–13 March) by his cousin Lord Louis Mountbatten, who assured him that his family would be attending his marriage. On 19 March came the good news that, in special proceedings before the President of the Divorce Court in which Mrs Simpson was represented (as at Ipswich) by Norman Birkett, the investigations of the King's Proctor – which had uncovered no compromising evidence – had effectively been brought to an end. 'I feel confident that we are now through our troubles,' Allen wrote to the Duke.

On 14 March the Duke was joined at Enzesfeld by Sir Godfrey Thomas, a faithful friend who had been his Private Secretary as Prince of Wales. A week later, Thomas wrote to George Allen of the life in Austria of his former master and King:

---

1. Having tactfully left Candé on 11 March, Fern returned there briefly twice that month at Wallis's own request – from the 19th to the 21st and for Easter week-end (27–28). She then joined her husband who was on business in London, and both of them returned to Candé on 30 April to help prepare for the Duke's arrival.

... All well here: like those who have preceded me at Enzesfeld, I haven't for many years known my host in such good form, or so easy from every point of view. But it is tragic to see the petty activities to which he has recourse, just to fill in the time. Still, whether it is counting the wine in the cellar, superintending the plucking of his dog, or examining the house books, it keeps him going till it's the hour for his next telephone connection with Tours. He is, more than ever, a charming and considerate host; & as a guide round the *Kunsthistorisches Museum* in Vienna, as good as any professional. What a strange mixture! You probably know that he moves from here on March 29th....

The correspondence resumes towards the end of the month.

Edward to Wallis
22.III.37   Schloss Enzesfeld

Sweetheart

Here is Mr Loo and a few eanum things I'm sending you by old Storrier. Only I cant say 'there WE are' yet and if you knew how terribly tempting it is to go to you too. I hate the waste of these four and a half months of our lives which are so vital and precious to us and which we'll never get back. Oh! poo when I think of it. On the other hand I guess it would give those mean swines a chance to hang us which they seem to want to do and we'll just show them that we can and will stick out this ridiculous and humiliating separation which has been imposed on us. God how I hate and despise the lot. I must say that the verbatim report of the proceedings in Court last Friday were very satisfactory and Norman Birkett was good – far better than at Ipswich!! I feel it really has cleared 'the legal air' a lot though why it ever needed clearing I dont understand. I'm so sorry you were worried and consequently upset by the newspapermen getting it all wrong before you heard anything reliable. I know it's easy to say take no notice of them darling but at the present tense pitch at which we are both of us bound [to] live until 27th April (much less now) it takes so little to upset us and drive us frantic. I hope one day to and I mean to get back at all those swine and at least make them realise how disgustingly and unsportingly they have behaved. If I ever hear another

275

word of that old bromide 'The English are a nation of sportsmen' I'll yell the place down!

Thank goodness all being well I'll be leaving here today week Monday 29th. That will complete fifteen weeks of Enzesfeld and its telephone service!! Maybe it will be worse where I'm going but anyway it will be a change for a boy which a girl has had. In separate cover is the new address, telephone and some post cards of the place. I also send a list of the things I'm sending by Storrier. Dudley Forwood (the equerry on trial) seems quite a nice boy – very young and needs keeping down but keen and efficient as regards traveling [*sic*] arrangements. I'm sending him back for his annual three weeks Special Reserve attachment to his regiment – Scots Guards – and he'll be able to get in touch with Ulick and Mr Carter and I'll tell Perry to have a talk with him too. He may suit us. I have just received this document from Allen. I have a copy relating to the formalities in France for our marriage. Ooh! how lovely that sounds and you'll see what we have to do. The eanum locket or charm with the silhouette of a boy's face is funny. Sam Gracie found it and gave it to Selby for me. Dont take any notice of these monograms on writing paper – I'm only using up some samples they sent from the shop till the proper blue ones come. I must make my 99th drowsel in Austria now. Oh! Wallis I love you so and please take enormous care and not play foolish games and hurt your knee as you've just told me you have. I'll write again from new place next week. Slipper will give you a dog kiss from your own

DAVID

List of things Storrier is bringing –

Mr Loo complete with collar and lead
brush and comb
dog biscuits
Bob Martin
His rug

One blue bag containing:
this letter
a legal document
new address
eanum charm of boy found by Sam Gracie
eanum comb of Easter Bunnies

the WE dressing set
the WE mirror (separate)
one powder box marked WWS
one packet of Gunsebrust
(don't make eanum pig)
your eanum stick
an egg from the Chicky Dees
one red belt
and a boy's enormous loving ooh and make 'pick up'.

Oh! darling one how long to wait and make come quickly.

A boy's new address: Landhaus Appesbach, St Wolfgang am Wolf-
gangsee. Salzkammergut. Telefon: St Wolfgang No. 9. 'Alle guten
Dinge sind drei.' 3 × 3!! Also some pictures of the Landhaus – not
'Pension'!!

Wallis to Aunt Bessie
[22 March]   Chateau de Candé

Darling
   I have just got your letter and have sent a cable to see if you can get
a later boat for several reasons. As I think I wrote you the Duke and
myself decided it would be more politic to have the wedding after the
coronation and as May is very booked for all members of the family
George VI has suggested June 4th as a convenient time for him to send
a member to the wedding. I see that is a Friday so am going to try to
change it to the 5th. We are going to have Bedaux trouble as they are
going to be running back from here to Paris etc. That means the
chateau is theirs most of next month. Then at the end of the month
the Duke arrives and proposes to try out secretaries and equerries from
here as it is simpler and cheaper from London than Vienna. He is not
going to the Duke of Westminster's house as they think it wiser for
him not to ever be in the same country where I am so up to the middle
of May I am afraid the place will be in confusion crowded etc so could
you arrange to arrive about the middle. I can't have Uncle Harry [to
stay] though I can certainly ask them all [to the wedding]. He wouldn't
have the proper clothes etc. nor know the form. It would all be very
awkward. As I have said before we mean nothing to the English or
the press and they wouldn't notice whether it was a member of my

family who gave me away. It is very pleasant to have the 'interviews' put out and I think very wise of the English Court to do it the way it does and again stop gossip etc. I heard that [Sir] P[atrick] Hastings doesn't think his client has much chance against Ernest[1] which is also good news. Let me know as soon as you can just when you can arrange to arrive around the middle of May. By then I should think I will be in ruin with this place and Norman Birkett having [had] to appear for me on Friday! I shall have some clothes for Sally to send back with you. Much love

WALLIS

Wallis to Aunt Bessie
Thursday the 25th [March]   Candé

Dearest Aunt Bessie

I have just heard from Mr Allen that to be married in France I have to have my birth certificate and my decree of divorce in Warrenton – the decree showing that the divorce was made absolute. To get the divorce decree you write to the Courthouse in Warrenton. It is quite simple. They send you the copy for a few dollars. The birth certificate I suppose is at the county seat where Montney is. You can of course take the papers to the French Consul in Washington. Naturally don't take them until you hear I get my divorce in London. Then go at once as they will have to be all gone over again on this side so I should have them here by the middle of May *at the latest*. I am sorry to trouble you but you are the only one that can do it. In sending them register the letter. Everything goes along here at great expense and not much amusement as I don't do anything but walk in the grounds and the weather is rotten. Aileen [Winslow] left yesterday after a week's visit. Foxy and Mrs Bedaux spent last week-end. Tomorrow the Grants and the Scanlons arrive for Easter and Saturday Mrs B comes back. Katherine spent most of last week in Paris and goes again after Easter. I have to have Paris come to me. Storrier arrived yesterday bringing me Slipper. It's divine to have him. The King has a new Cairn puppy to keep him company. I hope you will be successful in shaking Cousin Lelia for the return trip. The chapel here is most unattractive

1. Ernest had begun proceedings for slander against the wife of Colonel Arthur Sutherland, who had allegedly been spreading the rumour that he had been paid not to contest the divorce. The case – in which the defendant was represented by the celebrated Hastings, Birkett's great rival – was settled.

so it will have to be in the house. I get clippings from time to time all about the move etc. The Bedaux have taken it all very calmly. Much love

WALLIS

Wallis to Edward
The last of March   Candé

My darling
   I have been thinking all morning about your wretched brother. I think I should put in the letter that if he continues to treat you as though you were an outcast from the family and had done something disgraceful and continued to take advice from people who dislike you (I mean advising against doing anything for you but belittling you) that there would be only one course open to you and that would be to let the world know exactly the treatment you were receiving from the people (family) you had placed in their present position. You are tired of taking all the knocks and unfair publicity. You have made a great sacrifice and you don't regret it but you did not expect your brother to slip into your shoes and forget you completely not giving even any small help to the remaking of your life. Such an exhibition has been most hurting and you feel you must now take steps to protect yourself. Then you can bring in about no one to look after your interests in England the example of the Dukedom etc. a series of humiliations etc which you have taken and not attempted to resent. Then you make what you call last requests – the results of these will determine your actions for the future etc. Don't be weak, don't be rude, be firm and make him ashamed of himself – if possible. I love you and want you here so badly.

WALLIS

4 months of filthy treatment – rub it in – & the advisers. You might and should add that your introduction of him into his new life showed quite a different spirit from his introduction to your new life.

CHAPTER FIFTEEN
April~June

Edward to Wallis

2-IV-37   Landhaus Appesbach, St Wolfgang

Sweetheart: Here are a few snaps of Pookie (demus)[1] which you'll find in the new black bag. I hope you'll like as much as I do. I've addressed the parcel to Herman as usual and Godfrey will mail it in France tomorrow. The change of prison quarters is a great relief and its very peaceful and isolated here. Its such a lovely place and WE loved it too and I miss you so desperately more every day. You had that terrible cold here and THEY had their cape (hide face)! Its so wonderful to be able to say 'this month' now for meeting again but it makes one sick when one thinks that a whole third of this year will have been wasted away from each other. Oh! my darling one I'm so relieved you are listening to a boy and not moving until I come and having all the people down from Paris. Never mind the expense as its not for much longer now. I will be drafting a good letter for Mr Temple[2] and send it at the spycological [*sic*] moment embodying all your points which are flawless. Forwood is doing quite well and I think you'll be pleased with him but we must get Bernard [Rickatson-Hatt] to find us a good press liaison officer for May and June. Then I have the appointment of someone of standing in England in mind to watch after our interests there until we go back. God bless WE my beloved Wallis. I said an eanum prayer for WE in our dear little church last evening. I do love you so my darling one.

DAVID

1. The Duke's new Cairn puppy, replacing Slipper who had been sent to Wallis at Candé.
2. King George VI.

Wallis to Fern Bedaux
Wednesday, 7 April   Candé

Dear Fern

Oh my dear, such an awful thing has happened. I can hardly write about it. The Duke's and my beloved Slipper – he belonged equally to us both – was bitten by a viper yesterday afternoon and died last night. The vet in town did all he could but I found him too late and the poison reached his heart. It does seem cruel to have this added sadness. Herman is burying him near the gargoyle. It was his first walk here – he was bitten by the stream at the second hole [of the Candé golf course]. To add to all this despair is the English law, which it appears behaves in this fashion – though the 27th is the Day sometimes they don't what they call 'read' the Decree Absolute in open court till 10 days afterwards, and until such reading we must remain apart. I am sorry to write such a gloomy letter but I am sure you will understand the grief caused by Slipper's death – he had been so faithful through our many trials.

WALLIS

Wallis to Edward
Wednesday [7 April]   Candé

My darling

I have just given Herman Mr Loo's rug to wrap his little body in before Herman buries him. When you come we will get a little stone for him. Even God seems to have forgotten WE for surely this is an unnecessary sorrow for us. He was our dog – not yours or mine but ours – and he loved us both so. Now the principal guest at the Wedding is no more. I can't stop crying but we must be brave and suffer these next 3 weeks. You see we have had so much to bear for so many months that our resistance is low – so we must watch carefully and try and save our nerves. We are both feeling the strain – I can hear it in your beloved voice – that defeated sound. Perhaps your idea of getting off outside of Paris is a good one – naturally the train will be full of the press who will also jump off, but perhaps if [Douglas] Greenacre told them where you were going to descend they would be decent enough not to follow you. Herman and the cars can go up to Paris the day before. I think Hugh L[loyd]-T[homas] should meet

281

however no matter what the hour – arriving in a foreign country etc. I love you my darling one and this agony of separation is so immense.

WALLIS

Edward to Wallis
7th April 1937   Landhaus Appesbach

Oh! how utterly cruel that our darling Mr Loo should be taken from WE like this. My heart is quite breaking this morning my beloved sweetheart from sadness and above all from not being able to be with you and hold you so tight which is the only help when WE are unhappy. I have cried quite a lot too and I know what a ghastly night you must have had. I won't say any more about it all as that is too sad and too trying my darling one but I am sure you would like Mr Loo to be buried near one of the eanum paths I made for you at the Fort. If you could have him enbalmed and packed into an eanum lead box I will have Dudley Forwood call for him on his way back to England in his motor next week. He is very sympathetic and I know will be glad to do this for WE. I feel quite stunned and dread the remaining three weeks until I am to be with you never to be parted ever again my sweetheart. Please never that as I do love you so more and more. I suppose I must practice a little golf or do something this afternoon but I have'nt the heart to do a thing. For God's sake you be careful of those bloody reptiles and I promise you I'm taking care of myself for you so you're not to worry. A boy is holding a girl so very tight sweetheart. Your sad

DAVID

Wallis to Aunt Bessie
Tuesday the 13th [April]   Candé

Darling

Thank you for your wire. It really seems too much. The new dog is sweet[1] – but he is not Slipper. The latest legal news is that I apply for the decree absolute on the 27th but it is not read out in Court on English custom until the 3rd, therefore the Duke will not be allowed to arrive here until the 4th. They certainly can arrange the damnedest

---

1. On hearing the news about Slipper the Bedaux, who were in London at the time, had bought a Cairn of similar type and sent it as a gift to Wallis.

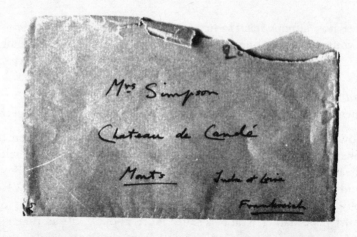

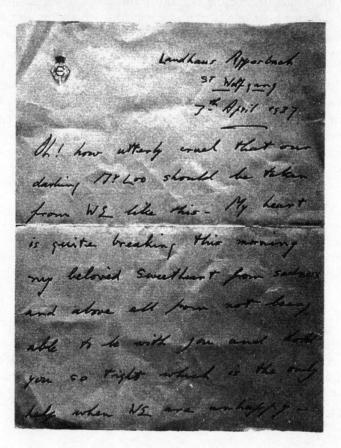

divorce laws. I hope you have been able to raise a birth certificate, otherwise some form of legal paper signed by you and Cousin Lelia showing I was born. The French want everything before you can be married. This is a long month and rain every day but I run a hotel. All the girls shopping in Paris come here for the week-ends. Impossible write much as am snowed under & no secretary. Will see you next month some time. All love

WALLIS

Wallis to Edward
Wednesday the 14th [April]

My darling
I am sure your letter is good and also strong. I have thought up a marvellous thing to say when you announce when our wedding will take place – this I shall save to tell you about when you arrive. You must now give your ammunition around a bit. I am so pleased with my other eanum gun and both Rogers think it OK and grand. WE don't care – but now we must protect WE and as we have been turned adrift we have an excellent chance. How stupid two camps. Well who cares let him be pushed off the throne. The minute the family split – danger. A fine history his will be after his behaviour to you. As you know a series of horrid books about you are appearing in England – and even the Daily Mirror has an editorial on how well they were behaving about you. You will of course have to write your side in self-defence. It is the most wicked campaign and it must not succeed. I love you more than ever my sweetheart. So much trouble WE have had together but it only makes my love grow stronger for you my dear. Please take care of yourself. I am always worrying in case something should happen.

WALLIS

Edward to Wallis
14.IV.37   Landhaus Appesbach

Oh! my beloved one
What a month of socks this April is turning out to be. Never mind it will all be over soon and they can sock us all they want to when we are together because then we'll be able to sock back at them wont WE

285

darling? Only they are eanum harder to take alone and the agony of drafting letters on the telephone. However the letter to Temple has gone with the messenger (he might have spared the public that expense!) and a boy is following to have his feets attended to. This is just a line to say I love you more and more my own sweetheart and praying that the next eighteen days and nights wont drag too interminably for WE. Poor WE – and there must be such a huge big store of happiness for us after all of these months of hell. A. G. A[llen] will show you a draft letter to Paul Munster tomorrow[1] – so please make any alterations and suggestions you think of. It will be lovely looking for our eanum new home somewhere or maybe we'll be able to afford to build one. Oh! God I love you so Wallis so please that HE may bless WE. Please take care of your precious self for your David like he is doing for a girl because its all he's got left in the World and its all that he wants.

Though there remained three weeks of separation, these were to be the last letters exchanged between Wallis and Edward before they became man and wife.

From the Duchess of Windsor's memoirs:
Finally, on the morning of May 3, there was a telephone call from George Allen in London. My divorce decree had now become absolute. I telephoned David in Austria. 'Wallis,' he said, 'the Orient Express passes through Salzburg in the afternoon. I shall be at Candé in the morning. . . .'

David arrived at lunch time [on the 4th] with his equerry, Dudley Forwood. David was thin and drawn. I could hardly have expected him to look otherwise. Yet his gaiety bubbled as freely as before. He came up the steps at Candé two at a time. His first words were, 'Darling, it's been so long. I can hardly believe that it's you, and I'm here.'

Later, we took a walk. It was wonderful to be together again. Before, we had been alone in the face of overwhelming trouble. Now we could meet it side by side. . . .

On the morning of the Coronation [12 May], David mentioned casually that he was going to listen to the broadcast of the ceremonies from London. It was a silent group that gathered around

---

1. They had decided to rent Wasserleonburg for their honeymoon.

the radio at Candé. David's eyes were directed unblinkingly at the fireplace.... The words of the service rolled over me like an engulfing wave; I fought to suppress every thought, but all the while the mental image of what might have been and should have been kept forming, disintegrating, and reforming in my mind.

When we were alone afterwards, he remarked only this: 'You must have no regrets – I have none. This much I know: what I know of happiness is forever associated with you.'

... Now came a cheering development. Herman received a letter from the vicar of St Paul's, Darlington, the Reverend R. Anderson Jardine, offering to come to France and perform the marriage ceremony. David was delighted and telephoned George Allen in London to get in touch with the clergyman and, if George thought well of him, to make the necessary arrangements for him to come to Candé. He arrived at the chateau the day before the wedding, a typical country parson in appearance and manner. I thought it brave of him to defy his Bishop in order to marry us, and David and I gratefully welcomed him as a man of God.

Somehow the preparations got done. Mainbocher made my trousseau. From his sketches I chose for my wedding gown a simple dress of blue crepe satin. Reboux made a hat to match. I asked Constance Spry, the prominent London florist, to come to Candé to do the flowers for the wedding. She was a person whom I knew and admired. She brought her assistant with her, and in a matter of hours they had transformed the atmosphere of the house.... This was her wedding present to me.

Other preparations, beyond our control, were also going forward. The press was congregating in the nearby city of Tours....

David hoped that, once the Coronation was over, his family might soften its attitude, and that at least some of them would attend the wedding. But another blow was in preparation, one especially humiliating to him. Sir Ulick Alexander, David's former Keeper of the Privy Purse and a steadfast friend, telephoned David to say that Walter Monckton was coming and would bring with him a letter from the King that would contain 'not very good news'.

In his letter [dated 27 May] the King said that he had been advised by the British and Dominion Prime Ministers that when

287

David had renounced the Throne he had also given up the Royal titles. As he was no longer in the line of succession, according to the King, he had furthermore lost his right to the title of Royal Highness. But the King wished him to enjoy this title, and therefore he was re-creating him HRH. However, he could not, he went on to say, under the terms of Letters Patent of Queen Victoria, extend this title to his wife. The King concluded by saying that he hoped this painful action he had been forced to take would not be considered an 'insult'. David would henceforth be known as His Royal Highness the Duke of Windsor, and I would be simply the Duchess of Windsor. . . .

The letter enraged David. He exclaimed: 'I know Bertie. I know he couldn't have written this letter on his own. Why in God's name would they do this to me at this time!'. . .

Our wedding day, the third of June, was beautifully warm and sunny. Herman Rogers gave me away, and it must have been with a profound sense of relief that he saw me become the responsibility of another.

Here I shall say only that it was a supremely happy moment. . . .

APPENDICES

APPENDIX ONE
Wallis's Commonplace Book

The Duchess of Windsor's papers contain a small, cloth-bound note-book, decorated on the cover with the Prince of Wales's feathers, half-filled in her handwriting with sayings and quotations. It carries no date; but, judging from the sentiments therein, it is reasonable to assume that she began it in 1934 at the outset of her romance with the Prince. The sixth entry may have been inspired by the cruise of the *Rosaura* in September of that year. The contents of the notebook are reproduced here as they were written.

To err is human, to forgive is divine.

A single, unquenched flame of lonely animation.

Mortality for others, immortality for oneself.

By thy long beard and glittering eye,
now wherefore stopp'st thou me?

Good Americans, when they die, go to Paris.

If your lips would keep from slips
Five things observe with care:
Of whom you speak, to whom you speak,
and How, and When, and Where.

Existence on the water is vastly restful to one's point of view. The past and the future are alike cut off; the present seems as interminable as the ocean itself, as endless as the line of the horizon; time stands still or rocks gently like the stars at night up in the rigging.

England: 'A nation gets old as a person gets old. One hardly notices it until it is there. Then one wakens to the reality that one's limits won't function as they used to and one's memory wanders and one's hearing is a little difficult and one's sight a bit hazy. That's what has happened to England. For a time your old age gave you caution – during that period you wisely seized the financial control of Christendom. But even your caution is deserting you now, and you cannot renew the freshness of your ancestors. If the populations and governments of Australia and Canada could change places with the p. and g. of G.B. there would be some hope for you. But as it is, in spite of your heroic qualities, your endurance, your chivalry, your unselfishness, you cannot last. Your brain is going, and you are going at the knees. The centuries bow you to the ground. Tradition fetters your limits. The past clogs the present. But we nations who have the sap of youth in us are grateful to you for giving us the strength of your stock. Your greatness will live on in us. America is England's immortality.'

Gloom follows at the heels of those too vivid to be pure.

Baudelaire: 'Always be drunk! With wine, with poetry, or with virtue as you will – but always drunk!'

Desire is too transient, perfection too much a matter
of mood.

Now that we two have met, would that we might drift forever
into the dream we dreamed tonight.

I have the wisdom of the serpent and the harmlessness
of the dove.

Champagne for courage, red wine for endurance.

Without a woman's love, no man is safe.

Oh! that it were possible
After grief and pain
To find the arms of my true love
Round me once again

Traditional British insularity, which neither travel
nor experience can ever wholly efface.

If people had no past, they would have no futures.

You must either aim to be very young or not young at all.
When you are very young, things are happening every day,
and when you are a little older, anything may happen.

A cold grey dawn of facts.

A time when it hurts to live – a green sore feeling inside,
and things outside seem to take a pleasure in going wrong.

But one thing I know to cry to my children:
Live your Life! (Daudet)

The man who makes a good lover is the man who
loves women first and *a* woman afterwards.

Tonight I love the whole pathetic, glorious,
ridiculous world, and you my darling most of all
and more than ever.

Pain under the ribs, under the heart; the struggle
between it and the brain to gain the upper hand;
the brain trying continuously to rationalise, to
mend, to put things in order to save the situation;
the pain clawing and tearing like a bird of prey.

Love alters not with his brief hours and weeks,
But tears [*sic*] it out even to the edge of doom. . . .

Why is absence so long and life so short?

We who are sailors' wives, next to sorrow what
we dread most is happiness.

Heaven only hates people who love each other;
it separates those who would be so happy.

A little pink hard-shelled woman with a habit of
making up to people only to say something
extremely unpleasant to them.

It is not an enemy who has done this thing but
mine own familiar friend.

How sad and bad and mad it was!
But then, how it was sweet!
(Browning, *Confessions*)

APPENDIX TWO
The Fort Guest Book

In her letter to Aunt Bessie of 14 January 1935 (page 111 above), Wallis wrote that she had given the Prince, as a Christmas present on her aunt's behalf, 'two red leather books' for the Fort, 'one for card accounts and one a guest book', the two of them costing a total of £3. The guest book was to become one of the Prince's most cherished possessions. It was a rule that all who stayed with him had to sign, with dates of arrival and departure; and for the next twenty years he took it with him wherever he happened to be. It accompanied him to France on his summer holiday in 1935; on the *Nahlin* cruise; to Balmoral and Sandringham in the autumn of 1936; to Austria after the Abdication; to Candé for his marriage to Wallis (where all those present at the wedding signed); back to Austria for their honeymoon; to the villas at Versailles and Antibes which they rented in the late 1930s; to Portugal, where they spent part of the dangerous summer of 1940; and to Government House, Nassau, their home for the rest of the war. The last pages of the book were signed by those who stayed with them at the converted mill house near Paris which they made their country home in the mid-1950s.

Reproduced below are the contents of this book up to the Abdication. In the interest of simplicity I have not given the dates of arrival and departure of each guest; rather I have grouped the names together according to the week-end or party in which they participated, giving the opening and (where useful) the closing dates of the week-end or party.

This list of guests is of considerable historical interest. Much was said at the time and has been written since about the Prince's 'circle', with the imputation that there was something raffish and disreputable about it. In a notorious broadcast delivered a few days after the Abdication the Archbishop of Canterbury, Dr C.G. Lang, spoke with 'rebuke' of 'a social circle whose standards and way of life are alien to all the best instincts and traditions of [the British] people'. In the Fort

Guest Book one sees exactly of whom this circle consisted. It was not large: only a modest number of visitors could be accommodated, and the same people signed again and again. It was an even mixture of his friends and hers, British and American. It is hard to see what general 'rebuke' could be levelled against what appears to be an innocuous, if fairly jolly, collection of courtiers and diplomats, American men of affairs and English Society people, garnished with a sprinkling of statesmen, sportsmen, soldiers and sailors.

1935

NAME	DATE		
Wallis W. Simpson	1 January	Mary Lawrance	11 January
EP		G. F. Lawrance	
Genevieve Bate		Gerald F. Trotter	
Fred B. Bate			
		Josephine Gwynne	18 January
		Javier Bermejillo	
Javier Bermejillo	5 January	Gwendolen Butler	
[two illegible signatures – 'Leatham'?]		Humphrey Butler	
Henrietta Worth Bingham		[Earl of] Dudley	

Marion Carrick   26 January
[Earl of] Carrick
Genevieve Bate
Fred B. Bate

[February was taken up by the holiday in Austria and Hungary.]

Gerald F. Trotter   9 March
Genevieve Bate
Fred B. Bate

Posy Guinness   16 March
K. W. Guinness
Poots Butler
Ulick Alexander

Hugh Lloyd Thomas   23 March
G. F. Lawrance
Mary Lawrance
Diana Fitzherbert

A. G. Menzies   30 March
Poots Butler
Winnie Portarlington
[Earl of] Portarlington

Colin Buist   6 April
Gladys Buist
Jack Aird
Katherine M. Rogers

Gladys E. Anderson   13 April
Patrick C. Anderson
Matesha Dodero
J. A. Dodero
Jorge Dodero

Sarah Woolley   27 April
Betty Lawson Johnston
J. O. Lawson Johnston

Rose Headfort   3 May
[Marquess of] Headfort
Aileen Devereux Winslow
James Dugdale

Kitty Hunter   6 May
George Hunter

Genevieve Bate   11 May
Fred B. Bate
Mary Lawrance
G. F. Lawrance

Walter T. Prendergast   18 May
James Dunn
Gerald F. Trotter
Aileen D. Winslow

Mary Dunn
Marianna Dunn

Patrick C. Anderson   25 May
E. N. Fielden
Poots Butler
Gladys E. Anderson

Aileen D. Winslow   31 May
Walter T. Prendergast
Diana Fitzherbert
James Dugdale

Genevieve Bate   7 June
Fred B. Bate
Matesha Dodero
J. A. Dodero

[for Ascot]
Gladys Buist   17 June
Colin Buist
Gerald F. Trotter
Poots Butler
Hugh Lloyd Thomas
Emerald Cunard

Louise Doeller   22 June
Wm E. Doeller

Kitty Hunter   28 June
George Hunter

George [Duke of Kent]   13 July
Humphrey Butler
Poots Butler
Walter T. Prendergast
Betty Lawson Johnston

Beatrice Eden   20 July
Anthony Eden
Emerald Cunard
Duff Cooper
Diana Cooper
Esmond Harmsworth

[The book then records the French holiday.]

Le Roc, Golfe Juan, A.M.
[Lord] Brownlow   5 August
Katherine Brownlow
Colin Buist
Gladys Buist
Jack Aird
Helen Fitzgerald
[Earl of] Sefton
Katherine M. Rogers
Herman Rogers

[*The record of the Fort
week-ends continues.*]

Katherine M. Rogers Herman Rogers	3–9 October
Kitty Hunter George Hunter	11 October
Genevieve Bate Fred B. Bate Sibyl Colefax Godfrey Thomas	25 October
Walter Prendergast Betty Lawson Johnston J. O. Lawson Johnston	16 November
Kitty Hunter George Hunter	7 December
Gladys E. Anderson Patrick C. Anderson Kitty Hunter George Hunter	14 December
Genevieve Bate Fred B. Bate Poots Butler Humphrey Butler	21 December

1936

| Kitty Hunter
George Hunter | 4 January |
| Robert Vansittart
Sarita Vansittart
Brownlow
Katherine Brownlow | 11 January |

ERI

Dickie [Mountbatten] Kitty Hunter George Hunter	25 January
Gwendolen Butler Humphrey Butler	31 January
Evelyn Fitzgerald Walter T. Prendergast Helen Fitzgerald	8 February
Duff Cooper Diana Cooper	15 February
Gladys Kemp Scanlon	21 February

Martin Scanlon
Kitty Hunter
George Hunter

[*Wallis was absent in Paris
in the first half of March*]

| Genevieve Bate
Fred B. Bate
Kitty Hunter
George Hunter | 14 March |
| Evelyn Fitzgerald
Duff Cooper
Diana Cooper
Helen Fitzgerald | 21 March |

[*There follows the week-end
in which Ernest and Mary
participated.*]

| Gladys Buist
Walter T. Prendergast
Colin Buist
Mary Raffray
Ernest A. Simpson | 27 March |

[*The first week-end in April,
Wallis and Edward along with
Mary and Ernest attended Lord
Dudley's party at Himley Hall.*]

Humphrey Butler Brownlow Walter T. Prendergast Poots Butler Sacha de Couriss	9 April [Easter party]
Genevieve Bate Fred B. Bate	18 April
Kitty Hunter George Hunter	1 May
E. D. Metcalfe Katherine Brownlow Brownlow Alexandra Metcalfe	16 May
Genevieve Bate Fred B. Bate	25 May
Gladys Kemp Scanlon Walter T. Prendergast M. F. Scanlon	30 May

DATE OF ARRIVAL	NAME	DATE OF DEPARTURE
1936		*1936*
March 29th	*Gladys Buist*	*March 30th*
"	*Walter T. Prendergast.*	"
"	*Colin Buist*	"
"	*Mary Raffray*	
"	*Ernest A Simpson →*	
Ap: 9	*Humphrey Butler*	*Ap: 12*

[*Wallis was absent in Paris again during the first week-end of June.*
There follows the 1936 Ascot party, consisting of a coming and going of guests from 13 to 22 June.]

J. O. Lawson Johnston
Betty Lawson Johnston
Emerald Cunard
Terence Philip
Ulick Alexander
Hugh Lloyd Thomas
Ewan Wallace
Evelyn Fitzgerald
Barbara Wallace
Helen Fitzgerald
Sefton

[*The last week-end of June, Wallis and Edward attended the Duke of Marlborough's party at Blenheim.*
The recital of the guests at the Fort resumes in July.]

M. F. Scanlon	4 July
Kitty Hunter	
George Hunter	
Gladys K. Scanlon	
Andrew J. Warner	
Edwina Mountbatten	10 July
Dickie [Mountbatten]	
Walter T. Prendergast	18 July
Aileen Devereux Winslow	
Helen Fitzgerald	1–8 August
Sefton	
Poots Butler	
Humphrey Butler	

[*There follows the
summer vacation of 1936.*]

S. Y. *Nahlin*
[*10 August to 6 September*]
Poots Butler
Humphrey Butler
Helen Fitzgerald
Godfrey Thomas
Jack Aird
Diana Cooper
Duff Cooper
A. Lascelles
Sefton
Katherine Rogers
Herman Rogers

Balmoral Castle
[*19-30 September*]
Ulick Alexander
Piers Legh
[Duke of] Buccleuch and Queensberry
Eileen Sutherland
[Duke of] Sutherland
Eva Rosebery
[Earl of] Rosebery
[Duke of] Marlborough
May Marlborough
Esmond Harmsworth
George [Duke of Kent]
Marina [Duchess of Kent]
Colin Buist
Gladys Buist
Katherine Rogers
Herman Rogers
Edwina Mountbatten
Dickie [Mountbatten]

Sandringham, Norfolk
[*The King's shooting party, 18-23 October*]
Ulick Alexander
Charles E. Lambe
[Earl of] Harewood
Samuel Hoare
Humphrey de Trafford
Harry A. Brown
A. Lascelles

[*The autumn guests
at the Fort follow.*]

Kitty Hunter	9 October
George Hunter	
M. F. Scanlon	
Genevieve Bate	

[*Wallis, accompanied by the
Hunters, was in Suffolk for the
next two week-ends, in
connection with her divorce
proceedings.*]

Kitty Hunter	30 October
George Hunter	
Sibyl Colefax	7 November
Sally Bonner	
Paul Bonner	
Charles E. Lambe	

[*There follows the King's visit
to the Home Fleet at Portland,
12-13 November.*]

H.M. *Yacht Victoria & Albert*
Edward RI
Samuel Hoare
[Admiral Sir] Roger Backhouse
Louis Mountbatten
Charles E. Lambe
[Admiral Sir] Dudley North

[*Then the final signatures at the
Fort up to the Abdication.*]

Bessie L. Merryman	13 November
Bessie L. Merryman	21 November
Kitty Hunter	
George Hunter	
Bessie L. Merryman	27 November to 3 December
Walter Monckton	3-11 December
A. G. Allen	4-11 December
Ulick Alexander	4-11 December
George	8-9 December
E. R. Peacock	9-10 December

DATE OF ARRIVAL		NAME	DATE OF DEPARTURE	
1936			1936	
Nov.	21st	*Willy Hunter.*	Nov:	23d.
"	"	*George Hunter.*	"	"
Nov.	27th	*Bessie L. Merryman*	Dec	3rd
Dec	3rd	*Walter Monckton*	Dec	11th
Dec	4th	*A. G. Allen*	"	"
Dec	4th	*Ulick Alexander*	"	"

DATE OF ARRIVAL		NAME	DATE OF DEPARTURE	
1936			1936	
December	8th	*Queen*	December	9"
December	9th	*E R Peacock*	December	10"

300

APPENDIX THREE
Note on the Value of Money

Throughout the period from 1931 to 1937, the value of the pound sterling was nominally fixed in London at a par of 4.866 US dollars. Its real value for exchange purposes fluctuated, falling below $4 in 1931-2 as Great Britain abandoned the Gold Standard, rising above $5 in 1933-4 as the United States did likewise, stabilizing in 1935-6 in the region of its par value.

Until 1970, a pound consisted of twenty shillings, a shilling in turn consisting of twelve pennies or pence. 4/6 meant four shillings and sixpence – the equivalent of twenty-two and a half new pence. Smarter establishments gave their prices in guineas (gns), a guinea consisting of one pound and one shilling.

In terms of its power to purchase everyday retail commodities, the pound in 1931 was worth about twenty times what it was to be worth in 1985. There was practically no inflation in the 1930s, so that the pound in 1937 had for most purposes the same value as it had had in 1931. During this time the average wages of the British working man also remained virtually static at about two pounds fifteen shillings a week.

The wages of domestic servants, however, were a notable exception, as the number of those 'in service' was decreasing as a result of social change. In 1931 a cook entering service in a middle-class London household could not expect to earn more than thirty-five shillings for a long week, plus board and lodging, while a young 'live-in' housemaid would be lucky to get fifteen shillings. By 1939 these figures had increased by about one-third.

INDEX